# GATECRASHER

How I Helped
the Rich Become
Famous and
Ruin the World

## BEN WIDDICOMBE

**SIMON & SCHUSTER**
New York   London   Toronto   Sydney   New Delhi

Simon & Schuster
1230 Avenue of the Americas
New York, NY 10020

First Simon & Schuster hardcover edition July 2020

SIMON & SCHUSTER and colophon are registered trademarks of Simon & Schuster, Inc.

For information about special discounts for bulk purchases, please contact Simon & Schuster Special Sales at 1-866-506-1949 or business@simonandschuster.com.

The Simon & Schuster Speakers Bureau can bring authors to your live event. For more information or to book an event, contact the Simon & Schuster Speakers Bureau at 1-866-248-3049 or visit our website at www.simonspeakers.com.

Interior design by Lewelin Polanco

Manufactured in the United States of America

10  9  8  7  6  5  4  3  2  1

Library of Congress Cataloging-in-Publication Data

Names: Widdicombe, Ben, author.
Title: Gatecrasher : how I helped the rich become famous and ruin the world / Ben Widdicombe.
Description: First Simon & Schuster hardcover edition. | New York : Simon & Schuster, 2020. | Includes index. | Summary: "A smart, gossipy, and very funny examination of celebrity culture from New York's premiere social columnist"— Provided by publisher.
Identifiers: LCCN 2019057334 (print) | LCCN 2019057335 (ebook) | ISBN 9781982128838 (hardcover) | ISBN 9781982128845 (paperback) | ISBN 9781982128852 (ebook)
Subjects: LCSH: Widdicombe, Ben | Gossip columnists—United States— Biography.
Classification: LCC PN4874.W543 A3 2020  (print) | LCC PN4874.W543 (ebook) | DDC 070.92 [B]—dc23
LC record available at https://lccn.loc.gov/2019057334
LC ebook record available at https://lccn.loc.gov/2019057335

ISBN 978-1-9821-2883-8
ISBN 978-1-9821-2885-2 (ebook)

For Pam and Owen

"Great minds discuss ideas; average minds discuss events; small minds discuss people."

**I have always loathed that trite little quote.**

# *Author's Note*

The contents of this book are entirely organic. They have been locally sourced from the streets of New York City, including gutters, red carpets, between the seat cushions of taxicabs, endless cocktail parties, and the occasional late night in a penthouse.

All of the personal events depicted in this memoir happened as I remember them. There are no composite characters, although names were changed for a handful of individuals who are not public figures, in situations where they may have had a reasonable expectation of privacy.

Most of the anecdotes relating to public figures took place in environments where I was invited as a working journalist, with the understanding that anything I saw could be reported upon.

There are some exceptions, because that is the nature of lived life, and also I couldn't resist.

# *Contents*

*Introduction*                                                      xiii

## PART 1  Fashion

  1  Hotel 17                                                    3
  2  Downtown '98                                               9
  3  Buffalo Hot Dogs                                          19
  4  T-Cells on the Specials Board                             27
  5  Party City                                                35
  6  "Chic Happens"                                            45

## PART 2  Fame

  7  Elevators of New York                                     71
  8  The Gossiplex                                             87
  9  Wanna Hold My Oscar?                                     101
10  The Buzz at Da Tommaso                                   125
11  Mar-a-Lago                                               159
12  Sunset Boulevard                                         179

## PART 3  Fortune

13  Trump Tower                          195

14  The Hamptons                        205

15  The Ponzi Palace                    219

16  Rockefeller Central                 253

17  "No Regrets"                        257


*Acknowledgments*                       273

*Index*                                 275

# *Introduction*

For much of the last twenty years, going to parties in New York City has been my job. I have stalked them as a gossip writer for the New York *Daily News*, flown to them by helicopter for *Vanity Fair* and *Town & Country* magazines, and just now I write a column about them in the *New York Times*.

As writing goes, it ain't Proustspeare. But I love the challenge of entering a room and uncovering the story that lies beneath the surface of each specific combination of people and place. The job requires the skills of a critic, detective, interviewer, and humorist, all balanced like a tray of mismatched glasses.

It has also provided a unique perspective on the political and cultural evolution of New York. Parties are a public performance space, and there is no better stage to watch as old taboos and pieties die out, and new ones take their place.

The broader fault lines in the culture over the past two decades are well-known. As income inequality worsened around the turn of the twenty-first century, a very few individuals amassed fortunes that exceeded any others in history. In New York, wealth once again became a public spectacle in a way not seen since the Gilded Age. But this time, something was different.

As the millennium turned, the rich began to perceive a value in publicity that previous generations of the American upper class, which modeled their reserve on old-world Protestant aristocracies, had rejected as vulgar. Publicity, after all, was a means to celebrity. And that realm belonged to the beautiful idiots who toiled in show business—long considered an inferior caste.

But for the new ultrawealthy, money was no longer enough. Now they wanted acclaim to go along with it. So the rich rebranded themselves as famous.

I did more than just watch this phenomenon. As an agent of the media, which had an interest in pumping up the spectacle, I helped push the whole show forward. And what a show it was.

No longer, as the old maxim went, was it acceptable for the elites to have their name appear in the newspaper "only three times": upon their birth, their marriage, and their death. Now nothing less than the front page would do.

But what, exactly, were they hoping to achieve?

The rich already enjoyed all the advantages that a capitalist society had to offer. So what else could they hope to gain by also being famous? The answer, quite simply, was more of everything.

In fin de siècle America, traditional twentieth-century battle lines between the lower, middle, and upper classes were being redrawn. In the twenty-first century, more citizens were concerned about the growing gulf of opportunity between the putative 99 percent of working Americans and the so-called 1 percent who were reaping benefits at the top.

Inside the snow globe of money that is New York City, however, even that view was quaint. Here, all the friction was happening within the 1 percent itself. In the arms race of the 1 vs. 0.1 vs. 0.01 percent, celebrity conferred three distinct benefits: more status, more money, and more political power.

Humans, as a hierarchical species, value the bump in status that fame provides. That renown can also be further monetized, adding to the elite's key competitive advantage. And fame, which is after all a popularity contest, thrives on a parallel track to democracy.

As the liberal establishment learned to its horror in the 2010s, celebrity can be weaponized to hijack the supply of information, win elections, and control governments. Who wouldn't want to be famous with all that on the line? All you need to enjoy the spoils is to dispense with the vulnerability of shame.

"Shame" is a useful word, because it covers everything from modesty to social embarrassment to remorse for serious wrongdoing. I mean all of those things when I say that in twenty-first-century New York, shame has become culturally obsolete.

Many writers examine our current moment of inequality through the experience of those it hurts the most. Millions of people are in debt and face a lack of dependable employment, barriers to accessing education and health care, and vulnerability to political interests that want to restrict voting rights.

But I saw its effects from the opposite end of the spectrum. I was rubbing shoulders with the rich guys who were benefiting from the new inequalities and, in many cases, enthusiastically pushing them forward.

I observed what inequality meant for people like Jeff Bezos, Rupert Murdoch, Donald Trump, the Koch brothers, and even the Hiltons and Kardashians. I visited their homes and socialized at their parties, all the while scribbling in my notebook. For twenty years, as a gossip culturalist and social writer, I have been in the rooms where it happened.

Party reporters occupy an odd position in that world. We slightly outrank the waitstaff but are still there to work, so we are not exactly guests, either. For the elites to be admired, however, there has to be somebody to admire them, so journalists are tolerated as a necessary evil. We are invited but not wanted.

Not that I started out being invited. In fact, I learned how the city worked from the ground up, as an underdocumented Australian immigrant, selling hot dogs on the streets of the Upper West Side.

But New York is a great elbow sharpener, and it rewards those willing to go through doors that are not yet open. What you find on the other side can change your life.

In my case, it was the squeamish spectacle of the emperor changing into his new clothes. Piece by piece, I watched the rich drop twentieth-century values to the floor like discarded silky underthings, to be replaced by the twenty-first-century principle of full exposure.

Shame was out, and celebrity was in.

# PART 1

## Fashion

# 1

## Hotel 17

**F**raud is the fun cousin of self-invention.

Knocking around Sydney in the mid-1990s was a character named Charles von S——, a minor grifter who claimed to be German nobility. In those pre-internet days, he managed to stay just ahead of his scams, the full extent of which I wouldn't discover until years later.

Charles was the son of Czech immigrants who had prospered in Australia following the Second World War. But through a combination of his middle-European surname and grand airs, he passed himself off as the heir to an ancient title. He was what the social gatekeepers in London, where I had lived earlier in the decade, used to archly call a "Perhapsburg"—a con artist posing as a blue blood.

One of his tricks, on forms like credit card applications, was to write his first name as Baron and use Charles as his middle name. He would then offer the resulting document, in the name of Baron Charles Perhapsburg, as proof of his aristocratic title.

Charles was patrician looking, if a little twitchy, and always slightly more sweaty than the weather warranted. He wore white shirts with khaki suit jackets, which complemented his complexion, and the extra half inch of flesh that spilled over his collar added an effect of Roman imperial luxury to his bust.

He could also be quite rude, which further bolstered his image of being some kind of colonial governor, inconvenienced by a secondment to the provinces.

Certainly, Charles hobnobbed with Sydney society, or at least its low-hanging fruit. He delighted in telling unflattering stories about the children of local wealthy families, including one young heiress who, on account of her ample figure, he liked to call "Janet the Planet." All while insisting that he was a gentleman with impeccable manners, of course.

In fact, the baron had a checkered past that obliged him to keep on moving. As a so-called banking consultant, he had been a bit player on the wrong side of a $132 million Australian financial industry fraud in the early 1990s, which sent the perpetrator of the scheme to jail.

Charles escaped that wreck with only a singed eyebrow, although he was called "a crook" in court proceedings quoted by the national newspapers.

"After the scam, he left for Germany, where he had relatives," another newspaper reported, before going on to note that police had "unsuccessfully sought his whereabouts."

Well, they didn't look in Sydney.

I met the baron there in 1997. He remained a figure of mild notoriety in the gossip columns, which reported on small court judgments against him and the various dubious business schemes that he would occasionally try to float.

Another odd thing was that he would always disappear from the city on weekends, to what he would vaguely indicate was his country property, or perhaps an opulent house party thrown at the estate of one or another of his society friends. More than once it crossed my mind he might in fact be serving out a sentence of weekend custody—a kind of adult school detention for minor offenders—at the local jail.

Charles was a friend of my handsome and naughty boyfriend Horacio Silva, with whom I was getting ready to move to New York City. It was an exciting time, full of going-away parties and arranging finances and wardrobes for our new life in the capital of the world.

But all these preparations seemed to discomfit Charles, for reasons that weren't quite clear. Eventually I got the impression that he didn't like the idea that someone else might have a grand plan afoot in which he didn't feature, let alone have the upper hand.

"I *love* New York," he said one day over a lunch table, an edge of possessiveness in his voice. "My family has an apartment that we're not using in the city, at the Dakota? On Central Park West? You absolutely *must* stay there when you arrive."

Horacio and I exchanged a look. In all the baron's boasting about his travels—at the same time as he told one newspaper that he was visiting Germany, he told another that he was seeing a sick aunt in London—he had never mentioned New York, let alone owning an apartment in one of its most prominent residential buildings. It seemed like a suspicious omission for a braggart of his caliber.

As we hesitated—doing some mental calculations as to whether this could possibly be true—Charles interjected.

"I'll get you the keys tomorrow," he said with an expansive grin.

This was about two weeks before we were scheduled to leave. After a couple of days, the baron realized—*ach, nein!*—that the keys to the apartment were in fact with his mother, who lived in a different Australian state.

"But don't book a hotel," he said. "You'll have the keys in plenty of time."

We booked a hotel.

But we also didn't give up hope that Charles might actually come up with the keys to the Dakota. Of course we wanted to get inside that neo-Gothic cathedral of Gotham wealth, famous from *Rosemary's Baby* and as the scene of John Lennon's murder, where the smallest garrets sold for several million dollars.

Anyway, wasn't the baron's claim too audacious to be a lie? There either was an apartment at the Dakota, or there wasn't. And if there wasn't, Charles had a 100 percent chance of being caught out.

Surely, they would have taught him to avoid odds like that at con-man school?

But the truth is, you can't con the willing. We kept ourselves on the hook because of the allure of luxury and status that staying in the Dakota promised. Also, neither of us knew enough about the ways of New York apartment buildings to say, "Just tell the doorman to give us the keys when we arrive."

So, on the hook like mackerel we stayed, not only right up until the day of our departure but also—unbelievably—throughout the duration of the twenty-two-hour flight.

"Sorry I didn't get the keys to you before you left," Charles said over the phone at the airport, as Horacio's Uruguayan family—his mother stoic, his father in floods of emotion—gathered to send us off. "I'll FedEx them to you at the other end."

We never heard from him again.

What still galls me about this con, more than twenty years later, is its sloppy technical execution. The baron set up the Dakota caper with no apparent chance either of personal benefit or even of getting away with it. His sole motive seems to have been telling a lie and seeing it through to completion.

Such amateurism is irksome. One always wants to deal with professionals, even when getting fleeced.

We landed at John F. Kennedy International Airport late in the evening of February 5, 1998, and took a cab to Hotel 17 on the east side of Manhattan. There, a double room with peeling wallpaper, whose shared bathroom facilities lay at the far end of a hall with torn carpet, had been reserved for one night.

The night manager—a deeply reserved, slender-faced young man, with drooping black hair and glasses—issued our key from inside a weapons-proof, reinforced-plastic booth in the lobby. It was like a big Perspex fridge and only really large enough for one person. But crammed next to him on a chair was Amanda Lepore, a star of the New York nightlife demimonde and muse of the photographer David LaChapelle, whose images had made her recognizable around the world.

Born thirty years earlier across the river in New Jersey, Amanda was a keen devotee of both cosmetic and gender-reassignment surgery, although she always rejected the term "transsexual." She enjoyed cheap accommodation at Hotel 17 because she had been dating the manager who checked us in; after they split, she never left.

But that night she was still as a sphinx, her architected cheekbones holding up kohled eyes rimmed with Venus-flytrap lashes, all framed by a cascade of straight magenta hair with its bangs curled upward like a breaking crest of surf.

It was an absurdly perfect first night in New York.

Even a sleep-starved twenty-seven-year-old getting off a flight from Australia couldn't fail to recognize Amanda as an avatar of the city's possibilities for self-invention. Built from the heels up out of silicone and maquillage, she was still infinitely more authentic than our fake baron and his nonexistent Dakota apartment.

But all that ridiculousness vanished with the first thump of the yellow-cab door at the airport. The city's twinkling skyline, visible from the Williamsburg Bridge going into Manhattan, was like a sign made out of flashing light bulbs saying, "This way."

You can live your whole life in London and never be accepted as a Londoner. In Sydney, they still use the word "Australian" as a synonym for "Caucasian." But all you need to be a New Yorker, equal with any other, is two feet on the ground in New York.

# Downtown '98

**T**he most significant emotional bond that any New Yorker has is with their real estate. Lovers, pets, even children, come and go. But finding the right New York apartment is a once-in-a-lifetime relationship.

After a few days at Hotel 17, Horacio and I moved into a Tribeca loft belonging to a writer and her photographer husband who were friends from Australia.

Lee Tulloch wrote a seminal novel of the East Village 1980s club scene, *Fabulous Nobodies*, that I had discovered on the floor, and devoured, in my first boyfriend's college dorm room. Tony Amos was a good-looking, blond surfer scruff from the beaches of Sydney. When not working on his art photography, he shot portraits for New York publications and had once, thrillingly, been featured as an eligible bachelor in a risqué Australian women's magazine.

We sublet their apartment for two months while they took their ten-year-old daughter, Lolita, back home for a visit.

Every new piece of knowledge about the city came as if we were being initiated into a secret society. Even learning that Tribeca is, as every New Yorker knows, real estate shorthand for the "Triangle Below Canal" felt like receiving some arcane and important wisdom.

We discovered that Canal Street, its northern border, is four smog-choked lanes linking traffic from the Holland Tunnel and New Jersey in the west with the Manhattan Bridge and Brooklyn in the east. There are whole countries less interesting than Canal Street. As a boundary common to Tribeca, as well as bustling Chinatown, picturesque Little Italy, and the fashionable lanes of SoHo, it felt like a Yellow Brick Road connecting all tribes of the new Oz.

Among New Yorkers, however, it is best known for the counterfeit designer accessories sold out of its bazaarlike storefronts. It was the place to go for hot-glued Prada handbags, rickety Chanel sunglasses, and Rolex wristwatches whose freshly printed numbers would smudge every time a hand swept by.

To the south, Tribeca petered out into municipal government offices and the charmless Financial District. With its large lofts and run-down lots available for redevelopment, the neighborhood would soon become a dormitory for wealthy creatives, particularly West Coast transients who worked in the film industry. But at the time, there was little to say about the area except that it had two famous restaurants.

The first was the Odeon, a fashionable brasserie that did a great hamburger that nobody ever ate—popular as it was with both cocaine-fueled brokers from nearby Wall Street and cocaine-fueled downtown writers, who featured the restaurant prominently in their eighties novels.

The second was Bubby's, a low-key lunch and breakfast spot,

where Horacio and I had our first bona fide New York celebrity sighting. Reading his newspaper over eggs one morning was John F. Kennedy Jr., who seemed to be made up of really great hair stacked over a really great jaw over a really great butt. He also had an overstuffed straight-guy wallet that clipped onto a belt loop with a length of silver chain, completely ruining the line—but we decided to forgive him that.

Despite these early bourgeois markers, Tribeca in 1998 was not yet the organic boutique for Hollywood producers' wives that it would become. Mostly it was still a ragtag collection of shops offering discount cosmetics in bulk, party supplies, used books, and really good Pakistani takeout.

Our building, a former industrial space on Chambers Street, had deep lofts with high ceilings. Inside each was an abundance of space not usually seen outside of sitcom New York apartments.

The nineteenth-century industrial architecture didn't admit much light, but its three front windows looked directly up at the matching towers of the World Trade Center. During the day, the metal-and-glass office buildings threw a shifting blanket of shadow over our street. And every night, they were mobbed by the wheeling white specks of dozens of seagulls, beglamoured and disoriented by its floodlights.

Seen from a distance, the towers were two enormous, out-of-proportion blocks whose weight threatened to tip lower Manhattan into the harbor. I remember thinking that it would be impossible to deconstruct buildings so large, and that they would probably just have to stand there forever, like goalposts for some forgotten sport of the gods.

Up close, they more closely resembled a 110-story pair of legs. And when low evening clouds settled over the tops of them like a skirt, it gave the disconcerting impression that if you were to look up, you might see a vast pair of knickers.

Their scale gave a thrill to life in the neighborhood. Scurrying around the toes of those giants, while their attention was absorbed elsewhere, in the important business of making money, it always felt like you were getting away with something.

Lee had a great feeling for the exotic characters who flourished in those streets. One of her discoveries was the future film actress and hell-raiser Paz de la Huerta. Lee profiled her as an up-and-coming style icon when she was still just a neighborhood teenager who liked to dress sloppily in hand-me-down court finery inherited from her father, a Spanish duke.

The shadows of lower Manhattan were full of such protean characters, like creatures living in the undergrowth. Often they were the children of loft-dwelling artists who had settled the area in its frontier years of the 1970s and '80s. Back then, a youngster could still be snatched on the way to school—like six-year-old Etan Patz, whose disappearance one morning in 1979 has been felt like a missing limb ever since.

So the menace of those streets was real, and its denizens had earned their wariness. Nonetheless, they flourished and grew colorful in the shade. Lee taught me that such fabulous nobodies could be found everywhere in New York, if you developed an eye for them.

Older people kept telling us we'd "missed" New York.

The generation who remembered the sixties and seventies was always talking as if New York had come and gone like a bus, carrying with it the last punk rockers and Greenwich Village folk singers and crusty second-wave feminists who had ever made the place interesting.

Some who remembered the eighties felt that AIDS had swept away the city's artists—and a large portion of their audience—leaving the city broken in ways that couldn't be fixed. Others blamed Rudy Giuliani, a right-wing former prosecutor who had become the first Republican mayor of New York since 1971. His conservative caprices included enforcing an archaic law, long ignored by his predecessors, that barred dancing in bars or clubs that hadn't paid for an expensive "cabaret license."

"It's over," they'd say, mourning not only the big, bygone clubs like Studio 54 and Max's Kansas City but also smaller neighborhood dens like Save the Robots in the East Village.

But the city, then as always, belonged to the young, and late-nineties New York was just as exhilarating as it had always been. Horacio was a great dancer, which was helpful—I dance like a teacher on prom night—since it impelled us to get out and discover the nightlife.

It was the twilight of the massive Manhattan dance palaces, which to a new arrival felt more like cities than nightclubs. Tunnel, a Notre Dame of dingy Tenth Avenue, was so big it had train tracks running down its main hall left over from its former life as a warehouse.

Inside, it had as many rooms as there were mirrors on a disco ball, including a retro-futuristic lounge designed by the artist Kenny Scharf, which felt like something out of the Jane Fonda sci-fi sex comedy *Barbarella*; a library; a dungeon; and bathrooms that were shockingly, transgressively, wonderfully unisex.

We also went to Roxy, an appealingly cheesy roller rink in Chelsea that turned into a dance floor on Saturday nights, and Twilo, a cavernous, aneurism-inducingly loud nightclub a few blocks away. Escuelita, a queer Latin nightclub on a dark block in Hell's Kitchen, had the best music and drag shows in the city. The Web, its complement on the east side, served the queer Asian community.

One night Horacio recognized Willi Ninja, an originator of vogueing and one of the stars of the 1990 documentary *Paris Is Burning*, working the door at Café con Leche, a Sunday dance party in Times Square. We got to chatting and took his number.

And we met Justin Vivian Bond, the gender-transcending visual artist and singer who, at the time, hosted a party called Foxy at the Cock, a gay bar on Avenue A. For a small cover charge, each participant was given a hundred dollars in play money, with a cash prize going to the person who had accumulated the most "Foxy dollars" by the end of the evening.

This inspired a fair number of transactional sex acts, not all of

them conducted in private. But there was also a performance component, where people would collect donations in exchange for committing outrageous feats onstage.

Some of them got repetitive—like the guy who came every week
because he liked drinking a mason jar of his own urine in public. But
only once did I see a young woman, naked except for a veil covering
her face, hold a Barbie doll between her bare feet and incinerate it
using an aerosol can and a Zippo lighter.

The cops raided Foxy almost out of existence, but not for the nu-
dity, the fire hazard, the drug use in the bathrooms, or even the sex.
They came because of the dancing, which the management insisted
on out of principle, even though they didn't have a cabaret license. In
Rudy Giuliani's New York, it was important to commit your radical
acts where you could.

In London, the most important thing about you is who your parents
are. In Sydney, your character is apt to be judged by what you do in
your leisure time.

But New Yorkers are judged solely by their jobs, and all anybody
cares about are the words under your name on your business card.
Without any connections in my new home, I was obliged to restart my
career from scratch, which felt a lot like coming into the city via the
tradesman's entrance.

Then there was the matter of the paperwork. Horacio and I had
both moved to Manhattan on journalist's working visas, which allowed us to report from the city for international publications but not
to hold down a domestic job.

And while my position as the New York correspondent for *Australian Art Collector* magazine was authentic, it didn't pay nearly enough
to survive. So, I started looking for work at places that neglected to
ask about employment status.

My first job that crisp spring was as a sales assistant at a store
called the Big Picture on West Broadway.

The Big Picture catered to tourists who wanted to have their faces Photoshopped onto New York landmarks, like the Statue of Liberty, or even works of art, like the *Mona Lisa*. Guests would stand in front of a green screen to get their portrait taken and choose some artwork or scenery from our stock of backdrops. Then the photographer would digitally extract their face from the portrait and drop it into the new image, for around $90 each, plus $10 a printed copy.

It was a relatively simple procedure that would go wrong almost every single time.

The shop was owned by an emotional husband-and-wife team, aged in their late fifties, named Steve and Sara Felder. The couple were not making a success of the business and existed in a constant state of financial stress.

Steve wore a halo of frizzy gray hair and was constantly peering over the top of his half-moon glasses. He had an impish, lopsided smile that could still excavate the dimples from his cheeks and evoke, for a blurry moment, the college lady-killer that he must once have been.

Sara liked to wear sleeveless cotton sundresses, over tights and a turtleneck when it got chilly. She tamed her tight gray curls with pins jammed in at different angles and was never without a pair of drugstore eyeglasses on a plastic chain around her neck, which clacked against a strand of colorful, chunky beads.

As the store didn't make any money, Steve and Sara would swoop upon any potential customer like prey. They would go in hard with radiant smiles and blistering charm, but anything less than full compliance from the target would quickly undermine their mood, which could degrade to bitter disappointment, and occasional verbal recriminations, in a matter of moments.

As the weeks wore on, the store's losses grew. And I was constantly running afoul of management by making faux pas—like the time Connie Chung, a well-known newsreader, came in, and I failed to alert the bosses in the back.

Steve almost throttled me with his half-moon glasses when he found out. The instructions were that whenever a famous person entered the premises, Steve and Sara were to be informed, so that they could surround the subject and expose them to their advanced sales techniques.

As the financial pressure mounted, Steve found solace in religion. He began consulting with an Orthodox rabbi, who became a regular presence at the Big Picture in his dark suit and smart, broad-brimmed felt hat.

The rabbi was a short, stout man with twists of black in his long gray beard. He drove an old-model sedan the size of a racquetball court, which he would park in the no-standing zone directly outside the store's front window. With tremendous effort he would push open the heavy driver's-side door and emerge from the belly of the car like a freshly laid egg. Breathing laboriously, he would then wobble around to the vast hood of the vehicle and prop it open with a strut, as if unforeseen engine trouble had caused him to pull over in this no-parking area where otherwise he would never have dreamed of stopping. He never did get a ticket.

The store was a hectic environment, but somehow the rabbi managed to dispense Talmudic wisdom in between tourists' grafting their faces onto Michelangelo's *David* or re-creating the pose on the *Charlie's Angels* poster.

A lack of privacy did sometimes get in the way, however. Once, I opened the supply closet to find the rabbi binding Steve's upper arm with tefillin, both of them jammed between the boxes of photographic printing paper and extra pens.

I apologized and stumbled backward, feeling that I had violated something private.

Sara noticed my embarrassment. "It's okay," she said kindly. "Don't worry about it."

One of my jobs at the Big Picture was to help customers select artwork into which they could insert their faces.

The number one seller was Raphael's *Sistine Madonna*, onto whose insouciant cherubs parents would drop their kids. We also did a lot of *Casablanca* movie posters, and middle-aged guys loved putting their own faces over Benjamin Franklin on the hundred-dollar bill. Many newlyweds chose Grant Wood's *American Gothic*, with its pitchfork-holding, stony-faced Iowans.

That's how I came to think of Steve and Sara, the first New York couple I ever got to study up close. They were neurotic, optimistic, indomitable, and inseparable: New York Gothic.

Sara was also in charge of the books, so the store's dire financial situation weighed on her particularly. That stress fed her tic of bringing the Holocaust into unlikely conversations, as a way of having the last word.

After one elderly customer had a particularly bad experience waiting for prints of himself as George Washington to be spat out, I gave him ten dollars' worth of free shipping.

Reviewing the invoices that afternoon, Sara asked why I had given such a discount.

I explained the customer had been made to wait a long time, "and he was such a sweet old man."

"Eichmann!" she suddenly responded, her eyes sharp.

From her tone, I inferred that she could only be referring to Adolf Eichmann, the Nazi death camp official who had been apprehended in 1960 while posing as a genial duffer.

"Eichmann was 'a sweet old man'!" she said with passionate disdain.

Not long after that, the Big Picture shut its doors—but not because I ever dared give another discount.

# Buffalo Hot Dogs

**R**eturning to life as a full-time foreign correspondent meant it didn't take long for the money to run out. But connecting with the Australian consulate-general, located in an office building across the street from Grand Central Terminal, helped stave off ruin for a few weeks.

Cultural affairs were handled by a gossipy, unflappable, and extremely helpful attaché named Robert Archibald. He helped pad my income by connecting me with a network of Australian artists and writers, residing in New York, whom I was able to profile for newspapers back home.

The consulate, a hub of Australian life in the city, threw regular

alcohol-drenched parties that ranged from the convivial to the apoca-
lyptic. After one event for the Australian American Chamber of Commerce deteriorated into a food fight—using the catered mini meat
pies and sausage rolls, dipped in tomato sauce, as projectiles—the
consulate sent an email to everyone on its list, threatening to imple-
ment a code of conduct. Thankfully they never did; barbarism is the
only thing that separates us from the British.

It was exciting to meet and write about the fancy Aussies in the
city, like Denise Green, a painter with a sun-filled studio on Laight
Street, and Judith Curr, an accomplished publisher. Another artist
with a studio in the woods of Connecticut promptly contracted Lyme
disease and had to teach herself to walk again by holding herself up
by the walls of a hallway and digging a shard from Uluru (the big red
rock in the middle of our country) into her hand so the pain would
keep her focused.

There was always a subtle dance around the power dynamic, since
Australians place great cultural importance on egalitarianism, which
can be hard to pull off when one party is highly successful and the
other is a nobody. And to have found that success among the nabobs
of New York gave some of the subjects considerable extra swagger.

"One of the things I take a little pride in is that I've done something of value to younger Australian artists, and that is come to New
York and survived," said David Rankin, a rather grand painter who
lived in SoHo with his equally famous Australian poet wife, Lily Brett.

And in their town house, located on the elbow of a Greenwich
Village street, I interviewed Alison Summers, a successful theater director. At the time, she was married to Australia's most famous novelist, Peter Carey.

Peter had just won the Commonwealth Writers' Prize for his
novel *Jack Maggs*, an award that was presented to him, in person, by
Queen Elizabeth. "She said, 'I always wish my children read more,
but they were never interested in books when they were growing up,'"
he recalled Her Majesty telling him during their brief exchange. "'All
they wanted to do was watch the television.'"

Being so close to such power, and the gossip it afforded, felt intoxicating. But despite the extra work, and the temporary access it gave me to refined society, there still wasn't enough money. In June 1998, it was clear that I needed to either get some kind of paying job in the city—immediately—or pack to go back home.

So, I answered a newspaper advertisement looking for someone to sell hot dogs on the street.

The newly opened Mellow Mouthful, as I discovered when I went for the interview, was a literal hole in the wall. A tiny kiosk embedded into the façade of a modern building on Columbus Avenue, it dispensed food and drink from a Dutch door that opened directly onto the sidewalk.

Its premises were exactly as wide as the door, and about sixteen feet deep, with a same-size storage space in the cellar underneath. It looked like a single-lane bowling alley.

Nobody who was legal to work in the United States responded to their ad, and of the applicants, I was the only one who spoke English. PS: I got the job.

The Mouthful's marquis menu item was the buffalo-meat hot dog, served on a potato-bread bun. They were delicious and—according to the upbeat sales pitch—had many nutritional benefits over traditional franks! But the kiosk also sold a choice of hot or cold soup; lemon and orange flavors of San Pellegrino mineral water; and vanilla, chocolate, or coffee frozen yogurt.

The yogurt was dispensed from a contraption that was almost Soviet in its inefficiency. Every serving had to be individually cut, by hand with a carving knife, from frozen loaves that were kept in a freezer in the cellar. Each slice would then be swirled, one at a time, by a rotating screw that was lowered by a hand lever into a funnel, which had been filled with berries or chocolate bars or whatever else the customer wanted mixed into their dessert. And both the funnel and screw had to be cleaned after each order.

The machine was like an old-fashioned printing press crossed with a post-hole borer and made more mess than both combined.

But the Mellow Mouthful was a passion project of its owner. Danny Hunt was a glad-handing entrepreneur in his early thirties, with searching brown eyes and a wide, flat smile. A former Wall Street trader whose grandfather had founded a famous brand of kosher food, Danny's sole ambition was to build an even greater franchise, this one on the back of the healthful bison.

Apparently, his earlier attempt at launching a food empire—a soup cart in Penn Station—had not gone so well. This time, however, he was sure it would be different. He even roped in Jon, one of his former trader buddies, as a partner.

Jon and Danny were a study in contrasts. Danny was looking for a girlfriend and commuted into Manhattan, while Jon lived around the corner with his wife and new baby. And whereas Jon was tall and handsome and used to stop by in his gym gear after work, Danny, invariably wearing a polo shirt that was spattered with yogurt and bison juice, had looks and a build that were more . . . relatable.

It was Jon's idea to go hippie on the branding. He came up with "Mellow Mouthful" as a name to invoke the good vibes of a bygone era. He also suggested the psychedelic logo and purple tie-dyed awning that announced the tiny store to the avenue.

"This is great," said Danny, posing with Jon for an owners' picture under the new awning. "It's going to be awesome!"

Manning the store throughout that summer was me—taking the orders and money up front, serving the hot dogs, and getting my fingers caught in the yogurt machine—plus a Spanish-speaking prepper in the back.

Most of the time we made ourselves understood to each other, although occasionally I would need to call Horacio from the wall-mounted phone to translate. The well-heeled Upper West Siders, stopping by on their way home for a buffalo hot dog and cold Limonata, seemed not to know what to make of all this.

"Is this your store?" they would ask first. The follow-up was usually, "Are you an actor?" After the second no, they would look confused and stop asking questions.

As middle management, I was on seven dollars an hour. But the various food preppers, on their unlivable wage of just four dollars an hour, tended not to stay very long.

The one I liked best was a slightly built twenty-year-old man from Mexico who suffered from alopecia. His name was Nagasaki, which was one of the situations that warranted a call to Horacio.

Passing the white plastic handset back and forth for translation, Nagasaki explained that he had been named after the target of the second atomic bombing of Japan in 1945. His parents were committed communists, he said, and had named each of their children after atrocities committed by Western imperialists.

To this day, I regret not asking the names of his brothers and sisters.

The work may not have been pleasant, but for a New York neophyte, it wasn't so terrible to be stationed on the street for that first summer, getting a feel for the passersby.

I noticed how Upper West Side women would go to lunch with their friends wearing designer workout clothes, something I'd never seen before.

Diamonds as daywear was also something new to me. Engagement rings tended to be modest in the Queensland beach towns where I grew up, but here, women wore ice rinks to the grocery store—often paired with those same stretch leggings and athletic fleeces.

Their husbands, by contrast, seemed more guarded on the streets. After work, the neighborhood men would add an artfully distressed Yankees cap to their suit, pulled low over their brows, like an "off duty" sign.

And everywhere were baby strollers that looked like sports cars and cost almost as much. There was even a triangular model with three wheels, so that you could push your child while you went jogging. What a town.

One day, Harrison Ford tipped me five dollars on a two-dollar-seventy-five frozen yogurt, sticking the bill into a plastic tub on which

I had attached a label reading "Medical/dental." Helen Hunt used to walk past but never ordered anything; I thought it was very sporty, how she pulled her long blond ponytail through the gap in the back of her baseball cap.

In the warm evenings, Jim, an older man who had befriended Danny and appeared to have nothing keeping him in his own apartment, took to hanging out in front of the store. After Danny started letting him have free food, he moved in by degrees, eventually bringing his own stool to sit by the window where I was serving customers.

Jim kept himself affable when Danny was around but behaved like I worked for him when he thought he could get away with it. He liked to call out and offer free food to any of his friends who might be walking by. Relations between us stayed civil enough, but it got to the point that when I saw him walking toward the store, carrying his stool, I would think, *Eichmann was "a sweet old man."*

Danny was thrilled with my work and used to talk enthusiastically about how I was in on the ground floor of what was bound to become a huge buffalo-hot-dog-and-frozen-yogurt chain. As an incentive toward corporate loyalty, he kept offering to take Horacio and me to the stage musical adaptation of the film *Footloose*, which was about to open on Broadway.

"Why is he so keen on taking us to that awful show?" Horacio asked one evening, after Danny had pressed us again to set a date.

"I think he sees it as LGBTQ employee outreach," I replied.

Still, it wasn't all five-dollar tips and free *Footloose* tickets. My first duty on the morning shift was to go into the cellar, which reeked of damp masonry and mold, and carve the blocks of yogurt into slices that would fit into the machine. With a blunt knife, and no guiding marks on the paper sleeve the yogurt came in, these tended to vary greatly in size, which the customers would invariably notice.

Next, I would use an ice pick to break up the frozen chunks of fruit and berries that were offered as add-ins. All that reaching into the freezer would numb my hands, and I often didn't notice when

I skinned my knuckles. When that happened, I just transferred to working on the red fruits, like strawberries and raspberries, until they stopped bleeding, and went back to the peaches and mangoes later.

Something else that wasn't mentioned in the newspaper ad was that the Mellow Mouthful—all hundred square feet of it—did not have a bathroom.

There was a noodle restaurant across the avenue that sometimes— but only sometimes—allowed me to use theirs. If they turned me down, there was a public restroom near Bethesda Terrace in Central Park that was a twenty-minute walk away. That round trip involved clocking out for almost an hour and leaving Nagasaki in charge while I was gone. The solution, as I eventually realized, was making sure the noodle restaurant manager got as many free yogurts, hot dogs, and Limonatas as his heart desired.

Danny maybe wasn't a marketing genius. In July, he put a sign on the sidewalk advertising that the kiosk sold both "kosher and non-kosher food." At the time, I didn't know that wasn't possible in a place the size of a closet that flouted kosher rules by preparing meat and dairy products side by side.

But this was the Upper West Side, so they knew. And they let me know. One tough-minded thirteen-year-old in a navy blazer from Gap Kids threatened to come back with his cousin to set me straight. "He's from *Israel*," the kid added with emphasis.

Later I whined to Danny: "I thought your family was in kosher food!"

But he shrugged and said the sign would be good for business. It stayed.

# 4

# T-Cells on the Specials Board

After subletting in Tribeca, we moved into the first of two apartments on West Fifteenth Street in Chelsea. Taking up an entire city block across the street was an art deco office complex, built in 1932 as a freight-receiving and manufacturing hub. Google—the company that would buy all 2.9 million square feet of it in 2010, paying $1.9 billion—had not yet been founded.

We were subletting from Maura, an artist who wanted to spend the year in Paris with her boyfriend. The reason for that plan did not become obvious until we moved in: the monster building across the street was undergoing gut renovations, involving all-day jackhammering, followed by private haulage contractors' collecting construction waste at unpredictable hours during the night.

What was being carved into the façade, directly outside our front windows, was an ambulance bay for a new urgent care facility. Knocking that into the side of the building took six months—which added a distinct realness to our experience of living in New York, since we were both writers who worked from home.

But we didn't care. There was too much else going on to distract us.

At the end of our block was the Meatpacking District, where sides of beef were unloaded from delivery trucks and hung on hooks beneath outdoor awnings, waiting to be cut into steaks for the city's restaurants.

Their dripping juices left the granite sidewalk slabs constantly slick with fat. Men with rubber boots and plastic coveralls would tread carefully back and forth, unloading pigs like logs from the back of mud-spattered vans.

But the meat trade in those blocks wasn't just at street level. Being almost devoid of apartment buildings, it was also popular with the kind of night visitors who value their privacy.

Jutting out into the Hudson River were piers that had been a popular gay meeting place for decades. Converted basements housed sex clubs with names like the Vault, the Anvil, and the Mineshaft.

And exactly once, I saw a trio of trans streetwalkers scatter, giggling, from a police car as it edged around a corner of the cobblestone streets. With their colorful skirts and shrieking laughter, they struck me as adult versions of the tropical birds that Australian schoolchildren used to be taken to visit on class trips. I was excited at the prospect of living next to such vibrant and oddly familiar neighbors, but I never encountered them again. In New York, the era when it was possible to find sassy hookers dispensing wisdom under streetlights was already over.

An only slightly more respectable scene could be found upstairs at Mother, a queer nightclub known for a party called Jackie 60. Once a year it hosted "Night of a Thousand Stevies," a national gathering of drag-queen Stevie Nicks impersonators who twirled in their crocheted shawls until dawn. On its dimly lit staircase one of those nights, I bumped past Kate Moss, the model, and Andres Serrano, the artist, as if the whole thing were a surrealist independent film with unexpected cameos.

But if the Meatpacking District had a heart—other than the ones you could find lying on the sidewalk, under a carcass—it was Florent, a twenty-four-hour French-American diner owned by an immigrant from the Loire Valley.

Florent Morellet, an HIV-positive artist whose framed maps of imaginary cities lined the walls, charted his up-and-down T-cell count on a row of numbers listed on the specials board. Next to the glass coffeepots, a framed black-and-white portrait of a young cop cheekily reminded patrons to support their local police.

In fact, the police commissioner was known to eat there—sitting alongside club kids who were drenched in glitter and higher than the price of rent. Actors like Johnny Depp and Keanu Reeves might run into designers like Calvin Klein and Diane von Fürstenberg, although they never ran into us. We did see Jerry Seinfeld once.

For all its cultivated chaos, everything at Florent was done correctly. It was spotlessly clean, and the sliced baguettes that arrived at the beginning of every meal were served warm from a heated drawer behind the counter.

Horacio, who was vegetarian, would order something sensible like couscous. But I enjoyed half a dozen escargots, followed by the cheeseburger, which came on a toasted English muffin beside a salad of bitter leaves and walnuts.

One night, when Paris Hilton was still only locally famous in New York as an underage heiress with an uncanny ability to get into nightclubs and dance on tables, we saw her pull up in a taxi. Horacio and I were seated in the back, and she came barreling toward us, headed for the restroom. Unfortunately, she didn't make it, vomiting on the linoleum floor in the middle of the crowded restaurant.

Her spokeswoman explained the next day that she had "eaten some bad fish."

That June, *Sex and the City*, an amusing trifle based on a series of sex columns in the *New York Observer* by Candace Bushnell, debuted on HBO. And Florent was exactly the kind of fabulous downtown hole-in-the-wall where the show's in-the-know characters liked to hang out.

Its impact on the neighborhood was subtle, at first—maybe a few more straight women dressed like drag queens than usual. But nobody minded.

Bill Clinton was in the White House, and that was the year Toni Morrison called him, admiringly, "the first black president." True, he threw the gays under the bus on same-sex marriage. But his otherwise liberal social policies were also dovetailing with a nice economic uptick, especially in the technology sector.

So what if a few elbows-out arrivistes, looking for an authentic "Meatpacking District experience," were bellying up to the counter? Wasn't I one of those, also?

N ot long after the jackhammering stopped, our landlady decided to return from Paris. So on October 31, we borrowed a hand trolley and bumped our scant possessions to a new place, one block to the east.

Every annual tradition in the city was still coming as a surprise to us, so we weren't prepared for the hundreds of people filling the streets in costume, heading to the nearby Village Halloween Parade. We trundled our stuff over Eighth Avenue, weaving between Smurfs and witches, Bill and Hillary Clinton pairs, and a swarm of bumblebees on roller skates.

Our new apartment was on the second floor of a stout, three-story carriage house separated by a courtyard from a taller building that faced the street. Insulated by larger apartment complexes on each side, it was marvelously quiet, especially compared to the construction site we had been living across from for the previous six months.

But while the premises may not have been loud, they were certainly quirky.

Constructed in 1905, the building was subsiding dramatically on its southwest corner, which lent a listing, shipboard quality to life inside the apartment. Anything dropped on the floorboards in the living room would roll noisily past the front door and come to rest against the wall behind the refrigerator. Set upon the coffee table, drinks would tip themselves to one side of the glass, and Scrabble tiles would migrate toward the edge of the board. You had to be drunk to have any sense of equilibrium at all.

Our landlord was an uncommonly handsome literary agent in his late twenties named Bill Clegg. He had an enormous dollop of light-caramel hair, like soft-serve ice cream, along with strong eyes and a nose that were drawn in quick, straight lines in the center of his face. When he met us to hand over the keys, all preppy-slouchy-sexy in khakis and a navy jacket, he kept his hands bashfully in his pockets.

"I hope you like it here," he said. "My girlfriend wrote her novel in this apartment."

Bill lived a ten-minute stroll away at One Fifth Avenue, a prestigious art deco co-op overlooking Washington Square, and each month I would leave our rent check at the front desk.

Entering the building, with its green canvas awnings supported by brass struts, polished wood lobby, and doormen dressed as South American generals, was like opening the pages of an Edith Wharton novel. To a freshly arrived immigrant, Bill's circumstances seemed to offer a model for the kind of orderly life that could be built in New York, if only you made the right decisions.

At the end of the twentieth century, Manhattan looked like a fortified city-state from a medieval illustration. The defensive perimeter of skyscrapers around its island didn't step down gradually on the other side of the river but abruptly fell away to a gentler, low-rise roofscape.

Nine months into our stay, Horacio and I still had never ventured across that river. But our first year, Willi Ninja invited us to a family Thanksgiving at the apartment of his mother, Esther Leake, in Queens.

We weren't prepared for the calm that falls over the frenetic city on Thanksgiving.

The streets in Queens, with their rows of neat brick houses with scalloped steel awnings over balustraded porches, were almost deserted. But at Esther's building, it soon became clear there was a party on every floor.

Children were playing on top of the elevator we rode up, clambering in and out of the moving car through a hatch in the ceiling. I watched nervously as their small white sneakers disappeared into the darkness, leaving only the sounds of their laughter echoing inside the elevator shaft.

Willi answered the door, beaming. He was wearing the high-waisted nineties-style jeans he favored, with a nylon long-sleeved top that hugged his dancer's torso.

Willi had the irresistible presence of a showman—tall and handsome with a body that moved like a fountain, as if his long arms and legs were jets of water. He had a strong, rectangular face and wore his hair long, with a pencil mustache that made him look like a musketeer.

The apartment was full of family, with young nieces skittering between rooms carrying armfuls of cups and plates. Willi, who was six foot three and had a back as broad as folded wings, smiled placidly as the girls ran around and between his legs, as if they were playing in a forest.

One of the children took me into the kitchen to explain the Thanksgiving dishes, some of which I had never seen, like the baking tray full of sweet potato under a layer of marshmallows.

"You never had that? That's candied yams," she said, excited to be introducing a visitor to something new. "You're gonna like that, I promise."

Esther, whose Parkinson's disease confined her to a wheelchair, conducted activities from the center of the living room. She grasped a camera tightly in both hands, grinning and waving it when she wanted a guest to come over so she could get a picture.

We had brought a bottle of wine, but there was no corkscrew in the house, so we went out to wander the streets of Queens until we found a store in Koreatown that was open on Thanksgiving.

When we got back, the cousins were looking at pictures of a recent family road trip to Disney World. Apparently, there had been a fair amount of farting in the car, the recollection of which shattered the nieces into shards of giggles.

After the meal—the candied yams were as good as promised— some of Willi's fellow dancers and *Paris Is Burning* costars came around, and we all rewatched the film.

They knew almost every word by heart, of course. But still, they searched each frame for their friends, many of whom had been killed by illness or transphobic violence in just the eight years since Jennie Livingston had released the documentary.

It made a strangely somber end to our first Thanksgiving in New York. I thought about how this volatile city seemed to be equal parts joy and danger, as we rode back down in the elevator, underneath a tiny pair of dangling feet, the sound of laughter echoing from the darkness above.

# 5

## Party City

very day working at the Mellow Mouthful, I would exit the subway at West Seventy-Second Street and pass by the front gate of the Dakota apartment building. I never did run into the baron.

Outside of serving hot dogs professionally, life in New York was pretty good. In the evenings, I'd wash the flecks of yogurt-crusted M&M's out of my hair and hit art-world and fashion-industry parties with Horacio.

The fact that we were rarely invited to these events was only a minor hurdle.

Gatecrashing is more than just an art form; it is a human right.

It is the fifth freedom. After all, who are these good times for, if not for you?

Or anyway, that was the kind of nonsense I told myself when there was a velvet rope between me and an open bar.

In the beginning, however, we had a mixed record. A notable early failure came in the first few weeks after our arrival in February.

Having transferred from the apex of summer in Sydney to the nadir of a New York winter, we were unprepared for the freezing temperatures, or the darkness that would arrive not long after four p.m. each afternoon.

Snow came down, and then a bitter wind blew it into dunes against uncollected trash on the streets, turning our block into a cold, wet antimatter version of a beach. But this snow was not like sand. I watched first in fascination, and then with growing horror, as it changed color daily from white to yellow to black. I didn't understand what caused that mysterious transformation, but it seemed to contain some warning about the underlying alchemy of New York.

The soles of my Australian shoes were too thin to protect my feet from the cold that radiated up from the sidewalk like deforming gamma rays. And Horacio and I independently bought the same Donna Karan winter coat from Century 21—the designer discount department store beloved of New Yorkers—leading to a nightly fight about who got to wear it when we were going out together.

One night early in our stay, we got word of a new bar opening on East Houston Street. It was called Idlewild, after the earlier name of John F. Kennedy airport, and had an air-hub theme. We weren't invited, but it sounded cool, so we decided to go and talk our way in.

At the time, Horacio was saying he was the correspondent for the Australian edition of *Rolling Stone* magazine. It was an economy of truth, to be sure, but it worked occasionally—most notably at the Blue Note, a jazz club in Greenwich Village, when we talked our way into a joint performance by the timbales virtuoso Tito Puente and the Cuban-born salsa queen Celia Cruz.

(Ms. Cruz arrived in a black limousine and stepped out of it like it was her dressing room—flawlessly made up, wearing a long sequined gown, and draped in a fur coat. As she breezed toward the stage, never breaking her stride, attendants levitated the coat from her shoulders like handmaid sparrows waiting on a Disney princess. The whole fluid movement repeated in reverse the moment her set concluded—the stride, the coat, the open limo door, its smooth acceleration into the night. It wasn't so much an exit as an assumption.)

Our arrival at Idlewild, however, wasn't so regal. We were unacclimatized and freezing, and the wind along Houston Street was slicing us to ribbons. We may have been just a little whiny and demanding.

Just our luck the door was guarded by an ice-blooded Canadian publicist. Norah Lawlor was gimlet eyed, impervious to the weather, and not having it from either of us.

"Australian *Rolling Stone*?" she said skeptically. "You're not on the list."

She asked us to step aside as she let in another couple, and then again for a party of three. If I stomped my feet, it was only to restore feeling.

It wasn't so much a strategic withdrawal as a rout. Denied and dehydrated, tears freezing on our cheeks as if we were plaster Madonnas, we returned home to warm up.

Slowly, I got the hang of it. I started writing a bar and nightlife column, "The Nightly News," for a free weekly Manhattan newspaper called the *Resident*. The paper offered a fee of $40 a column —which it rarely paid—but mainly met the criterion of not asking to see any work papers when I put myself forward for the gig.

That helped with access, to a point. But there was still no way of penetrating the better parties, other than breaking in. In fact, my first great gatecrashing success came by accident.

In the twilight of the twentieth century, W Hotels was a hot brand. So in 1998, when one opened on the northeast corner of Union Square, in downtown Manhattan, it was a big deal.

Casing the joint outside a party one night—keeping a few steps back from the velvet rope, like a wolf at a fence—I noticed the arrival of Lulu Johnson.

The daughter of Betsey Johnson, a well-known fashion designer, Lulu was having a moment as an in-demand socialite and arrived with a large entourage. A solicitous doorman unclipped the rope and let in the whole overdressed crew of gays and girls trailing behind her—including me, stepping smartly like a minor official at the end of a royal procession.

That night I learned the three golden rules of being a social stowaway: dress the part, act like you belong, and always be ready to sail with the tide.

The city's social ladder still extended far beyond what I could see from the ground. But at least I was starting to understand what happened at its lower levels. And the bottom rung of that ladder was the weeknight promotional party.

Above all, New York is a city of commerce. That means there isn't just one event touting some new product every night—there can be dozens. Book launches, film premieres, Broadway opening nights, art viewings, restaurant tastings, album listenings, fragrance sniffings—anyone can throw a cloth over a trestle table and spend a thousand dollars on snacks and alcohol to try to build buzz for their product.

At these events the drinks are free, the food is plentiful, and there's sometimes a celebrity or two in attendance, lured by the promise of photographers and the resulting publicity. Among New York's shiftless class of gawkers, gossips, and boulevardiers on a budget, they're a popular form of entertainment.

The entry level to this dubiously glamorous lifestyle is the store party. Typically held from six to eight p.m., they take place behind the square plate-glass windows of a street-facing shop—usually, but not always, some kind of fashion or accessories store.

There will usually be a young woman checking the names of guests at the door. Working the door at this kind of event is as low on the hierarchy of public relations as the party is on the hierarchy of parties.

Uncharitably, these gatekeepers are commonly known by the crashing community as "door bitches." But this is not just disrespectful; it is also sloppy taxonomy. There are many orders of guardian who might stand between an uninvited guest and his goal, and it pays to know your enemy.

An entry-level person in this role is known as a "clipboard." Her task is to check names off a printed list, keep out riffraff, and call the more important guests forward so they don't have to wait.

The next step up from being a clipboard is being an "iPad," which is the same job, but with more of a budget.

The third rank of door person is the "wristband," someone who dispenses those little shimmery bracelets that serve as keys to the kingdom of the moment. This role begins to have some discretionary power, beyond merely saying yes or no at the door.

Will the wristband deign to dispense a VIP bracelet, which grants access to the private lounge and free drinks? Or will she give just the regular kind, which dooms the second-tier guests to swimming around each other in circles, like carp in a pond?

Finally, after many years of diligent work and not letting in too many crashers, the wristband can aspire to the pinnacle of the profession. This is being a "headset."

The headset is a clipboard with superpowers. She stands at the threshold like Hecate, the Greek goddess of crossroads and entryways, linked to an invisible host of her fellow beings via radio-connected microphones.

There is no one more dangerous to a crasher than a headset, whose all-seeing network can instantly debunk dropped names or claims of misplaced RSVPs. The mere gesture of a young woman touching her earpiece is enough to send grown men scuttling backward, as if repelled by a force field.

Fortunately for them, the night protects such creatures—and there will always be another party. But even as some aspects of gatekeeping vary, others are remarkably constant.

The clipboard's uniform, for example, has not changed in decades.

It is a light cotton dress (usually a knockoff of a Diane von Fürsten-berg wrap) worn under a blue denim jacket, with strappy heels at the beginning of the night and ballet flats at the end.

If the doorkeeper has a boss who's on the ball, she will be banned from chewing gum while on duty. I have found that the presence or absence of gum in the clipboard's mouth is a pretty accurate indicator of the quality of the party you're about to crash.

Once inside, an experienced moocher can recognize other details that point to how well the event is being run. Serving red wine, which stains any surface it touches, is a rookie mistake.

Likewise—because no one hates to wait in line more than a freeloader—there should be no cocktail shakers, muddlers, or mixed drinks that will take a bartender longer than pouring two ingredients into the same glass.

For passed food, the longtime New York publicist James LaForce coined the rule "no sticks or dips; one bite." This means, don't serve anything:

a. on a skewer, as the party guest will then have to find some surface on which to set it down
b. that requires being dipped into a sauce, as that will drip, or
c. larger than one swallow, as that will leave crumbs.

Despite the small portions, many veterans of the weeknight party circuit will plan to eat their dinner from the trays of passed appetizers. Those you can spot, because they will be gathered by the door to the kitchen.

The menus of these events have not generally been regarded as significant sociological documents. There are no middens of New York City hors d'oeuvres for doctoral candidates to dig through, like mounds of ancient oyster shells, to track cultural shifts from year to year.

But anthropologists and journalists both know that every culture reveals itself in its trash. The evolution of the passed appetizer in New

York over the past two decades charts the shifting cultural values of the city as much as any record of election results, real estate transactions, or hemlines.

In the late nineties, growing in popularity with the dot-com boom and stopping abruptly with its bust in 2001, you sometimes saw caviar. This would typically be served on a bed of sour cream supported by either a blini or the sliced half of a finger-sized, boiled new potato.

When the market for tech stocks tanked, taking much of the economy down with it, brands started to economize on both party food and the staff to serve it. So, passed appetizers disappeared for a while, and in those lean times it became all about Parmesan cheese straws, stacked together like kindling in a beer glass at the bar.

As the economy recovered in the early 2000s, tuna tartare came to represent the hopeful new millennium. This could be a little gummy but was redeemed by being served on a crisp waffle chip of fried potato.

Then the times started getting overconfident. Wall Street had a run of good years, engorged by subprime mortgages on Pompano Beach investment bungalows, and somebody thought it was a good idea to celebrate this prosperous era by introducing lamb chops to cocktail parties.

That was a turning point.

No doubt the optics were seductive for a certain kind of event planner: confident men eating red meat, right off the bone. But lamb chops proved to be the ultimate hubristic hors d'oeuvre.

For a start, caterers were often confused about how to heat the lamb—were they supposed to cook it, in those little toaster ovens in the food-prep area, or just keep it warm? So, you never knew, when the tray came around, whether you'd be getting a tough flyswatter of mutton leather or a dripping lipstick of sheep's blood.

And forget messy cocktail sticks; suddenly there were actual animal bones being left around events, stuffed between the cushions of white party-hire sofas or tucked into the pockets of unsold jackets on their hangers.

It may not have been coincidental, after Lehman Brothers and its ilk took the global economy into a nosedive, that mini quiches started to become more popular. Eat that, real men.

Vegetarian options held steady over the years at a choice (if you were lucky) between mushrooms in filo pastry or herbed cream cheese spooned into the curl of an endive leaf. Vegan alternatives only started to emerge in the Obama years.

Not surprisingly, the two appetizers that speak the loudest about personal choice are also the most controversial: pigs in blankets, and mini hamburgers.

When pigs in blankets are served, it is the sign of a confident host.

Everybody loves them. But they also suffer from a stigma of being down-market and out of place at the kind of swank New York City party that might require someone to spell "soirée" on the invitation. Whatever party planner keeps pigs in blankets on the menu has to withstand the shade cast by snobs and anticarb activists, knowing they're doing the right thing.

And yes, the fact that they're best served with ketchup or a spicy mustard might be an infraction of the LaForce Law. But send a tray of pigs in blankets into even the most sophisticated Manhattan party, and it will be followed like the Pope around Saint Peter's Square.

In contrast, mini hamburgers are a cocktail party booby trap. They are likewise universally popular, and at first glance seem to lack the stigma of their frank-and-pastry fellow appetizers. In fact, they are bait set by mean girls.

A friend who worked at the Brazilian embassy in London once told me that while he was studying to be diplomat, the academy threw a dinner for the students in his program. It was full of all the meats Brazilians like to eat: top sirloin, rump steak, filet mignon with garlic. A pot of toothpicks sat innocuously in the center of the table. At the end of the meal, the trap was sprung: any student who took a toothpick and used it at the table had failed what was, all along, an undercover protocol test.

It's like that with sliders at fashion parties. They may look good, and you may be hungry, but there is no coming back from the slovenly spectacle of eating a hamburger of any size. It is etiquette Armageddon for anyone who hopes to have a career in fashion, and don't think you're not being watched.

And that was just at the lowest-rung store parties, where you'd be lucky if the gift bag contained a press release and a tin of mints.

But for a newly arrived novice who had not the first clue about the lethal currents and invisible riptides that ran beneath the surface of the city's social life, at least they offered a place to start.

# 6

## "Chic Happens"

**N**ew York in the late nineties was a confident place. Crime was down, the Dow Jones Industrial Average had been climbing at a forty-five-degree angle since the Reagan administration, and the New York Yankees won the World Series four out of five years in a row.

The symbolic gate to the city, in my mind, was not the Brooklyn Bridge or the Washington Square Arch but the giant, black-and-white DKNY mural on the southeast corner of Houston Street and Broadway. With the Statue of Liberty in the foreground (using considerable artistic license on perspective), the photorealistic city stretched south behind her, all the way down to the World Trade Center at the bottom of the island.

The tall buildings of Broadway itself perfectly framed those same twin towers, just to the west of the mural. Its unapologetic commercialism seemed to turn all the city's public space into a store display: here's an ad for the thing; here's the thing; now buy it.

I loved it. And how insouciantly New Yorkers wore their wealth!

The consumer internet was barely five years old, and the fortunes it funded were puffing up like soufflés. People were so self-assured, there was a trend for grown men riding children's scooters on the sidewalk.

It was a very specific look: it had to be a Razor-brand scooter, preferably red, and the man (midtwenties to midthirties) had to be impeccably dressed in a slimline suit, otherwise the ironic point would not be made. After all, an adult in a T-shirt on a scooter just looks like he's developmentally delayed. But a man on a scooter wearing business attire? He must be fearless but also playful, the sort of person who sees the world a little differently than you and me, to his vast and conspicuous material betterment.

These titans whizzed by bike messengers carrying large orange backpacks advertising something new called Kozmo.com, an online service that promised to bring any magazine or DVD right to your door, in under one hour. Seriously, what a town.

But for all its promise, the internet in 1998 was still like a communist-bloc department store, full of long empty shelves containing not much to buy. Even for the young, it was new; none of us had used the internet or "electronic mail" as students. In college, the closest thing to online porn was staying up until two a.m. to watch the Soloflex infomercial on basic cable.

Email was the first new communication technology since the invention of the fax machine. And just as when faxes came in, it was not uncommon to call the recipient of an email you had just sent to ask whether it had arrived.

This involved using a landline, which most people had just one of in their home. So to make the call, you had to turn off the internet and reconnect your telephone cable from the modem back into the phone.

(Taking care not to knock over the box of floppy disks you had next to your desktop computer.)

If your correspondent was still online, of course, their phone would be busy. But when they did pick up, and you asked whether they had received the email, the answer was usually, "Yes, but I can't open the attachment."

At least the novelty of email meant that spam wasn't yet ubiquitous. In fact, the most common kind of internet spam back then came to your actual physical mailbox: an unsolicited compact disc containing browser software to go along with a free month of dial-up access offered by AOL. The music of that dial-up, emitted by wood-burning 56K modems, epitomized all the excitement and anticipation of getting online—especially since it didn't always work the first time. The sound went through four distinct phases.

The first was ten R2-D2–like bloops as the modem dialed the phone number of your local internet provider. If you connected—and that was the part you sometimes had to try more than once, occasionally by switching to a different number—it was followed by several seconds of intensely unpleasant audio feedback, like a faulty microphone embedded in your ear canal.

Next came a sound like a cartoon pogo stick—two springy doinks—as the calling and receiving modems established the carrier frequency. If all that worked, the final phase was more feedback, like something metal being put through a meat grinder, which would finally smooth out into a kind of oceanic white noise.

Perhaps that aural illusion of crashing waves was why, in those days, we didn't browse the internet, we "surfed" it.

Even the word "blog" was still years away from being coined. But we did refer to the "information superhighway" on which we . . . um, surfed. And suddenly everything to do with the internet had the prefix "cyber-."

Once online, you could go "cyber-shopping," although for not much more than delivery of a magazine or a DVD, as long as you weren't in a hurry.

Or, you could hang out in a "cybercafé"—which meant online chat room, before it came to mean a sketchy storefront where you could buy warm cans of Coke while using gross public internet terminals. There, if you were lucky, you could engage in "cybersex"—an undefined pastime that was a leading techno-moral panic of the late twentieth century.

There wasn't much to read, however. Many print publications hadn't yet migrated to the web—suspecting that the whole thing was just a passing fad, like 3-D films or Smell-O-Vision.

What could they possibly publish on this strange new medium? Connections were too slow for video, and even photographs loaded line by line, as if they were being loomed into being by tiny weavers.

The moment favored writers, in a way we took for granted at the time. The internet was still more like a page than a screen, and a few lines of text were the perfect medium of entertainment.

It was a period when writing and imagery were still valued in their own right. Soon enough, conglomerates and social media overlords would decide that what was really important about the internet was its pipes and platforms—and that any words and pictures they conveyed could merely be supremely fungible "content."

But in 1998, the internet was still waiting for somebody to come along and drop a few gags on it.

**A**mong the dozens of parties held during the New York Fashion Week of spring/summer 1998, exactly two of them offered an email address through which to RSVP.

We weren't invited to either but responded to both. Only one—for an online fashion magazine called *Hint*—said yes.

Hintmag.com was one of the first internet-only fashion magazines. And as many of the best-known print publications, like *Vogue*, didn't have websites, online early adopters had the space almost to themselves.

*Hint* was founded in 1997 by Lee Carter, a young Californian with considerable flair who had moved east after performing in the clubs of San Diego and Los Angeles under the nom-de-drag Aesthetica. He lived across the street from our listing apartment in Chelsea, and we became close friends.

Like Horacio, Lee was a fashion autodidact who could read its images as clearly as if they were words. I knew nothing about fashion and used to repeat that as if it were dogma—mainly as a way to excuse myself from their conversations.

But by watching and listening, I picked up a few things. Such as, the correct way to parse a fashion magazine is to lay it on a flat surface and swipe the pages violently from right to left, at speed, as if you're angry at them. The ads are as important a text to understand as the editorials. Only ever refer to Alexander McQueen, the person, as "Lee." And fashion people don't wear pants. They wear "a pant."

Observing how they analyzed the industry and its media, I realized that the way to understand fashion is by deciding you understand it.

If you can look at a photograph and describe an outfit, even in the most rudimentary terms—its colors, the type of fabric, whether or not you like it and why—then congratulations, you understand fashion.

*Hint* published runway reviews, designer interviews, a shopping column, and party pictures. Melissa de la Cruz, who would become a bestselling author of young adult fiction, was then serializing her first novel, *Cat's Meow*, on the site. (And crashing parties by claiming to be the niece of the former Philippines president Corazon Aquino.)

Horacio suggested that *Hint* add a gossip column. The fashion industry was awash in money and privilege, enabling the most outlandish behavior by magisterial supermodels, entitled editors, and indulged multimillionaire designers.

We were going out most nights and seeing these antics firsthand, from the flagrant drug use to the public dressing-down by fashion's aristocrats of their perceived inferiors. A gossip column seemed like the perfect vessel into which to decant all the blood from the backstabbing fashion party scene.

Also, we had the field to ourselves. In addition to a relative lack of competition from the underdeveloped fashion internet, there weren't any rivals in print.

The late nineties were a strangely serious time in media. The brilliant, culture-skewering *Spy* magazine published its last issue in 1998, and mainstream fashion publishing was covering the industry with unctuous reverence.

The reason was advertising dollars, of course—*Vogue* never published a negative word about a designer or even a collection in case its house stopped buying pages. The fashion industry, and the outsized egos behind it, was going almost completely unexamined by its own media.

That wasn't our style. We found ourselves with access to this absurd world of wealth and celebrity, an Australian sense of humor, and nothing to lose. It seemed like the perfect opportunity to make some mischief.

Horacio came up with a name for the column: "Chic Happens." Lee designed it in a jaunty mix of watermelon, lemon, and peach hues, each item set on an alternating stripe of color. I did half the journalism and most of the jokes.

The first weekly installment of "Chic Happens" was published in August 1998. It kicked off with an item about Claudia Schiffer—a German supermodel not known for her intellectualism—under a headline that announced the tone of the column: "Schiffer Brains."

So yes, it was a bit snarky. And it was also an immediate hit.


People get a certain, very specific look in their eye when they're about to ask.

First, they search your face for clues. For what, I'm never sure—character, maybe? And often their brow furrows and their voice lowers as they get closer to letting loose that most commonly asked question: "How do you get your gossip?"

Then they don't believe the answer.

Because what nobody tells you about being a gossip columnist is how easy it is. When people know you're in the business of being indiscreet, they seek you out to tell secrets.

Knowing something of interest exerts a unique pressure on the human mind. The juicier the tidbit, the harder it pushes to be released, like an alien baby buried deep in the prefrontal cortex, desperate to come bursting through bone and flesh, singing show tunes.

Part of that is evolutionary conditioning—undermining a member of the tribe who has greater status can confer a competitive advantage. And part of it is brain chemistry—gossiping releases the feel-good hormone, oxytocin. The combination of those factors means that we are, as a species, hardwired to gossip.

That said, there are certain tactical considerations that can help you be a better gossip columnist when out in the field.

Standing by a large quantity of free alcohol (and, preferably, not falling in) certainly helps. For that reason, the humble store party, with all its underbaked glamour, was the essential forum for collecting gossip in New York City.

Its open bar serves the purpose of the fountain in the public square, attracting the thirsty townsfolk. And if there are people who can keep their secrets in the presence of a gossip columnist after two glasses of tepid, overwooded California chardonnay, then they are hanging out in better places than this.

Hygiene counts, too. From one veteran entertainment reporter who was known as much for attending every party as for his halitosis, I learned the importance of brushing my teeth before heading out to events in the evening. If you want people to whisper things in your ear, they need to be able to stand next to you without recoiling.

Finally, the sources need to know that, once they get the hormone rush of telling what they know, the information will actually appear. Nobody wants to stab Caesar with a banana—the satisfaction for the conspirator is in the spectacle of the outcome.

In fact, as a greenhorn gossip columnist, I often found that the ancient Romans provided a useful model. Their histories provide precedent for any outrageous act of human behavior you might encounter.

Whenever I was trying to decide whether to trust some anecdote that I picked up at a party, my first question was always, is it within human nature? Followed by, has it happened before?

Because most of the ridiculous antics of today's ruling class chronicled in the tabloids are right there in *The Lives of the Twelve Caesars*—copyright Suetonius, AD 121. And Tacitus's *The Annals* is a nonfiction *Game of Thrones*, only with more sex and violence, and better gossip.

Not only is the work of these historians highly entertaining to read, it also reassures us that human nature is constant over time and place—especially when it comes to the sins and vanities of the powerful.

Suetonius tells us that Julius Caesar was so sensitive about his thinning hair—"since he found that it was often the subject of the gibes of his detractors"—that he had a comb-over, which people only found funnier. And the reason he was so attached to that famous laurel wreath was that it covered up his receding hairline.

Tyrants and comb-overs, it seems, have gone together for two thousand years, and it's never not funny. Many other writers, over those same centuries, have adopted a similar approach to chronicling the celebrities of their time.

Gertrude Stein's 1933 success *The Autobiography of Alice B. Toklas* is nothing but gossip from start to finish. She is wildly indiscreet about the jealousies and infidelities among her set of writers and artists in early-twentieth-century Paris, naming—and annoying—Pablo Picasso, Henri Matisse, and Ernest Hemingway, among others.

The composer Ned Rorem continued the name-dropping in his frank series of memoirs, starting with *The Paris Diary*, published in 1966.

Stein and Rorem are themselves pilloried in Truman Capote's career-ending bonfire, *Answered Prayers*. That autobiographical novel was never finished, after the 1976 publication in *Esquire* magazine of two early chapters destroyed his relationship with the New York society women who were his patrons.

All writers, including journalists, novelists, memoirists, and play-wrights, betray their subjects. The gossip columnist is no more egre-gious an offender.

As with any other profession, it comes down to ethics. Taxi driver, nurse, president of the United States—any of these jobs can be done ethically or unethically. Gossip is no different.

Being an ethical gossip columnist means being truthful. It also means reporting in good faith, not to undermine another person for personal gain, including material benefit or emotional satisfaction. And it means punching up at those with more institutional power, not down at those already disadvantaged by the system.

At its best, gossip uses truth to hold the powerful accountable for their actions, preferably with humor. It is the modern equivalent of the jester in the royal court.

Lying in self-interest is human nature, and gossip's reputation as the most trivial form of journalism allows it to act like a canary in a coal mine, releasing a steady stream of news and anecdotes about the elites that illustrates their character on a human level. If this is done scrupulously, those small pieces of the puzzle add up to something far larger.

Is all that a post facto moral justification for something I did mainly because it was fun? Absolutely. It also may be a minority opin-ion: Dante reserved his ninth and direst circle of hell for treachery, for which being a gossip columnist probably qualifies.

But to answer the question "How do you get your gossip?": stand up straight, brush your teeth, and look like the kind of person who might be in the market for a funny story about a famous person.

Human nature will do the rest.

E verything about the city that first year was surprising and won-derful.

The subway was a revelation: an entire canal boat system, installed in the sewers. It was an adult version of the "It's a Small World" boat ride I remembered from a visit to Disneyland as a child in the 1970s, except with rats and knives instead of dolls and cultural stereotypes.

I loved the feeling of having textured subway tokens among the smooth change in my pocket. They were tactile proof of New York, and it was irresistible to keep rubbing them together like coins to pay the underworld boatman, Charon.

Certainly, in summer, the subway platform felt as hot and damp as a riverbank in Hades. And when they slithered out of their labyrinth, the trains bore mysterious names freighted with myth. Where was "Far Rockaway," and what marvelous things happened there?

The people in the cars hummed a constant human melody. You could close your eyes and hear Brazilian Portuguese, whose round vowels sounded like thick stew, bubbling in a pot, or the no-nonsense country French of the Quebecois. The subway mariachis, with their guitars and special-occasion sombreros, who brought such brief, intense bursts of joy. Learning to duck when someone from one of the wandering troupes of acrobatic dancers yelled, "Showtime!"

There was a particular kind of thin, middle-aged white man who brought his bike onto the train at rush hour and always looked angry. The Hispanic baby girls in their strollers, who already had their ears pierced. And all the young women on their way home to Harlem, each one wearing jeans or a puffer jacket by Baby Phat, or its cat logo in large gold hoops hanging from their ears. The subway is how New York explains itself to you.

Not every aspect of the city was such an open book, however. Celebrity, and specifically what it meant *here*, was something I had to learn how to read.

The first "famous" person I encountered closely enough to make small talk with was Monica Lewinsky. At the time, her affair with President Clinton was still the biggest story in the country, and she was at the height of her notoriety.

In Washington, fallout from Clinton's lying about the affair had led to his impeachment on charges of perjury and obstruction of justice. But in New York, Monica was courting the press to launch a line of handbags. One night, she held a party to promote the range not far from her apartment in Greenwich Village.

Beyond the occasional thrill of handing a hot dog to a movie star, I was not accustomed to meeting famous people. My first reaction, after Monica's publicist introduced us, was to be paralyzed by dissonance.

In that media-saturated, post-Warhol city, to encounter someone so famous was like meeting the ghost of her publicity. To my brain, which was lagging several moments behind events on the ground, Monica seemed more like a facsimile of her media profile than a human being.

And of course, she was selling her handbags, in that New York way. Here's an ad for the thing; here's the thing; now buy it.

At the party, Monica was constantly being photographed. She would pose with one of her handbags clutched high on her chest, so the label would be just under her chin in the picture.

She was great fun and had a wicked sense of humor. As we chatted, I made some joke and she good-naturedly smacked me with the bag she was carrying, which was by far the most exciting thing that had ever happened to me.

"Monica Lewinsky hit me with her handbag," I wouldn't stop bragging for months afterward.

That party rebooted my head in two ways. First, it got me over the jolt of strangeness that is so disorienting when a civilian meets a star.

Encountering a celebrity is like watching a film with 3-D glasses. The brain has to merge two stereoscopic images—the person and the persona—into the single figure who is standing in front of you. It's never not weird, and one of the joys of New York is watching tourists fall to pieces on the street when they spot some unemployed actor from a bygone sitcom. I just learned how to fall apart on the inside, and make it quick.

Second, more subtly, meeting Monica gave a seismic nudge to my unconscious prejudices about polite society. I had arrived with bags packed full of middle-class, twentieth-century values, which were not especially kind to so-called scarlet women.

Shouldn't a "girl" in her position, I thought, just crawl under a rock from sheer embarrassment? Surely, the only seemly course of action for the exposed mistress of a powerful man was to disappear.

But clearly, that was not how people did it here.

Meeting her was a lesson in how differently scandal and celebrity worked in this strange new culture. Rather than trying to avoid the spotlight, here she was running toward it, complete with a publicist and a plan to monetize her newfound notoriety with product.

Wasn't launching a handbag line a little shameless, under the circumstances? Not in this city, apparently.

Slowly, like I was puzzling over strange colors in the snow, I began to understand. She wasn't being shameless; she was refusing to carry the shame others were heaping on her. She was choosing to stand her ground, rather than be erased.

That's how it worked in New York. Here, behavior other places might regard as "shameless" is just refusing to be shamed.

Truly, this city operated on different rules than any place I had ever known.


D espite an increasingly interesting social life, I was still working for minimum wage selling yogurt and hot dogs. So there was plenty of time to ponder these new social mores while propped on my forearms, leaning over my Dutch door on Columbus Avenue. I would come to work in the day full of stories about the previous night's parties, and after my shift I would bandage my bleeding knuckles and go out to do it all again.

Surely there had to be a better way.

Finally, I saw an advertisement placed by an uptown gallery that was looking to hire an assistant. The art world, I hoped, might be a place where perhaps they didn't look too closely at employment papers.

A few months previously, I had profiled John Dugdale, a photographer who had gradually lost his sight until he was almost completely blind but continued to take pictures of himself and familiar objects from his home.

I had gotten along well with the owners of the photography gallery that represented him, so I contacted them and asked if they could give me an introduction.

"Don't go to work for them," came the response. "Come work for us."

It was an opportune time to leave the Mellow Mouthful. Not only was hand-cranked frozen yogurt not setting the food scene on fire, but the pressure of running a business was getting to the partners.

After arriving for the morning shift one swelteringly humid week in August, Nagasaki pointed to the white handset on the wall. "Call Horacio," he said.

Through translation, I learned that there had been a scene the night before. Danny and Jon had been hanging out in front of the store on a sticky night, the kind that sets everyone on edge. Danny felt Jon's wife wasn't being supportive of the business, went the story. And maybe he had said something unkind about her to Jon.

So, Jon took a swing at him. And Danny took a swing back. Neither connected, but there was a scuffle on the sidewalk—all under the tie-dyed good vibes of the Mellow Mouthful awning. I gave two weeks' notice and prepared for my new gig sitting in the window of a photography gallery in Chelsea.

The Wessel + O'Connor gallery, owned by business-and-life partners John Wessel and Billy O'Connor, on West Twenty-Sixth Street, was very, very gay.

Some of it was highbrow—like its exhibitions of works by Jean Cocteau. And some of it was less so, like Jim French, a photographer best known for his male nudes in *Colt* magazine.

In the middle was vintage work by artists including Horst P. Horst, Wilhelm von Gloeden, Peter Hujar, and David Wojnarowicz, plus a lot of fun physique photography from mid-century artists like Bob Mizer and Bruce of Los Angeles, who would meet young men just off the bus from the Midwest and persuade them to pose in G-strings for the camera.

Of the gallery's contemporary artists, its biggest seller was Dugdale, who created blue and white cyanotypes using large glass-plate
negatives from antique cameras.

It also represented Mark Beard, a multimedia artist who painted
in several different styles using various pseudonyms. His most popular works were large-scale canvases of male athletes that were purported to be 1920s sporting club portraits, made under the name
Bruce Sargeant, for whom he had created an extensive fictional biography.

As an assistant director responsible for selling them, I had to get
customers on the hook for their several-thousand-dollar price tag,
then tell them before taking the money that Bruce Sargeant didn't
exist. Despite the jazz-era dates on the wall cards, the artist had not
applied the final coat of varnish to many of the canvases until after
they were already hanging in the exhibition. Surprisingly, I don't recall
a buyer's ever backing out of the purchase.

Many of the more interesting artworks, however, were not on the
walls. Like a pet store that sold unicorns out of the back room, Wessel
+ O'Connor also did a discreet trade in items of gay culture that were
so esoteric as to be almost mythical.

For example, there was an artfully lit photograph of Marlon
Brando in profile—although not looking at the camera, he was clearly
posing for the picture—with his face in the crotch of a black man,
taking the full shaft of an erect penis deep into his mouth.

We also had a grainy copy of the underground adult film made by
Joe Dallesandro, the Andy Warhol superstar who starred in several
of his art-house movies, including *Flesh* and *Lonesome Cowboys*. Although now available on the internet, in the 1990s it was so unobtain-
able that it had begun to pass into legend.

Many wealthy men bought out of the back room, and not necessarily because they were buying erotica.

One of the four Koch brothers—billionaire oil heirs who engaged
in a fifteen-year lawsuit against each other, the victors of which became

the country's leading donors to conservative causes was a discreet collector of some of the more tasteful and expensive photography.

Although he never came into the gallery, one night I sat next to the gentleman at a friend's dinner party. Forty years my senior, he was large and plush and almost palpably stuffed with money, like the jumbo teddy bear that presided over the FAO Schwarz toy store on Fifth Avenue.

After a pleasant conversation, he asked if I would like to accompany him to a film the following week. Momentarily, a door cracked open onto a particular kind of New York future.

I imagined his luxurious Upper East Side town house, lined with the kind of art I knew he liked, as well as summers in the southern European resort city where he had a home. It seemed like an agreeable, jasmine-scented kind of life.

But the problem with waking up to breakfast at Tiffany's is that to get there, you have do what is required the night before. I thanked him for the invitation but demurred.

Not all of the gallery's high rollers were as discreet as Mr. Koch. Its most lucrative client by far was Elton John, who kept a large photography collection in his Atlanta apartment.

Elton bought a lot of Dugdales—he would walk around the exhibition and point at what he wanted, as one of us trotted after him with a notepad. But John and Billy were always trying to put other expensive things under his nose as well.

When he was in town, Elton stayed at the St. Regis hotel on East Fifty-Fifth Street. Once, the gallery dispatched me to his suite with a box of vintage prints by George Platt Lynes, a fashion photographer who died in 1955.

I remember feeling a little bit like bait. But it wasn't the first time that someone had served me up to Elton.

Five years earlier, when I was twenty-three, his longtime manager, John Reid, had approached me in a London nightclub and offered me a backstage pass to a show Elton was playing at the Royal Albert Hall. Greener than the grass in Hyde Park, I accepted.

After that performance—a double bill with the percussionist Ray Cooper—Reid met me in a large private lounge backstage. It was the green room, I suppose, although I remember it as being red, and there were maybe a dozen or so other people scattered around chatting, waiting for Elton to appear.

There was a weird frisson in the air; that night was the first time I experienced the latent, competitive energy of an idle entourage waiting for its star. They were like a bunch of oppositely charged atomic particles without their nucleus—each on edge, all trying to hang out on sofas and play it cool.

Reid had me line up in a row of about half a dozen other blond young men, all of us around the same age. It was only then that I realized that we were being provided to the talent as an après-show buffet. No wonder the other guests in the room were looking at us so strangely: I was a smörgås-boy.

When Elton arrived, however, he was a complete gentleman. He moved down the line, greeting us and shaking each of our hands like Her Majesty at a West End premiere. And if anyone got picked for personal time with the star, it wasn't me.

The afternoon I arrived at the St. Regis with the box of Lynes prints, it appeared that every other gallery and store in New York had arrived at the same plan. Young men were draped like silk scarves all over the room, shooting filthy looks at each new arrival.

I felt the same competitive crackle in the air as I had that night at the Albert Hall—and left the box and scrammed.

Sitting at the front desk of the gallery, rather than operating a yogurt machine, also made it easier to work on my new gossip column.

At the time, there was nothing else on the internet like "Chic Happens." The cheekier we were, the more popular we became, and the more people contacted us with information.

Our formula was to combine modest scoops with outrageous humor. We broke the news that the model Kate Moss was pregnant, observing that any child of such hard-partying fashion royalty would be born with a silver spoon in its nose.

We revealed that Anna "Nuclear" Wintour, the imperious *Vogue* editrix who seemed to hover above human foibles, was having an affair. (And then followed up with an eyewitness account from a Manhattan movie theater of her sharing a tub of popcorn with her new beau, *having not washed her hands in the ladies' room.*)

We wrote about the younger set of avant-garde designers, like Miguel Adrover (known for transforming found fashion into objects in his collections, like turning a Louis Vuitton handbag into a miniskirt) and Ben Cho, who liked to give his friends impromptu stick-and-poke tattoos at parties and died young of a heroin overdose.

Barely a week went by without something on Imitation of Christ, a label created by art students Matt Damhave and Tara Subkoff, who recycled and restyled clothes for downtown fashion plates like Chloë Sevigny. Everyone hung out at Seven, a cutting-edge boutique on the Lower East Side run by Joseph Quartana, who was the first to sell designers like Raf Simons and AsFour, an eye-wateringly hip quartet of perpetually glitter-covered designers. If there was an icon of that micromoment in downtown New York fashion, it was AsFour's circle bag—one enormous round of fabric with an arm hole three-quarters of the way up. All the cool girls with asymmetrical haircuts, pointed tongue studs, and Eastern European mononyms had one. (Later they excommunicated one of their members and had to change their name to threeAsFour.)

Gradually, led by the artists, the downtown scene started to unmoor from its traditional base in the East Village and on the Lower East Side and drift across the river in Brooklyn.

Manhattan was becoming too expensive, and in response, the first hipsters started to adopt a kind of ironic blue-collar cosplay. This included wearing trucker hats, growing déclassé beards, and serving Pabst Blue Ribbon beer at parties, which nobody particularly liked but had the benefit of being extremely cheap.

In response to mild snark about the upstart scene taking root across the East River, some outer-borough colonists started wearing a T-shirt with the silhouette of a Kalashnikov rifle and the words "Defend Brooklyn." Within its own set, it became as ubiquitous as the pashmina scarf, an essential fetish object for socially ambitious uptown hostesses in the early 2000s.

"Chic Happens" skewered both groups, as well as the designers and models who at that moment were crossing into mainstream culture as celebrities.

At Moomba, a celebrity hotspot of the day, we hung out upstairs with models and a moon-faced young man from New Jersey, Jonathan Cheban, who seemed to understand that embedding himself with the gays was the best way to get close to beautiful women. And we made sport of the rumors that Italian designer Miuccia Prada was having an affair with Rem Koolhaas, the Dutch architect in charge of the forty-million-dollar build-out of her brand's flagship store in SoHo.

The tremendous egos present in the fashion industry—combined with unlimited substances for designers and models to abuse—also provided us with a constant stream of feuds and bad behavior to report on.

In 2003, we ran an item about a benefit dinner for the HIV charity amfAR, held during the Cannes Film Festival, at which designer Calvin Klein attacked the insult comic Joan Rivers with a stream of invective.

"You're nothing but an old cunt, you cunt!" we reported his yelling, after she approached his table to say hello.

Joan didn't hear the remark, but she was accompanied by her daughter, Melissa, who told her what he had said.

"Excuse me," Joan said to Calvin, "but Melissa said you just called me a cunt."

Klein replied: "I sure did, and your daughter's an even uglier cunt!"

The designer then abruptly got up from the table to leave but hooked his foot on the chair and fell over sideways. Joan, who helped him to his feet, later acknowledged that Calvin—who would go to rehab later that year—had been "a little tipsy."

Occasionally, "Chic Happens" broke actual news. A patchwork vest the twenty-five-year-old Balenciaga creative director and fashion-world darling Nicolas Ghesquière sent down the runway in 2002 caught the eye of our young intern, Sameer Reddy. He identified it as an almost exact copy of a piece by a lesser-known San Francisco designer, Kaisik Wong, who had died in 1990.

The item caused a minor scandal and started a conversation about plagiarism in fashion. Ghesquière was forced to acknowledge his "inspiration" in an interview with the *New York Times* two weeks later.

Not that he let it dull his glorious Gallic hauteur. Asked whether he thought his reputation might suffer as a result of the incident, the designer replied: "No, I'm known for many things."

We weren't making much money out of "Chic Happens," but it garnered attention. Even as the column gained popularity with readers, the response from its targets was mostly inertia.

We were protected by the newness of our medium and the old guard's not knowing whether something written on the internet was worth responding to. It also helped that we had fans throughout the institutions we were needling.

Certainly, from all the insider tips we were getting, the big fashion houses leaked like Steve Bing's condom. (That vintage "Chic Happens" joke refers to a wealthy businessman who dated several models, as well as Nicole Kidman, before finally impregnating Liz Hurley. We wondered aloud whether that miracle had been entirely intentional on his part.)

"Chic Happens" was one of the earliest successes in the first wave of web-only publications. It had a notable antecedent in "Supermodels Are Lonelier Than You Think!," written by the pseudonymous "Patrick" in Paris, who scanned and critiqued the pages of European fashion magazines long before they had their own websites. We loved Patrick's arch and insightful commentary, and just as he influenced us, we noticed our own style being picked up by others starting out in the wide-open space of online gossip.

Our snarky tone caught the attention of Mario Lavandeira, a young man who was fired from his job at the celebrity weekly *Star* magazine for running a personal gossip blog, *PageSixSixSix*, on company time. When lawyers from the *New York Post*, publishers of the "Page Six" gossip column, warned he was infringing on their trademark, Mario changed the name of his blog to his nom de plume, Perez Hilton.

A young reader in the Philippines emulated "Chic Happens" some years afterward with an anonymous gossip blog called *Chikatime*. Manila proved to be too small a stage for his talents, however, and later Bryan Yambao abandoned gossip for self-performance as the globe-trotting fashion personality Bryanboy.

And "Chic Happens" was a model for the tone of *Gawker*, a New York gossip website launched by Nick Denton in 2002, which quickly became the flagship of an online media empire. Horacio and I, neither of whom had particular interest in running a business, could only marvel at Nick's talent for monetizing what we did as a hobby.

For us, the column was never more than a lark, and we continued to rely on day jobs to survive. Horacio found a position as digital director of *T*, the style magazine of the *New York Times*. And after winning a green card through the Diversity Visa Program—commonly known as the lottery—I left the art gallery to work for a web start-up.

One year after moving into the lopsided apartment, Horacio and I amicably split, moving easily from lovers to friends and still putting out a column every week. We began getting press attention of our own, including mentions in the *New York Times*, and profiles in *New York* magazine and the *Guardian* in Britain.

A picture accompanying a story about us—titled "Gods of Gossip"—even made the front page of the *Australian*, our national newspaper. My mother, who was never a fan of the gatecrashing thing—she felt it was behavior beneath our family station—said: "That interview was very embarrassing."

Elton John's filmmaker boyfriend, David Furnish, flew over from London to interview us for a fashion documentary he was shooting. Between takes, we bonded over how Sting's wife, Trudie Styler, always seemed to lean forward to make sure she was in the pictures when she sat in the front row of fashion shows. And apparently David forgot to turn on his sound equipment, because a month later he flew back and we filmed the same interview again.

With our increased notoriety around the turn of the millennium, we also got invited to better parties. Slowly the clipboards gave way to wristbands.

In the early 2000s, Marc Jacobs was the hottest designer in the world. With his fluctuating weight, struggles with drug addiction, and fondness for dating porn stars (some of whom were, shall we say, commercially available for companionship), he also made great copy.

On the night of his spring/summer 2002 fashion show, a thunderstorm rolled through the city around six p.m., cleaning up what had been a hot and sticky day. But the rain stopped in time for his evening presentation at a converted industrial pier in the newly trendy Meatpacking District. I sat—or maybe stood—somewhere toward the back. Peering over the heads at the front row, however, I could tell it contained by far the most glamorous lineup of any show at New York Fashion Week. In addition to the powerful editors, like Anna Wintour of *Vogue* and Tina Brown of *Talk*, there were around two dozen celebrities of the kind normally seen at a Hollywood awards show.

Sarah Jessica Parker, then the reigning queen of television, was there, along with Chris Noth, who played her *Sex and the City* love interest. They sat near Hilary Swank, who had won her first Academy Award for Best Actress the year before, and her husband, Chad Lowe.

Gretchen Mol, an It girl of the moment, was lined up with Debbie Harry, Sofia Coppola, and Christy Turlington. Monica Lewinsky, newly trim and glam from her contract as a Weight Watchers pitchwoman, arrived with long silver drop earrings and dark curls cascading over bare shoulders.

Jacobs lived up to his reputation for keeping audiences waiting. Finally, as anticipation and celebrity wattage threatened to cook the room like a toaster oven, the lights went down and the music went up.

The collection featured many of the star models, like Karolina

Kurkova, Natasa Vojnovic, Stella Tennant, and Erin Wasson, whose comings and goings filled our column each week. It was a moment when Eastern European models, who embodied the fashion industry's fascination with dangerously thin women, were coming into vogue, and every season there was a new sensation stepping out from behind the old Iron Curtain.

Both men and women walked together, showcasing a season of sixties-inspired solids, stripes, and floral prints in colors like lilac, marigold, and dandelion. By then I knew enough to understand what he was selling was retro-optimism, a style that gestures forward but is actually rooted in the safety and familiarity of bygone days. In this way, fashion is like politics: people say they want the future, but they buy the past.

But it *was* a gorgeous collection. And the response from the crowd was over-the-top fashion-luvvy rapture.

The models trooped back out in their final parade, to thunderous applause. As they disappeared from the catwalk, the designer himself emerged from backstage, wearing strangely ill-fitting black pants and a blue shirt, with his long, stringy hair pulled back behind his neck.

He applauded in return, as was the custom. And after his bow, the wall behind him parted in the middle, opening to reveal an after-party space with long bars, waiting to receive the crowd.

It was a coup de théâtre worthy of his spectacular show. The budget was especially large that year, since the party was also a launch for his first women's fragrance, a sideline that had the potential to generate as much revenue as the fashion.

Among the hundreds of guests who streamed into the cavernous space were yet more celebrities: Zoe Cassavetes, David Copperfield, Natasha Lyonne, Rosanna Arquette in a black Sex Pistols tank top, Tara Reid, Maya Rudolph, Kimora Lee Simmons, Stephen Dorff—even the fading talk show host Sally Jessy Raphael.

Even by the hyperbolic standards of New York Fashion Week, it was a star-studded room. In the throng, I sidled up to Donald Trump, who was between marriages and had been dating a string of models.

That night he was with his Slovenian model girlfriend, Melania Knauss, one of the new girls who had been swept into New York on the tide from Eastern Europe. I watched the couple as Donald chatted with Tina Brown—he was grinning and expansive, Tina cocking her chin as she listened, while Melania silently watched.

She was a closed book and he was a comic book, I thought. That could be enough for a column item.

But there was too much going on to linger anyplace for long. The vibe in the room was frantic and strangely competitive, like a sample sale where the product was celebrity. Everyone was fighting for some limited supply of something, even if nobody quite understood what that something was.

Perhaps there was also some self-satisfaction mixed in with that sense of magic. To be among that crowd felt like a moment of arrival, a vindication of our decision to move to New York. There never had been a party like this, and as it turned out, there never would be again.

It was the night of September 10, 2001.

# PART 2

## Fame

# 7

# Elevators of New York

I n New York, relationships are just real estate by other means.

After splitting with Horacio I needed to find somewhere to live commensurate with my finances, which could have danced on the head of a pin. Fortunately, an artist from the gallery where I worked was looking to rent the top floor of her East Village town house. The lease was cheap, the apartment was unrenovated but had two bedrooms, and it was available for seven months. I stayed for thirteen years.

The apartment was a third-floor walk-up in a hundred-year-old building, with high ceilings and windows on three sides. In the front, it looked out at the treetops of East Fifth Street. At the rear was a courtyard containing one huge old tree facing a redbrick wall covered in climbing ivy, from which roosting songbirds would sing loudly each day at dawn and at dusk.

The 1970s kitchen featured one long, mustard Formica counter-top, which had a section that flipped up to access the fire escape. From there you could climb either down into the yard or up onto the blacktop of the gently sloping roof—"tar beach," New Yorkers call it—which was perfect for sunbathing in the summer.

The apartment had no insulation, so it was stifling in hot weather and frigid in winter. In the warmest months, curtains had to be hung between rooms to compartmentalize spaces small enough for the ancient, dusty air conditioner that hung in a front window to effectively cool.

As I walked through the apartment in summer without any shoes, the crumbling parquet floor would come away in small pieces and stick to the bottom of my sweaty feet. The white lath-and-plaster walls had been painted many times over the preceding century, covering various layers of brilliantly colored lead paint. Chunks of it would break off overnight, so that in the morning, the floor could look like it was strewn with seashells, white on one side but turquoise or pink on the other.

In cold months, the fire escape could be used for extra fridge space, and during parties, we'd chill bottles of wine in snow scooped from the windowsills. The heat came in unpredictable gusts from a centrally controlled boiler elsewhere in the house, carried through bare pipes that tore through the floorboards, leaving holes convenient for the visiting mice.

This was good news, because mice and rats are incompatible. It's a New York adage that if you have mice, at least you don't have rats.

For the first few years I had a wonderful housemate from Sydney, Clare Drysdale, who had moved to New York to start a career in publishing. When she got married at a nearby Gothic-revival synagogue—built in 1849 and restored by a Spanish painter, Angel Orensanz, as an arts center—I ordained myself as a minister in an internet church and conducted the ceremony.

Our neighborhood was full of art and artists. Justin Bond, the trans performer, lived nearby, as did Randy Jones—the gregarious original cowboy of the Village People—who still had his trademark mustache, wore a cowboy hat every day, and was quite likely to be listening to the Village People on his headphones when you passed him on the street. One warm night at Wonder Bar, a local gay dive, I met the young designer Prabal Gurung—impossibly sexy in pale jeans shredded to reveal a stars-and-stripes Speedo underneath.

CBGB, the punk club that defined the East Village's anarchic spirit, was then still open on the Bowery. And actual punks could still be found in Tompkins Square Park, the neighborhood's muddy green heart, reclining on benches under their colorful plumes of hair like Vegas showgirls relaxing between numbers.

Love Saves the Day still sold vintage toys and fan magazines on Second Avenue, and singing drag queens would still serve you dinner at Lucky Cheng's one block over. Most miraculously, there was even a store—Menuditis—devoted entirely to selling memorabilia relating to the Puerto Rican all-teen boy band Menudo.

Up in my new apartment, my bedroom overlooked the Fish Bar on the other side of Fifth Street. Every night around closing time, its drunken patrons seemed to get into exactly the same raucous argument outside its front door.

"FOCK you," the first guy would yell.

"No, fock YOU," the second guy would roar back.

It was the same thing every night, until they were broken up by a cursing neighbor or the arrival of the commercial garbage truck that came to pick up the bar's empty bottles. But I never minded: I didn't want to live someplace quiet; I wanted to live someplace loud.

At a sunny two-top in the window of the Cooper Square Diner at the end of the block, I sometimes had lunch with an elderly neighbor named Quentin Crisp. Although he never became especially famous in the United States, he was a legendary wit in his native Britain.

His memoir of mid-century life, *The Naked Civil Servant*, contained advice against doing housework, on the grounds that, after four years, the dirt didn't get any worse. And he warned social climbers: "Never keep up with the Joneses; drag them down to your level. It's cheaper."

Quentin had been the inspiration for Sting's song "Englishman in New York." He moved to the city in 1981 and lived across East Third Street from the Manhattan chapter of the Hells Angels motorcycle club. In his croaky, high-camp English accent, he liked to describe the bikers who loitered on the block as "tall as trees and twice as shady."

Just before the turn of the millennium, when he was ninety, I interviewed him on the subject of what he remembered about the twentieth century. Despite its being a very hot day, he was dressed in a blue velvet jacket and black leather cowboy hat, a silk scarf knotted at his throat.

"My earliest memory is of the First World War, when soldiers were driven through the streets and girls threw them sweets," he said. "And I thought, They're going to die, what good is a toffee? But I didn't say so, because I was only six."

Over a fried-egg sandwich, he continued: "When I was born, the automobile existed, but I don't think anything else did. I never listened to the wireless. The wireless as entertainment came into existence while I was at school. But I do remember another wonderful invention, which also came into existence while I was at school. It was the crossword puzzle. I still do them."

He also recalled reading Virginia Woolf's *Orlando* in 1928, the year it was published. But the raciest decade was the 1930s.

"The greatest scandal of the century was the scandal of Mrs. Simpson," he said of the woman who would become Duchess of Windsor. "No one spoke about anything else. When you went into a shop and ordered half a pound of tomatoes, before the woman said, 'We haven't any,' she said, 'What do you think she said today?' Everyone was talking about Mrs. Simpson, and I regard her as the first American martyr. Because

Edward VIII had told his father he would never ascend the throne, so all that business about 'I go to join the woman I love' is rubbish."

During the Second World War, he watched the Battle of Britain being fought in the skies above London. "By 1940 the raids had begun, and the east was bright pink with doom, because they set the docks alight and they burned for days. And the ground shook with antiaircraft fire and you could hear the shrapnel falling through the trees and tinkling on the pavement," Quentin said.

"But you knew it was no good standing there, you were as likely to be hit as standing here. So in the end you ignored the war and you went about your business."

He had unexpected and sometimes lacerating views of celebrity. Princess Diana, he said, was "trash who got what she deserved." And the most attractive man he ever saw was Raymond Burr, who played Perry Mason and Ironside on television in the 1960s. "He was so large, and people are lovable by the pound."

And the most interesting person he ever met?

"I think everyone is interesting. Nobody is boring who will tell the truth about himself. And when we say people are boring it is ourselves we criticize, because we have not made ourselves into that wide-open vessel into which people feel they can pour anything," he said. "And in America, everyone talks about themselves. People will tell you the story of their lives while waiting for the traffic lights to change."

Quentin was then preparing to return to Britain to promote his latest book. But he was frail and had hardly any money —he cadged fifty dollars from me to fill a prescription for heart medication—and had stopped cutting both his hair and his fingernails, giving him a witchy appearance underneath his wide-brimmed black hat.

Three weeks later, just after arriving in Manchester and a month before his ninety-first birthday, he died.

The unwanted contents of Quentin's apartment were put out on the street. Miguel Adrover—the designer who had turned that Louis Vuitton handbag into a miniskirt—retrieved his rolled-up mattress from the curb and made a frock coat out of the heavily stained ticking.

He showed it the following season, and later that year the Council of Fashion Designers of America gave him its award for best emerging talent. The coat is now in the permanent collection of the Museum of Modern Art.

The morning after the Marc Jacobs party, I was woken by sirens. That was not unusual downtown, but there did seem to be a lot of them. I was still lying in bed when Horacio called and told me to turn on the television.

My apartment was just over a mile and a half from Ground Zero. I knew I would be filing stories about the attack for Australian news outlets, so I dressed quickly and began walking south on the Bowery.

Forty minutes after impact, the streets of lower Manhattan channeled a human tide, flowing away from the site in every direction. They were plodding in shock as the Bowery homeless missions scrambled to open their doors to offer the refugees water and first aid.

The great cloud of concrete dust that enveloped the neighborhood as the towers came down had covered everyone in uniform shades of brown and white. Occasionally a face had been washed clean by a bottle of water. But there were surprisingly few injuries among the walking—only once did I see a man, the arm of his suit jacket shredded, with bright red blood overlaying the soot that covered him.

Many other observations, however, never made the newspaper reporting. Shock was affecting people differently; I saw one man, caked in ash from head to toe, grinning and mugging for pictures with a pair of spotless tourists.

Shortly after crossing Canal Street into Tribeca, I was stopped by a police cordon, just then being strung across West Broadway. It was a beautiful, cloudless morning, unhumid, with the trees in full leaf. Any bars and restaurants that had staff were throwing their doors open, supplying the first responders.

The last thing I remember before heading back uptown was seeing three firefighters at a tall bar table on the sidewalk, heavy gear discarded around them, drinking beers and laughing. Because they didn't know.

The frivolous end of the media spectrum—like fashion gossip columnists, for example—didn't know either. But we did understand that it was not a moment we were needed.

Snark and irony disappeared from the culture overnight; Horacio and I took an extended break from "Chic Happens." But it was not just the media that lost a layer of froth: adults on Razor scooters and hipsters in "Defend Brooklyn" T-shirts also vanished from the streets.

Three days later, twenty-five hundred meters from where I lived, George W. Bush stood on a pile of smoldering rubble and spoke into a megaphone. Other days, according to the wind, my East Village apartment would be within the smoke plume emanating from the ruins, which continued to burn for months to come.

Many small businesses failed while the fires burned, including *Jalouse*, the fashion magazine I was writing for. And yet, the scene came roaring back to life relatively quickly. After a month of trauma, the parties started up again, and "Chic Happens" returned.

For a year after the event, any New York firefighter in dress uniform could walk through the velvet rope into any fancy party in the city. They weren't just heroes but sex symbols, devoured whole by women.

During a fashion party at the Bryant Park Hotel six months after 9/11, I watched as one physically unassuming fireman, mustached and middle-aged, sat on a banquette between two young women in tight party dresses, necking with each of them like a teenager. It was the city's yin and yang, the balance between sex and death, restoring itself.

As the traumatized culture lurched back into equilibrium, the demand for the kind of silliness Horacio and I purveyed seemed to be greater than ever. Around this time, we were contacted by a London-based television production company called Shine. Two producers, Christa and Angus, would be visiting New York, they said, and could they take us out to dinner?

We met them at Pastis, a clattery French brasserie clad in noise-amplifying white tile that had opened in the gentrifying Meatpacking

District. It drew a mixed crowd of celebrities and Eurotrash, as well as side-eyed glances from the motley patrons of Florent, farther down the block.

Christa, the senior producer, entertained us with stories from her career—she had been responsible for a top-rated British daytime talk show, whose high-strung host she had to calm down before they went on air each day by trilling dolphin noises. She also had a new boyfriend who believed in the health benefits of drinking his own urine and was trying to introduce her to the lifestyle.

About thirty minutes into the meal, they made us an offer. Shine wanted to turn "Chic Happens" into a daily, hour-long show for British television.

These two were clearly insane. They'd known us for half an hour and were already offering us five hours of television a week. Also, we were "bloggers"—that term had only just come in—not TV talent.

This was going to be a disaster, and obviously we wanted to be present for every second of it. So yes, we said, we are available to become British daytime television stars.

That's great, they responded. There was just one more formality. We had to meet the owner of the production company, Elisabeth Murdoch, to get her sign-off.

As luck would have it, Elisabeth would soon be visiting New York, and we could go over to meet her at her family's apartment. She'd be staying with her father, Rupert.

There are an estimated eighty thousand working elevators in New York City, and each ride in every one of them is like a psychodrama from a Bret Easton Ellis novel.

All of them smell funny. The dirty ones are like being locked inside a dumpster, with grime on the walls divided by weird rivulets of moisture, oozing down from the ceiling.

The clean ones are even worse, with stainless-steel interiors so washed with chemicals that passing through them can feel like being disinfected after work at a nuclear facility.

But even having a chance to think about the smell is a luxury. Because that would indicate you're in the car by yourself, with the leisure to notice things. Which you won't be.

You'll step in just as some thirty-year-old guy with a beard and a Herschel backpack is pressing the "close door" button (which does nothing) so obsessively that coffee is spilling from the sippy-lid cup he's holding in his other hand.

The door will be closing just as you enter. It will knock your shoulder, causing you to take one step to the side, then jolt open again. Backpack Dude will shoot you a dirty look and then glare meaningfully at his phone, furious at the wasted seven seconds.

But, just as the doors are closing a second time, a new man will appear. He will be thirty years old and have a beard and a Herschel backpack. He will furiously start pressing the "close door" button the moment he steps into the elevator.

This guy will not be holding coffee. Except he will clock you with his backpack in his important mission to swing rapidly around and attack the button like a woodpecker on a tree.

Phone Dude will appreciate this attention to the task. They won't actually bump fists, but it will be understood.

Sometimes, in New York, you might find yourself riding in an elevator with a celebrity. This is a whole other level of terrible experience.

First, your face will betray you. Your eyes will narrow for the fraction of a second it takes to remember why this person looks familiar. The celebrity will notice you doing this, and you will notice their noticing, and then you will feel like a fool.

The poor celebrity now has to do a little quarter smile of acknowledgment. Not enough to engage with this random person she has found herself stuck with in a confined space, but enough so that you don't go on social media immediately when your phone signal comes back and call her snooty for ignoring you just now.

Julianne Moore is excellent at this smile. I have spoken to her many times at film premieres, and she is one of the most pleasant and patient actresses ever to walk the red carpet. She also gets her hair done on the tenth floor of a building where I once worked.

Julianne is very small and light on her feet and tends to waft, so that being in an elevator with her is like being stuck in a phone booth with an endangered butterfly. There is no corner to retreat into fully enough that you can be sure you won't swat her into extinction with a sneeze. It's completely nerve-destroying.

The next level of hell is being in an elevator with a celebrity at an event where it's your actual job to get quotes from celebrities. This is misery for both parties. What are you supposed to ask them in the time it takes to go two floors? What are they supposed to answer?

One year, while covering the Grammy Awards, I found myself smooshed next to Robbie Williams. At the time he was so famous in the United Kingdom that, like David and Victoria Beckham before him, he had been forced to move to California out of self-defense.

"How's America treating you?" I asked weakly.

"With kid gloves," he replied.

The Pulitzer Prize for investigative reporting eluded me that year as well.

Once, in the early days of "Chic Happens," when I was especially broke, Horacio and I were invited to a fancy party at Soho House, a private club in the Meatpacking District.

Our friend Laura Brown, a young journalist who would later become the editor in chief of *InStyle* magazine, had a birthday that was a few days apart from fellow-Australian fashion model Sarah O'Hare's. They decided to celebrate together.

Horacio and I got to the party early. The other two people who arrived at the party right on time were Sarah and her husband, Lachlan Murdoch, the younger son of Rupert.

The four of us rode up in a small elevator together. Two Australian gossip columnists and two Australian celebrities, sharing the same fish tank of New York oxygen for six floors. It felt like going through a difficult pregnancy.

First, we did the double take. Then, they did the quarter smile. Lachlan in those days still had dimples.

The Murdochs were clearly trying to work out who we were. We were heading to the same floor, but they didn't know us. Were we following them? Maybe we'd just gotten on the elevator and decided wherever they were going was more interesting than our own plans?

As the elevator ride entered its second trimester, I squirmed and moved closer to one corner. Sarah moved closer to the opposite corner. Lachlan's dimples faded.

By the time the doors finally opened, it felt like my water breaking.

I flowed into the room with relief, where *Hint* publisher Lee Carter was already waiting, and went to get us drinks from the bar. The party was held in a space called the Library, which held no books but did feature wallpaper with a bookshelf pattern.

I was pondering this when the bartender handed me three glasses of champagne and asked for thirty-six dollars. Open bars, it seemed, were only for common-folk parties; billionaires didn't roll that way.

At the time, I had forty dollars to my name, and fortunately all of it was on me. I opened my wallet and slowly handed over the bills, watching each slip of paper leave my hand like a novelist tossing a life's-work manuscript into the sea.

As I skulked back with the drinks, I couldn't help but calculate that that round had cost almost the same as I would have made during a six-hour shift back at the Mellow Mouthful.

That day I learned one of the cardinal truths about being a civilian in high orbit. As glamorous as it may look, hanging out with rich people is mainly just stressful and expensive.

There was another elevator to deal with when we arrived at Rupert Murdoch's apartment to meet his daughter Elisabeth.

He was then two years into his fourteen-year marriage to Wendi Deng. The couple had just had the first of their two daughters and were living in a former chocolate factory on Prince Street in SoHo.

The building stood on a block lined with newly planted trees and zigzagging wrought-iron fire escapes. But when Horacio and I arrived at the address we'd been given by the Shine producers, I realized with alarm that I hadn't remembered to ask for the Murdochs' apartment number.

"I can't believe we don't know what apartment it is," I moaned.

Horacio rolled his eyes. "Just press the top buzzer," he said, and, well, yes. Rupert had the penthouse.

Inside the dark lobby was a vintage steel-cage elevator with worn floorboards and a rickety accordion door. It seemed eccentric, even by the standards of SoHo's ostentatiously bohemian billionaires, but what did I know? Maybe all the oligarchs were going steampunk that year and flying zeppelins to Davos.

We got in, and the contraption slowly rattled its way to the top floor as if it were pulling itself up with ancient, bony fingers.

Elisabeth opened the door to greet us, smiling warmly. Then she asked politely, "But why did you take the freight lift?" and gestured very slightly to a shiny new passenger elevator, whose presence on the dimly lit ground floor I had failed to notice.

The penthouse was a triplex, with rows of windows facing north and south, as well as a roof deck on which the original water tower had been converted into a novelty dining-cum-meditation space. The eleven-foot ceilings had exposed wooden beams and were supported by molded cast-iron columns, set off by redbrick walls.

I was struck by the warm blend of Australian and Chinese décor, which seemed very specific and personal. Rupert had renounced his native citizenship in 1985, but here, oil paintings of outback scenes and shelves of Australian books dominated the space. Even the muted brown, gray, and pale green color scheme evoked the parched hues of the Australian countryside.

In contrast, bright jade sculptures in traditional Chinese forms popped against this subdued backdrop. A folded stroller, stashed under the baby grand piano in a corner of the living room, added a welcome messy, human detail to all the curated taste on display.

The couple's daughter, Grace, was barely one at the time. In a small bathroom under the stairs was a gag front page mocked up by Rupert's staff at the *New York Post*, with a paparazzi picture of him holding the baby accompanied by a headline accusing him of kidnapping her.

Such personal touches can be unusual in a city where high-end decorators conspire to make billionaires' homes look alike. The default style of Upper East Side finance moguls, who are some of the richest people in the city, is chintz-covered sofas arranged beneath impressionist oil paintings by the most famous names they can afford.

The other big money in town comes from real estate. Those billionaires, perhaps living out their Ayn Rand architect fantasies, often favor the orthopedic silhouettes of expensive mid-century art combined with shin-height Eames furniture. I was pondering all that and probably looking blank when Elisabeth interrupted to ask what we'd like to drink.

"White wine," we said.

Elisabeth said, "Sure," and picked up the phone.

Cool, I thought. She's calling the butler.

"Is Dad there?" she asked whoever answered. After a very brief pause, she said, "Hi. Where do you keep the wine?"

Before that, I had never thought much about how Rupert Murdoch filled his day. I suppose I pictured him starring in his own Fritz Lang film, casting dramatic shadows inside the lantern crown of an art deco skyscraper, monitoring a constant stream of ticker tape while barking orders into a gramophone horn.

But apparently, Rupert does the same thing as any other parent. He fields questions from his children about the location of common pantry items that are in exactly the same place as the last time they asked.

"Thanks," Elisabeth said. "See you then."

Our hostess rose from her low sofa and found a paneled door in the wall, which gave at the touch of her fingertips. She rustled inside for a few moments before retrieving a room-temperature and rather grand-looking bottle of white Burgundy.

Then she asked me, "Would you open this?"

I took the bottle and wandered into the large kitchen. The first thing I noticed was a square window directly over the sink, which perfectly framed a view of the Empire State Building. Wendi was not a woman I could picture wearing rubber gloves, but whoever was responsible for the washing up in that apartment had a very pleasant spot in which to do it.

There were many drawers full of gleaming kitchen utensils, and it took me several minutes to find a corkscrew. In the living room, I could hear Horacio keeping up his end of the conversation.

I peeled the foil from the neck of the dusty bottle, and then, disaster.

The ancient cork disintegrated at the first touch of the corkscrew, crumbling to dust into the vessel. It was like watching a mummy take a swim. All I could do was hold the bottle in horror as the cork dissolved into the honey-colored wine.

I was already on edge from having arrived in the service elevator like I was delivering a donkey, and now I'd ruined Rupert's bottle of wine. I started to panic.

Frantically I rifled through the Murdoch kitchen cabinets, trying not to slam doors, looking for anything that could help. Finally, I found a glass pitcher.

Over that I placed a paper towel and started to pour the wine through it, trying to filter out the cork pieces. The sheet kept slipping and dropping the brown crud back into the pitcher, but I was not deterred. I would re-decant the wine and try again.

It was while all this was happening that Elisabeth walked into the kitchen, wanting to see what was taking so long.

I can't remember what she said—something gracious, no doubt. But the look on her face was as if she'd just found me standing in front of an open birdcage, eating her favorite parrot.

She made gin and tonics.

After another hour, and a second round of cocktails, Rupert himself showed up. He didn't arrive via the freight elevator.

Elisabeth introduced him, and he smiled and said, "I've heard of you guys," which was fabulous but also a little chilling.

I shook his hand and was struck by the softness of his skin—it was like squeezing a baby's face.

Rupert's arrival was our cue to leave, so we gathered our things and gave the passenger elevator a spin. Back down on Prince Street, Horacio and I managed to hold off until we weren't standing directly under the Murdochs' windows before bursting into laughter.

Unbelievably, and surely ill-advisedly, Elisabeth green-lit the show.

# 8

## The Gossiplex

**W**hile the prospect of a "Chic Happens" television show meant that we might finally make some money out of our hobby, I was still obliged to have a day job.

For the first year I had a green card, I worked at the website of a magazine geared toward the wealthy. While the print version was a dour publication full of practical advice for money management, its online sibling was more of a lifestyle guide for the rich.

The first lesson was, don't call them rich. The polite term, I quickly learned, was "high-net-worth individuals."

And the stinking rich? They preferred to be known as "ultra-high-net-worth individuals."

It was a moment when being wealthy was becoming embraced as a subculture. Until then, the media had treated it mostly as a sideshow, exemplified by Robin Leach's appealingly awful eighties gem *Lifestyles of the Rich and Famous.* Or else it was seen as a niche market that was mostly off the radar, served by the likes of the *Robb Report,* an unreadable glossy devoted to Monopoly Man trophies like six-figure watches and yachts with helipads.

But around the turn of the millennium, something was changing. Immense wealth was rebranding itself not as some arbitrary privilege linked to sex, race, and class but as a bold lifestyle choice. And the rich were coming out of the closet, loud and proud.

At the website, I had a marvelously idiosyncratic boss named Laura. An observant Orthodox Jew who was unfailingly home before sunset each Friday, with the lights already on and no other device she needed to operate before the end of the Sabbath, she somehow managed to also be the WASPiest person I ever met.

Laura had a chic blond bob, wore a lot of Ralph Lauren, and favored understated but expensive European handbags. Whenever a task came up that was mildly irksome, she would quote her father: "As Daddy always said, that's why it's called 'work' and not 'gee-oh-ell-eff.' "

She cast a similarly broad net for spiritual advice, consulting an Eastern mystic about how to meet a husband. He told her that in order to get married, she must feng shui her home. She did, and it worked.

Not only did a handsome businessman roll up at her door, but with the adviser's help, blessings kept coming. Laura was overjoyed when, after getting married for the first time in midlife, she became pregnant.

Humbly, she returned to the master for further guidance. He reflected and told her the child must be named "Kingly Wongmo."

Well, he may have been right up until then, but there were limits.

So when I gave Laura a stuffed toy for the nursery, she named that Kingly Wongmo instead and cut off the guru.

Unfortunately, the website was not going as smoothly as Laura's personal life. For a brand devoted to "high-net-worth individuals," its managers were terrible at handling cash. Within a year it went broke and shut down, putting me back in the market for work.

But I didn't mind. After all, I was about to be a television star.

A couple of months after we met Elisabeth, Shine flew us to London and put us up for a week at the St. Martins Lane Hotel. Waiting for us in our rooms were gift baskets containing organic bath products and vintage hardcover books; mine was a 1929 edition of *When We Were Very Young*, by A. A. Milne.

Tucked inside was a postcard of a saucy nude taken around the same era. "Dearest Ben, Here's to taste and decency," wrote Christa. "Watch that _tone_!!"

It was weird being proto television talent and treated so much better than the world treats writers. It was the professional equivalent of having two-inch lifts suddenly placed in our shoes.

Not that Horacio or I knew what to do with it. A helpful employee of the production company put our names on the list of the Shadow Lounge in Soho, the hottest nightclub in Western Europe. We sat in the VIP room, where the only other person was Graham Norton, and didn't say a word to him. Clearly we didn't have this VIP thing worked out at all.

During the day, we filmed test segments. I managed to annoy my ex–life partner by coming up with the tagline "We're Ben and Horacio. One is smart, one is good-looking, and the other one's him."

The premise of our show no longer had anything to do with gossip, which had proved too risky for Shine's legal department. Instead, we were going to be fashion makeover experts for housewives.

This was about as far from my area of expertise as it was possible to get. One of the tests involved our going up to strangers on the street and giving impromptu makeover advice.

I approached one middle-aged tourist who was accompanied by two young children. She had an enormously enhanced chest and was wearing a tight T-shirt with writing on it that couldn't be read, since it disappeared under the shelf of her breasts. And then it turned out she didn't speak English.

But she responded well to the camera and mugged along with the gag of trying to read her T-shirt. I found the pantomime to be excruciating, but Shine was thrilled with the test. If this was what daytime television viewers demanded, I thought, no wonder its hosts needed to be narcotized by dolphin noises.

*Chic Happens TV* was going to be filmed daily in New York but aired in Britain. We got as far as posing for photos outside the vacant storefront in SoHo that was to be converted into our on-the-street studio. They even pointed out where in London they were planning to put billboards promoting the show.

It seemed that Shine wanted to expand into America on a tight timeline and needed to put an international show—anything—into production as quickly as possible. But finally, mercifully, someone in London realized that none of this made sense.

We were canceled two weeks before we were to start filming, notified by a call on the first anniversary of the September 11 terrorist attacks.

Since being terrible on television was not an experience I had been especially looking forward to, but nevertheless seemed unable to decline, I wasn't too upset. Plus, I had gotten to ruin a bottle of Rupert's good wine and see the Empire State Building from Wendi's kitchen sink.

So, I came away feeling that I got pretty good value out of the Murdochs. And in fact, my next gig was within their media empire.

Even though I still thought of myself as a sensible arts journalist who had a fun sideline writing about fashion, as a result of the success of "Chic Happens," the world saw me as a gossip columnist—and those were the jobs I was offered.

Around 2000 I started filling in occasionally on "Page Six," the gossip column of the *New York Post*. The tabloid newspaper is headquartered in a forty-five-story skyscraper at 1211 Sixth Avenue that also houses Murdoch's other media properties, including Fox News and, when he bought it later, the *Wall Street Journal*.

A parlor game played inside the building is to size someone up in the elevator and guess, based on fashion choices and personal hygiene, where they work.

Fox News employees were unmissable: puffed-up white men in shiny suits and shoulder pads, their female counterparts mostly blondes in short, tight skirts. Everything about their appearance was emblematic of the culture of sexual harassment that festered at the network for twenty years under the leadership of its toad-king chief executive, Roger Ailes.

"Posties," by contrast, were the archetypal ink-stained wretches. They reveled in their tabloid dishevelment. For men, the uniform was a loose tie over an untucked shirt, worn under a jacket with a sweat-stained collar, sometimes with a trench coat that could be balled up and used as a subway pillow after a late night drinking at the *Post*'s favorite bar, Langan's.

From the tenth floor, the *Post* was putting out the mightiest gossip column in America. "Page Six" was created in 1977 but found its stride in the mid-1980s, when Richard Johnson began what would be a twenty-five-year run as its editor.

"Page Six" was about power, and as befitted the column that bestrode the city like a colossus, it took itself very seriously. While the occasional joke was unavoidable, readers understood it was there to lay the smackdown on celebrities, not to have fun.

It was the first time I had ever set foot inside a New York daily tabloid, and based on the fearsome reputation of "Page Six," I was nervous to meet its four writers. They sat near a wall of windows at the end of the *Post*'s newsroom, overlooking a bank of industrial fans.

As I approached, I passed a photocopied notice on the men's room door, reminding employees that it was illegal to take drugs on the premises. I wondered what kind of workplace had to remind its own staff not to shoot up before they went home to their families.

Richard was away when I started—it was him I was filling in for, albeit from the other end of the totem pole. The other staples included Chris Wilson, who was a talented shoe-leather reporter. Scruffy and permanently hungover, he would come in late, having been drinking with celebrities, and his stories from the previous night would often fill the daily sked. (The "sked"—or schedule—was the daily list of the column's stories. It would be filed with the rest of the paper at a daily "sked meeting," so that editors across departments didn't step on each other's toes.)

Paula Froelich was the pit bull. She worked the phones on leads and terrified sources into submission. That first day, she took to calling me "Booger" as a nickname, which I had no idea how to take and made me flush with nervousness.

Ian Spiegelman was a street-smart guy from Queens who was on the next rung up from me as a stringer. But the other freelancer was the most intriguing: a good-looking, prematurely gray young man who dressed in zoot suits and spoke in a 1940s wiseguy patter named Jared Paul Stern.

The costumey *Guys and Dolls* schtick was laid on thick: Jared wore spats on his feet and fedoras on his head, and pinstripes in between. He often featured his wife, Ruth, in his writing about nightlife, referring to her as "Snoodles."

Jared was also the column's number two officer, whose name appeared at the top of the page when Richard was away. Such authority was unprecedented given that he was not on staff but was a freelancer— an unorthodox arrangement the *Post* would come to regret.

Sitting at Richard's desk was an education. His phone rang all day, spewing information like a gossip cornucopia, filling the column without anyone's having to leave the room.

Having the number of his direct line—which I was now picking up—was a status indicator among the city's elite. I learned to disguise my accent when answering, because the conversations with people who thought they were speaking with someone powerful were such fun.

The best part was when they realized they weren't speaking to Richard. Some—usually the women—having begun the conversation solicitously, would stay polite. Others—usually the men—would become testy when they placed me, correctly, at the very bottom of the power structure. These were the kinds of people who were rude to their waiter in restaurants. They had a limited amount of goodwill to spend in the world, and they weren't going to waste any of it on someone unimportant. It is exactly this type of personality that gossip columns exist to skewer.

Answering Richard's phone also taught me about the primacy of the "Page Six" brand. In New York City, it was synonymous with gossip. Whenever anyone, whether celebrity or civilian, heard some juicy little thing that was just squirming to exit their brain via their mouth, it was the *Post* they called.

But on my first day, all I wanted was to be asked to look up a phone number, so I could lay my eyes on the column's legendary Rolodex. In the gossip business, this was a fabled artifact, akin to the Library of Alexandria stuffed inside the Ark of the Covenant. It contained contact information for every politician, movie star, athlete, musician, and celebrity of any stripe who had ever had the misfortune of appearing on the page in its forty-year history.

Finally, somebody needed a number for Liza Minnelli's spokesperson.

"I'll get it!" I squeaked, much too quickly.

I approached the low filing cabinets, which backed onto the row of desks where the gossips sat. Slowly I opened a drawer and gazed upon the mother lode: hundreds upon hundreds of yellowing paper cards, alphabetically organized on rows of spindles. They glittered like gold and smelled like mildew.

After a moment's prayerful reflection, I retrieved the number of Liza Minnelli's publicist and closed the drawer as if I were resealing a reliquary. It was a satisfying first day in the tabloid gossip business.

Picking up irregular shifts over the following months, I gradually found my way in the newsroom. From the more senior "Page Six" reporters, I had feared resentment, hazing, and jealousy over turf. But I learned that gossip writers, like the rest of the city's journalists, are mostly a collegial bunch, even across rival publications. Competence is the price of admission, but if you have that, you will be treated like you earned your place.

I even relaxed enough to realize that "Booger," if not exactly a standard compliment, was at least meant affectionately.

Hanging around the *Post* newsroom was great fun. I was completely enamored with the gruff allure of the reporters, like Dan Mangan on the city desk and Lisa Marsh, a glamorous blonde working the fashion beat whom Dan had his eye on. Very occasionally, the crown of a Murdoch head would be glimpsed bobbing on the other side of a set of filing cabinets.

Sometimes, even more rarely than a Murdoch apparition, the alcoholic star columnist Steve Dunleavy would visit his office next to the gossip desks. Legends sprouted around him like weeds under the park benches he was notorious for falling asleep on after a night at Langan's.

Dunleavy liked to claim Elvis Presley died while reading his own tell-all book about the singer's drug-taking and womanizing. In 2000, he was thrown in a Des Moines drunk tank after causing a scene at the airport on his way to cover a presidential primary. And a reporter who covered a high-profile celebrity trial alongside him told me he once turned up to the courthouse so pickled that he forgot to tuck himself back in following a visit to the men's room, flashing everyone waiting in the corridor outside.

For all its tawdry glamour, however, the *Post* was not the place to set right anyone who had a low moral opinion of gossip columnists. It was hard not to notice that "Page Six" had an ethics problem.

Many of the reporters had side incomes sourced from the same powerful people they wrote about. Jared operated a clothing label called Skull & Bones, which consisted mainly of polo shirts bought in bulk from China. They were available to purchase in large quantities, should you be a wealthy person in need of presents for your staff.

Other would-be authors had deals with the publishing arm of

Harvey Weinstein's film company, Miramax Books, which provided large checks as an "advance." Likewise, Hollywood studio heads would pay writers for ill-defined script development deals. Sometimes the scripts and books would be delivered, and other times they didn't have to be.

Richard accepted at least one cash bribe, a thousand-dollar "Christmas gift" from the restaurateur Nello Balan, who liked the city to know whenever celebrities were seen at his establishment. It was depressingly possible to conclude that such corruption was just how the gossip business worked at big-city newspapers.

Certainly, influencing the gossip columns appealed to a specific type of very rich man who liked to feel as if he were an unseen puppet master, pulling the strings. These men tend to own private jets and large houses in Florida and are often close friends with Bill Clinton. They like to date a lot of models without having to marry any of them.

Jeffrey Epstein was one of them. A mysterious financier with huge houses in Manhattan and Palm Beach, he was constantly on the prowl for young women.

Quite how young, we didn't realize—he would later be unmasked as a serial rapist of minors, including teenagers he lured into employment as "masseuses." Epstein's criminality put him in a different class to his fellow wealthy womanizers, who merely gave the impression of being constantly on the prowl.

Steve Bing, the serial celebrity-dater and Liz Hurley baby-daddy who was heir to a $600 million New York real estate fortune, was a little like that.

Another was Ron Burkle, usually described in the tabloids as a "supermarket billionaire," who at this time was ranked by *Forbes* magazine as the 335th-richest person in the world. Like Bing and Epstein, he was a large donor to the Democratic Party and operated in the same miasma of sexual innuendo and ambient money that seemed to engulf the forty-second president wherever he went.

Journalists referred to Burkle's private jet, which often ferried VIPs across the country in the company of unknown other parties, as

"Air Fuck One." And his liberal politics were enough to put him in the crosshairs of the right-leaning *New York Post.*

He and Jared should have been smart enough to stay away from each other. But they weren't.

Sick of being made fun of in "Page Six," Burkle set up a sting operation. He arranged a meeting with Jared, which he secretly recorded with cameras, during which he offered the reporter a large bag of cash, purportedly in exchange for ending the negative coverage.

Jared did not take the bag. But he did enthusiastically discuss the possibility of Burkle's becoming an investor in the Skull & Bones fashion brand, in exchange for payments totaling $220,000.

Burkle shared the tape with federal prosecutors, and also the *Post*'s rivals, who delighted in running the story over several front pages.

Jared claimed, plausibly, that Burkle had kept anything that would have exonerated him—specifically, his telling the billionaire: "You can't pay for protection, you can't buy it, and I'm not selling it"— out of the edited tape extracts that he provided to authorities and the media. And despite Burkle's best efforts, Jared was never charged with any crime.

Still, it wasn't a great moment for anyone invested in defending the ethics of the gossip profession.

The "Page Six" bribery scandal was simmering while I freelanced at the *Post* but erupted after I had been poached by its competitor, the New York *Daily News.* An editor named Colleen Curtis, who enjoyed "Chic Happens," asked me to be an assistant on their rival gossip column, "Rush & Molloy."

The *News* then had the largest circulation of any newspaper within New York City; the *Times* beat it when national sales were added, but within the five boroughs, the *News* reigned supreme.

Founded in 1919, the paper had occupied an iconic mid-century Times Square skyscraper with a giant globe of the earth in its lobby. With the globe transposed to the roof, that building became the inspiration for Clark Kent's employer, the *Daily Planet.*

But by the time I got there, that piece of prime real estate had long been sold and converted into apartments. The *News* then resided in an unlovely modern building on the corner of Tenth Avenue and West Thirty-Third Street, the last vestige of its history being the beloved newsroom clock, a four-faced wooden box carted from headquarters to headquarters like a picture of Mother.

The offices, on the undeveloped western edge of midtown, were built on top of rail tunnels serving nearby Penn Station. In summer, diesel fumes from the trains idling below permeated the building. In winter, chunks of ice would break off its fifteenth-floor parapet and accelerate down the sloped façade, firing across the sidewalk at exactly head height. And there was nowhere to eat except a demoralizing canteen in the basement called Deli Grandville, which sold watery roast chicken slices and cabbage from steam trays, or else artery-cement sandwiches like "meatball heroes" on white sub rolls soggy with red sauce.

I'm not complaining, I'm bragging: it was tabloid heaven.

Although the paper's staff was not especially diverse, its politics were to support the working class, immigrants, and people of color. This odd disconnect was captured by a maxim among the journalists: "The *Daily News* is read by one million people every day, none of whom you'll ever meet."

The floor of the newsroom was laid with gray carpet squares, lifting at each point, with rodent traps placed in high-traffic areas along the walls. Once I was speaking with the television editor when he opened his desk drawer to discover that mice had eaten all the chocolate from inside his box of Raisinets but left the raisins behind, still in their plastic bag.

Despite a downward trend in the paper's glory, there was still plenty of old-school tabloid lore to be absorbed.

It was public knowledge that the Mafia, through its grip on the unions, had long controlled newspaper printing and distribution in New York City. Some of the otherwise all-male *Daily News* editors were so scared of the printers they would make Colleen call when their pages were running late, in the belief "they wouldn't yell at a girl." And there were a few characters around the newsroom, known only by mob-sounding nicknames, whom I never did get the courage to ask what they did.

Phil Roura, a veteran editor whom I adored, would delight in cornering me in his office and giving me the saltier version of the paper's oral history. "That sofa you're sitting on right now?" he would say, "Mickey Mantle sat on that very sofa and told me how he once went on a date with Angie Dickinson, took her home, and was so drunk that he threw up while he was . . ."

As with many of his stories, that punch line is best left to the imagination.

George Rush and Joanna Molloy, the married duo who penned the *News*'s marquis gossip column, had both come up through "Page Six." There, Joanna had landed scoops like Woody Allen's romantic relationship with his girlfriend Mia Farrow's adopted daughter Soon-Yi Previn, a seemingly unbelievable story that she trusted because caller ID showed the source was telephoning from within their household.

It was a relief to be at the *News*, where journalists weren't taking money from their subjects. Nello also once messengered George a literal bag of cash, which George promptly returned—only slightly miffed at having been offered less money than Richard.

Such ethical calls were not hard for George, a gentleman scribe who had attended the august Columbia Journalism School after growing up in Chicago. He had great patience for listening to sources drone on in their own self-interest, responding to especially useless information with only a polite "Good to know." I made a mental note that this column wasn't as rude to people as "Page Six" and started using the phrase myself.

Joanna was an Irish-American firebrand whose politics landed somewhere between progressive and Bolshevik. She was passionate about using the gossip column as a platform for social justice, including the redistribution of celebrity wealth.

Joanna had grown up on the same block in the Bronx as Jennifer Lopez who was then styling herself as "Jenny from the block." They even attended the same school, Holy Family, some years apart.

Lopez, despite her growing wealth and fame, had never contributed to the school, even though her mother had worked there as a teacher. This was an affront to Joanna's sense of fairness. For years, "Rush & Molloy" ran items pressuring the singer to donate a scholarship, a CD, anything. As far as I know it never worked, but it was refreshing to work for a gossip column with a visible moral compass.

Joanna drilled into her assistants that the purpose of attending these fancy parties and speaking with celebrities was not to be a guest but to represent the reader, the average person, who was not invited.

That is still some of the best advice about practicing journalism I have ever heard.

# 9

# Wanna Hold My Oscar?

In 2003, Horacio and I wrapped up "Chic Happens" after a five-year run.

Toward the end we had grown lax about posting regularly, which irritated our readers, and we in turn were feeling less obligation to produce free content every week. But the column had served its purpose, which was to establish us with paying jobs in New York.

Fortunately, at the *News*, "Rush & Molloy" sat right next to the fashion section. I quickly fell in with its editors, Alev Aktar and Amy DiLuna, which smoothed my entry into the new workplace.

Amy was something of an anti-fashion editor, in that she was far more interested in food than clothes. I admired her perversity. Food was the negative corollary of the fashion industry, the unspoken element that needed to be subtracted in order to create merchandisable people.

There was always a cooking show playing on the television in Amy's office. I would go in to gossip about gossip, as she edited runway photographs from the wire services, and we both picked up tips for caramelizing bacon.

And there was another perk of the job: George had me accompany him on a reporting trip to Los Angeles for the 2003 Academy Awards.

Our first stop that weekend was the Independent Spirit Awards. A daytime awards show for independent films, it takes place every year on the Saturday before the Oscars in a large white tent on Santa Monica Beach.

The Spirit Awards are laid-back in that studied Angelino way, which hints at hours of stylist agita behind the selection of each pair of sandals. As a breeze raked in from the Pacific Ocean, Scarlett Johansson and Daniel Day-Lewis mingled with Julianne Moore, Mark Ruffalo, and Christina Ricci; Halle Berry presented an award, and there was much interested chatter about two young actor siblings new to the scene, Jake and Maggie Gyllenhaal.

I remember the sea of jeans, halter tops, and wrap skirts parting when Sissy Spacek made her entrance wearing a dark velvet pantsuit, peacock-blue sash, and John Lennon–ish dark glasses. That's how a Hollywood legend arrives at the beach, I thought.

It was also the only time I ever encountered Brad Pitt and Jennifer Aniston as a couple, in the golden flesh.

In retrospect, it is hard not to see them as the Adam and Eve of twenty-first-century gossip culture. They became the foundational myth for so much of the celebrity fiction that would follow, with their imagined reconciliations and love children and secret rendezvouses.

But even then, when their marriage seemed secure, they were so famous they created their own weather system, moving through the tent in a vortex of flashbulbs and gasps.

For the second time, I experienced the same dissonance as when meeting Monica Lewinsky, seeing them as a weird double-exposure of both person and persona. Watching the visceral effect they had on people in the room also offered some insight into how they could be mistreated so badly by the gossip media. In a battle between person and persona, the person didn't stand a chance.

The next night, at the Academy Awards, Nicole Kidman and Adrien Brody won the top acting honors. But the biggest overall winner was *Chicago*, which took six Oscars, including Best Picture and Best Actress in a Supporting Role for Catherine Zeta-Jones.

*Chicago* was made by Miramax Films, the small but powerful studio run by brothers Bob and Harvey Weinstein, who were at the peak of their influence. Harvey had aggressively reinvented how studios campaigned for Oscars, scoring a string of successes throughout the 1990s.

His signature achievement before then had been the 1999 Oscars haul for *Shakespeare in Love*. The film took Best Picture along with Best Actress in a Supporting Role for Judi Dench and Best Actress for Gwyneth Paltrow, whose tearful acceptance speech became an indelible pop-culture moment.

Industry rivals grumbled that Harvey's brazenness bordered on cheating. Certainly, the Academy was playing catch-up with his tactics, scrambling to close loopholes in their lobbying rules after he profitably exploited them for win after win.

Nevertheless, the place to be after the Academy Awards broadcast in 2003 was the St. Regis Hotel in Century City, where Miramax was holding its after-party.

The windowless ballroom was strangely dowdy and corporate. But Harvey, who was bursting out of his tuxedo like a small moon, exerted such gravitational pull in Hollywood that stars swarmed the party like comets.

Matthew McConaughey, Marcia Gay Harden, and David Carradine were there. Catherine Zeta-Jones, who was nine months pregnant, swept in wearing a flowing black gown—hanging onto her gold statue with one hand and her husband, Michael Douglas, with the other.

Diane Lane and Josh Brolin arrived, arm in arm. I passed Salma Hayek chatting in Spanish to Diego Luna and Gael García Bernal, whose careers had recently been bolstered by the Mexican hit film *Y Tu Mamá También*.

There was a star or an artist seemingly in every direction: Patti LaBelle; Caetano Veloso; Julie Taymor; Joan Rivers.

Even the dancer Cris Judd was there, a few months after the end of his yearlong marriage to Jennifer Lopez, taking his last lap as a celebrity.

Shortly after George and I arrived, a live charity auction began. One of the last items was a diamond necklace, for which Harvey ostentatiously bid up to tens of thousands of dollars.

After winning the object, he announced that it would be a gift for his wife, Eve. She shot him a look, and something unsaid passed between them; I got the impression she was not expecting to ever take delivery of it.

George broke off to chat with Harvey and garner quotes from the ranking stars. Wandering through the room, I soon ran into Marty Richards, whom I knew slightly from New York.

Despite being flamboyantly gay, Marty was the widower of a Johnson & Johnson heiress who left him a reported $50 million fortune. This funded his career producing Broadway musicals, which won him a handful of Tony Awards, and he had also optioned Miramax the rights to *Chicago*.

As a lead producer on the film, this allowed him to claim the Best Picture Oscar as his own.

Marty shot me a flirtatious look. "You wanna hold my Oscar?" he asked.

Well, of course I did.

So I grabbed the little fellow and did a couple of curls with it like an eight-and-a-half-pound barbell. It wasn't life-changing, but I will admit: it is fun to hold an Oscar, especially one for a freshly minted Best Picture.

Marty, the belle of the ball, was in high demand. He was surrounded by young people who seemed to be aware, as he was, of an Oscar's aphrodisiac qualities. So he soon floated away and trilled, "See you back in New York!"

In fact, the whole room seemed to be on a high, engorged by Miramax's success. I noticed Harvey on a banquette, leaning in close for conversation with Salma. Eve was nowhere to be seen.

After another loop of the party, I spied Sean Connery and his wife, Micheline Roquebrune. They were chatting amiably on a sofa, slightly removed from the throng.

The Scottish actor was wearing full Highland dress, including a doublet and ruffled white lace jabot. After waiting for Peter Boyle to pay his respects, I motioned with my notebook, indicating I'd like to speak with him.

He smiled and shook his head.

But I didn't mind. For a novice on the Oscars circuit, even being turned down by Sean Connery was more exciting than scoring an interview with any other star in the room.

W riting for "Rush & Molloy" every day, I continued to be surprised at people's efforts to keep themselves in, rather than out of, the gossip columns. This was a city that ran toward publicity, not away from it.

Even people who weren't famous would tell incriminating stories about themselves, just to have their name appear in bolded ink on the same page as those of Hollywood movie stars.

One anonymous tipster with an AOL address used to email the big tabloid gossip columns with such accurate inside scoops about Madonna—which were always interesting, were never uncomplimentary, and inevitably dropped just when there was an album or tour to promote—that I always believed it to be coming directly from her publicist. And if it wasn't her publicist on the other end, then maybe I have Madonna's secret email address.

Many celebrities would let paparazzi know their daily schedules, so they could be sure of being photographed. And some would just pick up the phone and call the columnists themselves.

Courtney Love used to call out of the blue and talk for hours, while I filled a yellow legal pad with her stream-of-consciousness stories about her celebrity friends. I would twist my legs into a braid trying to guess whether, if I set the phone down long enough to take a bathroom break, she'd even notice I wasn't there.

"Troy said I could trust you," she said at the beginning of her first very long and wildly indiscreet monologue, leaving me to wonder forever after who that was.

Then she dished stories about her daughter, Frances Bean Cobain, who, when Courtney was talking to herself, would ask, "Are you talking to the drugs in the room, Mommy?" and Courtney said she would reply, "Yes, honey, I'm talking to the drugs in the room."

Courtney also described how she was part of a secret clique of Hollywood celebrities who were caring for Elizabeth Taylor in her final years; how she, Liz, and Donatella Versace liked to make funny voices and pretend their diamond rings were having sock-puppet conversations with each other; and how she would go shoplifting in tony LA stores with her pal Winona Ryder.

"She'd get caught by the store detectives all the time," Courtney said nonchalantly. "But they always just let her put the stuff back."

Donald Trump was another local figure who never passed up the chance to speak to a reporter. He was slightly cool on the *News*—our paper had backed his first wife, Ivana, in their 1991 divorce, while the *Post* had taken his side—but he adored being in the gossip columns. I buttonholed him at parties for small-bore items about his plans to buy a Scottish golf course ("We're going to make a Trump tartan!") or the launch of his latest brand extension.

For the christening of Trump Vodka, which came in a heavy gold-leaf bottle, the rapper Busta Rhymes performed in the atrium of Trump Tower. Donald was then five seasons into his NBC reality show *The Apprentice*, and the building was filled beyond capacity with hundreds of his suburban fans, jostling to catch a glimpse of the star.

"Lotta ladies here tonight," Busta said into the microphone. "That's how Trump do."

Finally, Donald appeared in the lobby's mezzanine restaurant like Evita on the balcony of the Casa Rosada. The crowd cheered and surged forward, spilling their chocolate martinis. They couldn't get enough of the spectacle, either the gold and pink-veined marble of Trump Tower or the gold and pink-veined man himself.

The vodka was served in flimsy plastic cups that cracked in the grip, and much of it ended up on the floor, creating a sticky slick. Unable to move, tired of getting shoved, and worried about my shoes, I headed out early to retrieve my coat.

Working the coat check that night, and as overwhelmed as everyone else by the crowd, were Trump's two young-adult sons, Eric and Donald Jr. They were struggling but doing their best and being polite to everyone. I was impressed. It gave me a glimmer of hope that, despite the unrelenting bombast of their father, they might actually have had a normal childhood.

LOL.

Prowling such palaces each night felt like being a spy infiltrating Venice at Carnevale, cloak, dagger, and all. Every room was a lock that needed to be picked to give up its secrets.

At least, that's the romantic take on being a party reporter. Many serious journalists regard it as the waitressing of our profession: unprestigious, lowly paid, and with unreliable hours.

I understand that view but do not share it. To me, the events beat is like being offered the key to the city. Parties are a great equalizer of opportunity, especially for an immigrant with no existing networks to exploit.

It's practically a cheat code to win the game of New York: here's a room full of the best-connected people in the city; go get 'em.

Of course, once you're in front of these characters, you have to work out what to say to them. This presents a new set of challenges, particularly as you don't always know who you'll run into.

Fortunately, Americans are highly susceptible to foreign accents. As a dual Australian and British citizen, I toggle between those two as the situation demands.

Australian is useful for confrontations, like when paparazzi are trying to push me aside on the red carpet. British tends to emerge when I need to conceal the fact that I don't know what I'm talking about, or to whom.

This happens more often than journalists like to admit. Julia Stiles and Erika Christensen, two unrelated but near-look-alike actresses who came up around the same time in the 2000s, confused an entire generation of red-carpet reporters.

Likewise, I once had a long and very pleasant conversation with either Joan Allen, the dramatic actress, or Joan Cusack, the comedian. We both realized at the same moment that whoever it was, I had mistaken her for the other.

Sometimes the confusion is semantic rather than visual. Peter Gabriel, Gabriel Byrne, and David Byrne are all kept in my same mental kitchen drawer, and any time I go rummaging in it I invariably pull out the wrong one. Any combination of Dylan McDermott, Dermot Mulroney, Patrick Dempsey, and Jason Patric coming down a red carpet makes me break into a cold sweat.

And while I no longer confuse Laura Dern and Laura Linney, I'm embarrassed to admit it took some practice.

To deal with these situations, the experienced party reporter develops a list of questions that are a covert way of asking, "Who are you again?" My go-to is usually: "You've had so many marvelous roles—do you have a favorite?"

Sometimes you know who the person is but have no idea what to ask them. If they're in the film/TV show/play that is the subject of the occasion, I usually ask if they have any funny behind-the-scenes anecdotes from making the thing.

But sometimes you get red-carpet randoms who are nothing to do with the production and are just there to be photographed. My question of last resort in those days was, "What jobs did you do before you became famous?"

Only one person has ever come close to being even mildly offended by that gambit: the great Broadway diva Bernadette Peters. Her eyes swelled like spotlights adjusting their aperture, she drew herself up to her full five feet three inches in height, and she replied: "I have *always* been an *actress*."

One of the events each year that required maximum preparation for dealing with an unpredictable combination of movie stars was a viewing party thrown by *Entertainment Weekly* magazine on the night of the Academy Awards.

It was held at Elaine's, a steak-and-martini restaurant on an unfashionable stretch of the Upper East Side, frequented since the early 1960s by actors, athletes, journalists, and authors.

Its patroness, Elaine Kaufman, was a squat, formidable woman who had smoked so many cigarettes that her voice could be read in braille. She was a Yankees superfan and on special occasions would don chunky diamond earrings in the team's logo that, she liked to say, were a gift from its owner, George Steinbrenner.

Her vast and varied clientele was the subject of a 2004 book, *Everyone Comes to Elaine's*, which established through a catalog of her brittle quotes that she was equally rude to all her guests, from Norman Mailer to Sylvester Stallone.

True to its reputation, watching the Oscars at Elaine's was like being dropped in a bucket of random celebrity names generated for a game of charades. Angela Bassett, Matt Dillon, Candace Bushnell, Tatum O'Neal, Liza Minnelli, Liev Schreiber, Jane Krakowski, Katie Holmes, and Alan Cumming would all cram into the tightly packed room, where the overtaxed waiters spilled sauce on each guest equally, without regard to rank.

One year, my dinner place was next to Shannen Doherty, the spit-fire television actress. In retrospect, I should have asked what job she did before she became famous. Instead, my opening question was about her former husband, Rick Salomon, who was best known for costarring in Paris Hilton's career-making sex tape. She promptly moved chairs.

Another year I shared a table with Anne Hathaway and her boy-friend Raffaello Follieri. A charming Italian, the young man was an investing partner of Ron Burkle, who moved in Bill Clinton's inner circle. Eating at Elaine's may have prepared him for the food he got in federal prison, since he was sentenced to four and a half years on fraud and money-laundering charges shortly afterward.

The Oscars broadcast often ran late. Toward the end of the evening, after the drinks had been flowing for several hours, some celebrities felt comfortable enough to powder their noses with cocaine in the tiny restrooms, which afforded little privacy. This kind of detail tended to be left out of the gossip coverage, however, partly as a courtesy and partly as future leverage. Then everybody received a gift bag worth thousands of dollars and was kicked back out into the chilly night.

But it wasn't all staying out late and getting drunk with George Clooney. (Although I did that after the premiere of *Confessions of a Dangerous Mind*, the first film he directed. Even the biggest stars will sometimes wallow with the fourth estate when promoting a passion project.) It may not come as a complete surprise that the geniuses of the gossip press are not too hard to manipulate. All you have to do is lie to them.

I cost "Rush & Molloy" a doozy of a correction after receiving an anonymous email tip, purportedly from a bartender eyewitness, about a catfight between two C-list media personalities. One was a model then promoting herself as "the most downloaded woman on the internet," the other a moderately famous Hollywood actress with a reputation for public sloppiness.

I called the bar, and the manager confirmed the fight. I called the model's spokesman, and he confirmed the fight. I called the ac-tress's rep, and she didn't get back to me. With a neutral witness plus confirmation from one party and silence from the other, that was good enough to go with the story.

Except. What the model's rep didn't say was that he and she co-owned the bar where the alleged incident took place. He, his manager, and the "bartender" tipster, if that person even existed, were lying in concert in order to drum up coverage.

And the actress's publicist turned out to have been on a plane to Hawaii and genuinely out of contact. It wasn't just the usual unreturned phone call, which, in the gossip business, we tended to take as a tacit admission of guilt. So, oy.

The day that ran, as my old boss Laura might have said, was definitely work and not gee-oh-ell-eff. The correction was longer than the original item.

Another time, there was a young guy hanging around the scene, claiming to be the son of *CHiPs* actor Erik Estrada. He would drop the name in order to get into nightclubs where he could meet models.

For a Father's Day column, he told me an entertaining story about being a kid in Los Angeles, driving around with his dad in the car. The highway patrol would always give them special treatment, he said, and it wasn't until years later that he worked out why.

It made great copy, until the actor's wife called to say there was no such son. So I ran a correction, adding, "The little louse made it up."

Shortly afterward, I ran into the guy at a party. With true con-man moxie, he marched up to me as if I'd done something wrong and stuck his finger in my chest.

"Listen," he said, leaning into my face. "I don't appreciate you calling me a louse."

W e got great hate mail in the gossip business.
Before an entire generation learned its manners from reality television and social media, with its culture of nonstop insults and permanent outrage, receiving hate mail was an occasion. And writing it could be an art form.

Two or three times a year, a small white envelope used to arrive at the *Daily News*, addressed to the gossip column. The envelope and single sheet it contained were from a set; the paper stock was ivory and of high quality.

The correspondent had an elegant, old-fashioned hand and wrote in flowing cursive with bright green ink from a fountain pen with a narrow nib. The emerald letters popped against the creamy paper.

There was never a return address, but the postmark read Waterbury, Connecticut. The letter itself would be just a brief, unsigned note to the gossips—maybe only twenty words long—telling us how stupid we were.

Although the performance of cultural superiority was grating, I had to admit our correspondent had style. Right down to the last, meta flourish: "green ink" is obscure British-journalism slang for hate mail.

When the *Daily News* gave me my own gossip page, in 2006, I called it "Gatecrasher," in homage to my days of crashing parties. It also came with a new email address for tips, gatecrasher@nydailynews.

The day the new column debuted, I sat and waited for the first email to come into the empty account. Minutes ticked into hours as I stared at the screen like a dog watching the front door for its human to come home.

Finally, an email arrived. It was from a man named Anthony, from whom I would hear a number of times over the years, who wrote a few crisp sentences about how terrible the column was and ended with the line "You'll have to do better than that."

I wrote back and thanked him for reading, which is what writers say when we're trying to irritate a critic.

I liked that response, because often those who wrote to criticize would open with the claim that they didn't read gossip. This obliged them, in the second sentence, to perform a kind of midair triple axel, in which they outlined the circumstances by which *just this once* they had glanced at the gossip pages and were so appalled by what they found they had to let me know.

This type was surprisingly common. I even had a private nick-name name for them—"Bugs Bunnies," after the cartoon rabbit who was constantly popping his head up in the wrong place, having missed "that left turn at Albuquerque." How strange it was for these intellectuals to suddenly find themselves in a land of idiots! And how urgent that I be informed.

But people have always fibbed about what they read. I learned that in the pre-internet 1990s, while working at an LGBT community newspaper in Sydney, which made most of its profit from romance classifieds.

Those advertisements were free to place, and anyone wanting to reply would mail five dollars in cash with each response. The Sydney *Star Observer* made a small fortune every week from their personals section—even allowing for Bubble, the receptionist who opened the mail, who had a sizable party-drug habit and was skimming at least 30 percent off the top.

And yet, in our annual readers' survey of which sections people valued and which they ignored, we got the same result every year: absolutely nobody ever admitted to reading the dating ads. If the paper had been into making "data-driven decisions," as Silicon Valley types like to say, it would have ditched the personals and gone bankrupt within a month.

The lesson was that people will lie about their media tastes in order to feel better about themselves. Navigating this as a new columnist was something I had to learn on the job.

The relationship between journalist and reader before the advent of social media now seems positively quaint. When people were still sending hate mail through the post office, they didn't include a return address, so that was the end of it. But with email, the recipient could always reply, so the experience became a dialogue.

Because I would always write back to critical emails, I discovered something remarkable: far more often than not, I'd get a friendly response, completely at odds with the tone of the original message.

Some would apologize, explaining they were just having a bad day. Others would say that they had thought more about whatever issue was on their minds and could see both sides.

What the writers had in common was a need to be heard. And

perhaps, when writing to a newspaper, they felt they had to use particularly aggressive language to be noticed. But mostly, the validation of being recognized was what they wanted—and what came back from replying to a hostile note was often friendliness.

This strategy did occasionally backfire, however.

Once in "Gatecrasher" we ran a picture of the Chinese American actress Lucy Liu wearing a red-string kabbalah bracelet, which was trendy with celebrities at the time. The caption opened with an ill-advised canard: "That's funny, she doesn't look Jewish."

Two people wrote in to complain. One woman said that she had adopted a child from Asia, was raising her in the Jewish faith, and was hoping her daughter would grow up in a world where it was okay for people who looked like her to practice Judaism.

It was a persuasive message that made me understand why the caption had been wrong. So I thanked her for writing and apologized for causing offense, and we had a cordial exchange of emails.

The other guy who emailed was more . . . rabid. But I did the same thing: thanked him for writing and apologized.

The next person I heard from was my friend Paula at "Page Six": the writer had forwarded my email to the *Post* and encouraged them to run an item using the apology against me.

Paula was just warning me about the guy. Few outside the business realized that, although our newspapers were constantly at war, the city's rival gossips largely cooperated. We would sometimes even give juicy items to each other if, due to our own relationship with the subject, we couldn't use them ourselves. Notwithstanding the occasional publisher-ordered strafe, we mostly had each other's backs.

Soon enough, however, even receiving a hostile email would feel old-fashioned.

In July 2006, the year "Gatecrasher" started, a San Francisco company called Twitter went live as a platform for "micro-blogging," something nobody had ever heard of. And in September of the same year, Facebook opened its membership to anyone over the age of thirteen who had an email address.

Now the readers were publishers too. And once opinions were content, they needed to be even more vehement in order to stand out.

It turned out that until then, people had only been communicating privately because there hadn't been an option to do it publicly. When the open forum replaced interpersonal messaging, all sides shifted to war footing.

There would be no more responding to an angry email and working it out with the person on the other side. On social media, replies were received not as invitations to common ground but as fresh outrages for users to define themselves in opposition to.

All that would become clearer to me in hindsight than it was at the time, even though I thought of myself as a tech-savvy upstart who had made his name on the internet.

In truth, I thrilled to the throwback charm of having a daily column in messy, pulpy newsprint. There was nothing headier than the whiff of ink and sawdust that puffed into the air when you snapped open a fresh copy of the paper. I even didn't mind the *News*'s notoriously wonky printing, which misaligned color photographs into unreconciled layers of red, yellow, and blue. Or the smudges of black ink from the copy, which would soon find their way from your fingertips to the buttonholes on your shirt and the corners of your eyes.

And every so often, an exquisitely poisonous green-inked letter would arrive on creamy stationery from Waterbury, Connecticut. What website could give you that?

Perhaps I was also lying about my taste for the internet in order to feel better about myself. I said I wanted the future, but what I bought was the past.

It is a cliché of journalism that "news is whatever somebody doesn't want you to know; everything else is advertising." In the columns, we had the same maxim for the relationship between gossip and publicity.

Journalists flatter ourselves that we are warriors for truth. But to paraphrase another cliché: every time a journalist makes plans, a publicist laughs.

In New York media, gossip columnists and publicists existed in a state of codependent mutual antagonism comparable to the old *Spy vs. Spy* cartoon in *Mad* magazine. It may have seemed like we were constantly at each other's throats, but like the eternal yin and yang, gossip and publicity could not survive without each other.

Just how influential publicists can be among the city's establishment was impressed upon me at a fiftieth-anniversary party for the PR firm Howard Rubenstein and Associates. It was held at Tavern on the Green, a chintzy holdout of the old guard in Central Park whose early-eighties power-lunch aesthetic made it look like a first-class lounge on the Love Boat.

The firm's eponymous founder, then aged seventy-two, was besieged three deep by well-wishers. But I needed a quote for the column, so I fought through the scrum.

It was only after I had literally elbowed my way into the middle of the tightest circle that I realized I was surrounded by George Pataki, who was then the New York governor; Hillary Clinton, then a New York senator; and Rupert Murdoch. I don't know who copped the point of my elbow in their rib cage, but one of them did; I squeaked out my question and scrammed.

Howard was held in such esteem because he understood how to create equilibrium between the opposing forces of client and journalist. It was a talent all the top publicists shared.

Another leading Hollywood flack once told me that none of his clients ever cared what was written about them in the gossip columns, as long as the accompanying picture was large and flattering. For any writer, hearing that the words don't matter is like being told there's no Santa Claus. But it's a truth that has been brought home to me many times.

One morning "Gatecrasher" led with an item about Tyra Banks, the model and television host, having lunch with Jay-Z at a midtown restaurant. They left without paying the check.

The story was illustrated with an almost full-page glamour shot of Tyra, which she gleefully held up that morning during a live appearance on *The View*. To her, it was all just promotion. And she got her picture in the column again the next day when she went back to pay the bill— trailed, of course, by a photographer.

If you wanted the monsters to perform, you had to feed them—and they ate publicity.

Another outsized personality who occasionally cropped up was Princess Diana's former butler Paul Burrell. He had made a living out of exploiting his connection to her since her death in 1997 and came to New York to perform a one-man show based on his memoir of royal household gossip.

I interviewed him for a cheesy article of tips on how Americans could incorporate palace etiquette into their own home. Don't lay out a fish knife, which the British royals consider to be a vulgar Europeanism—that sort of thing.

Although he had a wife and two children back home in Britain, Paul was clearly gayer than a conga line of Liza Minnelli's ex-husbands. He turned up for this article on good manners, held over tea at the tony Four Seasons Hotel in midtown Manhattan, in an oxford shirt unbuttoned to his navel.

While I was asking him questions about how the queen arranges her forks, the shirt was gaping open so wide that his nipples were uncovered. I was nervous that his chest hair was going to shed onto the buttered scones.

Paul came to tea with a portly male companion who, he explained, was a Disney superfan, and the pair were planning to travel together to Disney World. The friend was dressed head-to-toe in Disney-branded clothing and looked like he might manage boy bands out of a motel in Orlando.

All this was at odds with the very straitlaced conversation we were having about English country house manners, such as whether to add the milk or hot water first when pouring tea.

"A famous duchess visited Buckingham Palace and asked, 'Does anyone put milk in the teacup first?'" he said, nipples erect. "'That's what the common people do. We call them the MIFs, you know. The Milk-in-Firsts.'"

Another Brit who could be relied upon to supply bizarre copy whenever she came to town was Naomi Campbell. One Fashion Week, I covered an event promoting racial diversity in the fashion industry.

"I've never been on the cover of British *Vogue* and I've asked a million times and they've always refused me," she said at the Bryant Park Hotel. "They'll put the same white model for half the year—I swear, like six times—but wouldn't put me on once in my own country. But I still want my British *Vogue* cover!"

They were powerful comments about an important problem, and I was excited to get them for my column. The only problem was, in the twenty years since her professional debut in 1987, Naomi had been on the cover of British *Vogue* eight times—twice with other models, once posing with Sean Combs, and five times by herself. (I ended up running the quotes with a disclaimer.)

Another time, her publicist called to ask me if I knew any gay bars in Manhattan that had a secure but highly visible VIP area. It seemed that Naomi needed a little pick-me-up in the form of some public adulation.

I happened to know a bar in Chelsea that had a private space on its balcony, overlooking the rest of the room. Like the scene in *Soapdish* in which Sally Field's character travels to a suburban mall in order to be recognized and mobbed by fans, Naomi duly turned up that evening and the place went nuts. The publicist reported later that the experience had improved her mood significantly.

Models could often be a tough interview, and I once found myself struggling during a sit-down with Jerry Hall. She was between partners, having split from Mick Jagger—whose lawyers successfully argued, much to her surprise, that despite their sunset wedding ceremony in Bali, the couple had never actually been legally married.

So now Jerry was starring in *Kept*, a forgettable reality-dating show whose premise was that she would select, from a cast of much younger applicants, a boy toy to keep at her beck and call. The implication was that the guy would win a lifestyle of penthouses and limousines, in exchange for—what, exactly? Being available as some kind of sexual lapdog? That part was unclear.

She and the contestants were marshaled for a promotional party on the second floor of a decrepit, marked-for-demolition building facing the Soho Grand Hotel. Jerry had been given a plumped sofa on which to recline, like a languid odalisque, for the benefit of press and photographers.

Barely ten minutes into our conversation, the interview was already hopelessly bogged down. I just wasn't finding any questions that elicited an interesting response. In desperation, I asked about her hair.

Jerry thanked me for my interest and told me she had just had it feng shuied.

"Excuse me?" I said.

"I have my hair feng shuied," she repeated, flipping one of her long blond tresses with the backs of her fingers. "It gets the negativity out."

She added that she went to her hairstylist, a man in Dallas by the name of Michael Motorcycle, once a month to have the procedure done.

Gossip writing: also not Proustspeare. When a supermodel tells you she feng shuies her hair, you have what you came for.

Each night on the beat was a blur of brief interactions with superfamous people. The job of a reporter on the celebrity page is not to surprise famous people when they're off duty but to speak with them at prearranged press opportunities, so mostly they're expecting to talk to journalists and manage to be delightful.

Meryl Streep has the ability to fix you in her gaze as she's speaking as if you are the most fascinating person she's ever met. When Jude Law decides to be "on," it's like interviewing a tanning bed.

Hugh Grant and Kate Winslet still manage to give thoughtful answers to red-carpet questions they must find utterly banal. Hugh Jackman is even more charming and sincere in person than he appears on camera; so is Tom Hanks.

But sometimes I found that embodying your on-screen image is not always a good thing. In the flesh, Robin Williams was so much like his manic, desperate-to-entertain persona that it seemed to be eating him up from the inside.

Occasionally there was schtick. To drum up interest in the gossip pages, publicists promoting the romantic comedy *Something's Gotta Give* put it about that there was a real-life romance taking place between its leads, Jack Nicholson and Diane Keaton.

This seemed highly unlikely. Nevertheless, when I interviewed the stars at the Boathouse in Central Park following the film's New York premiere, Diane, then aged fifty-seven, conducted the entire conversation sitting girlishly in the lap of Jack, who was then sixty-six.

The scene was uncomfortable for everyone. But the redoubtable Hollywood publicist Pat Kingsley sat nearby and didn't take her eyes off them, as if she were their parole officer.

At the other extreme were those stars who just hated dealing with journalists. I've never tried to get a quote from Liam Neeson, Leonardo DiCaprio, or Robert De Niro, even at their own film premieres, without being completely sure they'd rather be anywhere else on earth.

Other times the person you get simply depends on the day they're having. I've spoken to Cate Blanchett both when she wasn't in the mood to be interviewed and also when she was so at ease she complained about her bunion.

Unfortunately, I learned early on with Australian stars that attempting to ingratiate myself as a compatriot wasn't always a winning strategy. Take it from me that trying to warm up Guy Pearce with an appreciative reference to Mike Young, the teenage heartthrob he played in the 1980s on the Australian soap opera *Neighbours*, is not the right way to start an interview.

The most reliably professional stars to deal with were the so-called divas. Jennifer Lopez, Beyoncé, Madonna—they'd give you exactly what you needed in a two-minute interview, as long as you behaved yourself and didn't try any "gotcha" questions.

Mariah Carey was the same. I remember interviewing her after an appearance, when she was wearing a very low-cut top over a push-up bra that could have doubled as a medevac device for large marine mammals.

Although she's only five foot eight, her six-inch platform wedges elevated her bust to just beneath my chin. Her face was caked with thick stage makeup, which crumbled as she spoke and fell in great chunks down the cleft of her bosom, like a glacier calving into the sea.

I maintained an unnatural eye contact with her throughout the interview, since I dared not look down, even at my notebook. Afterward, when I reviewed my notes, they were just illegible loops of handwriting and one pinkish-brown explosion where a chunk of Mariah's foundation had hit the page like a meteor strike.

Paul Newman enjoyed going out, even near the very end of his life. Once, while we were speaking at a party, a fan came over and asked for an autograph.

Slowly and gingerly, he grasped the longneck beer he was holding in his mouth, in order to have both hands free to sign. The actor was very frail, and I was worried the weight of the bottle would pull his teeth out. But he was so graceful, even in that awkward gesture, that his charisma was like being bathed in radiation.

I also had a few enjoyably nutty encounters with Jerry Lewis when he was in his eighties. Whenever he visited New York City, he would stay at the Waldorf-Astoria Towers, luxury apartments adjacent to the famous hotel. I interviewed him there in a room strewn with old publicity images of him with Dean Martin that he was approving for a DVD release of their greatest hits.

Jerry responded best to a tone that was somewhere between respectful and obsequious, and that's what I gave him. It was important for him to feel like he was being treated as a major figure.

The more comfortable he was, the more expansive he became.

When he learned I was Australian, he telephoned a friend who owned a casino in Tasmania—waking him up in what was the middle of the night there—to tell him he was being interviewed by a fellow Aussie.

Some of Jerry's showbiz stories were a little tall, however.

He told me that, in the early 1950s, he had been staying in one of two large penthouse suites at a hotel in Las Vegas. The other, which had an adjoining terrace, was occupied by John F. Kennedy, who then represented Massachusetts in the United States Senate.

At the time, Kennedy was framing the book that would become *Profiles in Courage*, the winner of the 1957 Pulitzer Prize for Biography. With a serious cast to his brow, Jerry told me the future president asked for his help.

He gestured to make sure I understood how close their penthouses really were. They would meet to discuss the themes in the book, he said, and pore over pages.

Jerry chose his words carefully, but there was a sparkle in his eye. The message was clearly that he was too modest to come out and take credit for his work on the book, but a prudent person, on hearing his account, would conclude that he was largely responsible.

The modesty itself was suspicious. Some people found Jerry to be a kind man, and others did not, but nobody ever described him as humble.

The authorship of *Profiles in Courage* is, in fact, contested. It is now generally acknowledged to be the work of Kennedy's speechwriter, Ted Sorensen.

Having heard it straight from the horse's mouth, however, I know better: the person who deserves credit for *Profiles in Courage* is Jerry Lewis.

With the column giving me access to some of the biggest names in Hollywood, sometimes I tried to be strategic and develop a relationship with a star. That never worked, not even once.

Around that time, Tom Cruise fired his longtime and fearsomely effective publicist, Pat Kingsley. It was rumored that he blamed her when he did not receive an Academy Award nomination for his film *The Last Samurai.*

But Pat was generally regarded as the top PR in Hollywood, and she played hardball. If a journalist crossed her on one of her clients, she would block their publication's access to her entire roster, which included titans like Jodie Foster, Al Pacino, and Will Smith.

Pat had also managed to keep Tom on a leash, shielding some of his crazier antics from popular scrutiny. But after the split, he decided to transfer public relations responsibilities to his sister, Lee Anne De Vette, a fellow congregant in the Church of Scientology.

Suddenly, after years of being muzzled on the subject of his faith, Tom started speaking about it to the press. It was not well received.

Shortly after he changed publicists, I received a tip from a staff member at the Prada store in SoHo. Tom had come in to do some shopping, and as was the protocol for a major star, the store was closed to the public for the duration of his visit.

What Miuccia Prada got for the forty million dollars she spent with the architect, Rem Koolhaas, was a wooden halfpipe, leading down from the main entrance on Broadway into the belly of the store, which served both as stairs for the customers and display shelves for the merchandise.

But it was made out of slippery zebrawood, and although the feature looked great, it could be treacherous to navigate.

Sure enough, says the staff member who was present that day, Tom slipped at the top and bumped down the stairs on his Oscar-denied behind.

When I called Lee Anne, she asked me not to run the item. Sensing the opportunity to get her on my side as an ally, and salivating at the lifetime of Tom Cruise scoops that would surely follow, I agreed.

Needless to say, I never heard from her again.

# 10

## The Buzz at
## Da Tommaso

**T**he thing about writing a daily gossip column on a print deadline is that the bus leaves every day at six p.m., and somebody has to be under it.

The first deadline of the day was the ten a.m. sked, when my likely stories were shared in a meeting with the paper's various section heads. An updated sked was due at two.

Sometimes, if the tips I chased down turned out not to be true, my sked fell apart. Fortunately, when that happened, I was able to rely on an assistant, a talented young reporter named Laura Schreffler.

Laura had a miracle new device called a Sidekick that she operated with her thumbs and which seemingly connected her with every other twenty-four-year-old woman in America. Gossip came out of it like water from a spigot.

But if that didn't work and we still didn't have a lede—jargon for the top item—by four p.m., it was time to panic.

As a less-established columnist, my phone didn't ring with tips the way it did for Richard Johnson or George and Joanna. I relied on going out at night for my information.

In those days, the celebrity hangouts were Bungalow 8, a small club in west Chelsea, and Beatrice Inn in the West Village. Snowdrifts of drugs ran through both clubs.

Beatrice attracted a younger, hip, downtown set, like Heath Ledger, Mary-Kate and Ashley Olsen, and Chloë Sevigny, whose brother, Paul, was an owner of the club.

Bungalow was run by Amy Sacco, the nightlife queen of the moment. She brought in a slightly more conventional Hollywood crowd, like Owen Wilson, Matthew McConaughey, Jeremy Piven, and Lindsay Lohan. It was a great place to get gossip.

One night at the bar, an actress I knew casually dropped that her friend, Ethan Hawke, had started dating his kids' nanny right after splitting from his wife, Uma Thurman.

"What, you didn't know that?" she said, after my jaw hit the floor. "It's been a couple months now."

So that made a lede.

But not every night filled the next day's column so handily. And when the well was still dry at four p.m., it was time to work the phones.

The first calls were always to publicists, who would happily tell what they knew in exchange for favorable coverage for one of their clients. Each had their specialty.

Brad Zeifman and Lisette Sand-Freedman of Shadow PR repped Richie Akiva and Scott Sartiano, impresarios behind two of the city's popular night spots, 1Oak and Butter. Those clubs were good for items about rappers, bankers, and the so-called "models and bottles" crowd: susceptible young men who could be persuaded to spend $300 on a bottle of Absolut vodka just to feel like they were in the proximity of beautiful women.

Steven Rubenstein, next on the call list, ran politicians and other New York City power-players at the right hand of his father, Howard. Shawn Sachs and Ken Sunshine had top-tier movie stars, including Ben Affleck and Leonardo DiCaprio.

For model gossip, I called Full Picture. It represented Victoria's Secret talent like Adriana Lima and Alessandra Ambrosio, as well as Heidi Klum and her fashion reality hit, *Project Runway*.

Lizzie Grubman, whose father, Allen Grubman, was the country's top entertainment lawyer, represented a mix of celebrities and night spots. She self-immolated in 2001 after driving through a line of people waiting to get into a nightclub in the Hamptons and became front-page tabloid fodder herself.

But like a true New Yorker, Lizzie had no use for shame. After serving a jail term, she went straight back into business and fronted her own MTV reality show.

Nadine Johnson had luxury clients, including the country's most fashionable hotelier, André Balazs, owner of the Standard chain as well as the Chateau Marmont in Los Angeles. Being married to Richard Johnson of "Page Six," however, she wasn't a great source. (Until their split, which unsurprisingly was not covered by "Page Six.")

But the godfather of New York publicists was Sy Presten. He was the last press agent still in the game who had worked with Walter Winchell, the most powerful columnist of newspapers' mid-century golden age, who died in 1972.

Sy's clients, who often had been with him for decades, were not exactly fresh young things. His pitches arrived through the mail, on pages soundly thrashed by a manual typewriter. And speaking to him on the telephone was like reaching a 1950s radio announcer.

He had a talent for double-dipping on items by locating news about a client in an unrelated Italian eatery that he also repped. A signature Sy Presten pitch would always include the phrase "according to the buzz at Da Tommaso restaurant"—which often made it into print, surely to the befuddlement of readers.

(The last time I had lunch with Sy, in 2019, he was ninety-five and had just been written up by the *New Yorker* for a feud he was having with Cindy Adams, the *Post*'s eighty-nine-year-old gossip columnist.)

If the daily call-around failed to generate a lede, it was necessary to get creative. One of the arts of tabloid news writing is finding an angle on big stories even when you have no access.

A week or so before the wedding of Prince Charles and Camilla Parker Bowles, for example, I called the White House to ask if President George W. Bush and the First Lady would be sending an official gift.

For Charles's first wedding, to Princess Diana, Ronald and Nancy Reagan had sent an engraved bowl. This time, however, a White House spokesman said no gift was planned. The Bushes passing on the future King of England's second trip down the aisle was more than enough for a lede on a slow news day.

Sometimes the ledes even came from a competitor. In those ancient times, before as much content was available for free on the internet, book publishers and even celebrity magazines saw a benefit in previewing their stories in the gossip columns as a way to stimulate sales.

That's how "Gatecrasher," in 2005, became the first place to run pictures of Brad Pitt and Angelina Jolie vacationing on a beach in Kenya together with her son Maddox. The photographs caused a sensation, confirming rumors that they were indeed the world's hottest new couple.

*Us Weekly* owned the images, which looked to me as if they had been staged by the actors, although the circumstances of the photo shoot never became known. But the magazine was content to let my column break the story in return for a plug.

Once those two went public with their relationship, there were a lot fewer slow days in celebrity news. In fact, the spring and summer of 2005 ushered in a golden age of gossip that would last several years.

Brad divorcing Jennifer Aniston and taking up with Angelina played out a primal human fear to which almost everyone could relate, that of losing one's partner to a more competitive rival. Never mind that the so-called love triangle was embellished into fiction by the tabloids; the narrative is so powerful that it is still on the cover of magazines, fifteen years later.

(The weekly celebrity magazines and the gossip-hungry daily newspapers were often lumped together under the term "tabloids." The difference was that the weeklies sometimes made up stories, while the newspapers did not.)

Also in 2005, a pleasant young actress named Katie Holmes, who often talked to the gossip reporters when we ran into her at parties, married Tom Cruise.

By then, the public had grown suspicious of his ties to Scientology, and what pressures the secretive religion may have put upon his previous wife, Nicole Kidman. So the story that played out in the celebrity glossies was of a powerful and potentially sinister man controlling a young innocent who was in over her head.

Like the Brad-Jen-Angie "triangle," it was as much mythmaking as journalism. But the narrative resonated so strongly with ordinary people, it was doled out in weekly installments by the gossip magazines as an inexhaustible soap opera.

Covering the media circus as much as the principal players for the *Daily News*, writing a gossip column started to feel like an actual job.

G atecrasher" came out every weekday, and life ticked forward like the newsroom clock.

When Democrats unseated enough Republicans to win a majority in the House of Representatives in the 2006 midterm elections,

Joanna Molloy cut the headline from the *New York Times* and pinned it to her cubicle. When the same thing happened in the Senate a few days later, after a slower count, she added that headline underneath.

Horacio and I gossiped on the phone about our boyfriends and hookups; Clare moved with her husband to Brooklyn and then to London. Willi Ninja died, of AIDS-related complications.

For two summers I had a delicious affair with an ambitious politico who had advised Michael Bloomberg in his mayoral campaign. He was probably slumming to date a mere celebrity-chaser, and the fact that he hung his framed Pulitzer Prize certificate by the bed certainly added an edge to the sex.

But I was gratified that the gossip from the corridors of power was just as absurd and entertaining as any nonsense out of Hollywood. He had often been called upon to stand behind Bloomberg during speeches, for example, to indicate the support his boss enjoyed among African Americans. He explained that in political theater, this was called being "the black-drop."

His studio apartment in a modern high-rise had no curtains, which always made me concerned about privacy, but he would insist no one was watching. Outside his floor-to-ceiling plate-glass window was a classic New York view: West Side warehouses, stacked like shoeboxes before the mountain range of buildings that formed the midtown skyline. Each one was speckled with bright, square windows like the compound lenses of an insect eye.

I always thought it was strange, his conviction that no one was watching. This was New York City, after all. Why bother even coming here, if not to watch?

One night I went to cover an event at the Four Seasons restaurant, a modernist redoubt of corporate power in east midtown. Paris Hilton charged out of the ground-floor restroom and past me on the stairs, wearing a sequined cocktail minidress and high heels as slender as chopsticks. Halfway up, she lost her balance and floated back like a feather, right into my arms. As a meet-cute, it was wasted on me, but it made for a snappy line in the column.

After the politico I dated a blogger, a start-up executive, and a mafioso named Tony. Tony's stated profession, of managing a Brooklyn pizzeria, in no way accounted for the luxury condominium he occupied next to the High Line in Manhattan, nor his Porsche Cayenne SUV. Tony's way of telling me to shut up when I was being too mouthy, which was all the time—growling *"never mind"* in a low, guttural register—was so sexy that sparks shot out of my toes.

Laura moved on after a year, and later I was helped by Kelly Will and Nancy Kane. In an arrangement that was perhaps not ethically immaculate, Nancy was also a freelance publicist for some of the stars we covered in the columns. One day George asked his new assistants, Chris Rovzar and Jo Piazza, if they could find a rep for Cuba Gooding Jr., and she swiveled around in her chair and raised her hand.

Coming into work one morning, I took sick on the subway. After about an hour doubled over my desk in pain, I asked Jo to take me in a cab to St. Vincent's hospital in Greenwich Village.

The American health care system is one of those national institutions, like deep-fried Oreos and mass shootings, that many people are curious to observe from a distance but would prefer not to experience personally. And as a dystopian theme park ride, St. Vincent's did not fail to deliver.

At the hospital, a clerk had me fill out a thick sheaf of insurance paperwork and directed me to take a seat in the waiting room. Taking my place on the plastic chairs, I was surrounded by a cross section of New Yorkers reading the paper or checking their phones, in no particular hurry, as if they were waiting for a bus.

The clerk stared at me impassively from the other side of knife-proof glass, with no apparent intention of introducing me to a doctor, while I clutched my stomach and struggled to stay upright. A man sitting next to me, wearing a trench coat buttoned to his neck, noticed my distress.

"You took a cab here?" he asked in a no-nonsense Brooklyn accent. I nodded.

"If you wanna get admitted, you gotta come in a ambulance," he said. "You want my advice, go outside and call 911. Then they gotta take you."

I considered his suggestion, of walking out the automatic glass doors and calling an ambulance to take me sixty feet. Absurd systems require absurd solutions, so I had to admit the plan had a certain elegance. But the downside was that it would add unknown hundreds or thousands of dollars to my bill.

Instead, I said to Jo, "I need you to make a scene."

And she did, so effectively that I was promptly moved into the emergency room, and she was escorted out of the building by security. An astute study, Jo would later ape my symptoms to gain admittance to a different ER, on assignment for the *Daily News* to track down a shooting victim.

Once inside, I was diagnosed with appendicitis, issued a paper hospital gown, and stuck with an IV drip. The man in the next gurney, who was handcuffed to a railing, thrashed and bellowed through a psychotic episode as his two teenage sons waited patiently for the storm to subside.

After another hour, as I was pushing my drip to the bathroom while awaiting surgery, a public affairs officer for the hospital bounded up and handed me his card. My editor, Colleen, had called and told them to look after me.

The gown didn't have a back, let alone any pockets. So I clutched his card in my free hand and tried not to think of the breeze on my buttocks while he ran through his "anything I can do for you" spiel.

Within a few years, St. Vincent's would be gone, razed to the ground to make way for luxury condominiums. But at that moment, the hospital was so broke that it had run out of basic supplies, including gauges for the IV lines.

I asked if he could do anything about the plastic tube in my arm, which was backed up with blood almost to the saline bag. He said he'd get right on it, and I never saw him again.

While this medical comedy was playing out, at another hospital elsewhere in the city Lisa Marsh and Dan Mangan from the *Post* were having their first child. I have always liked the fact that Lillian is exactly the same age as my appendix scar.

R ecovered and back on the party circuit, I met a nice-seeming, if somewhat wet, young man named Jared Kushner, who had started dating Ivanka Trump. He used to wander around the city like Macaulay Culkin's character in *Home Alone 2: Lost in New York*, gormlessly walking into Manhattan landmarks as if he owned them—which, like the Puck Building in SoHo, he sometimes did.

"I took my dining room table out about eight months ago and replaced it with a Ping-Pong table," he told me at a party there. "More people come over to hang out and play Ping-Pong than they do to have dinner."

That made a harmless item for the column, under the headline "Jared Kushner's Ping-Pong diplomacy."

It was funny, because this guy, a diplomat? Besides, Ivanka always made for good copy—everybody loved her.

It was a gossip item for a complacent time. Liberal New Yorkers liked to grumble about the Republican in the White House, but a promising young Illinois senator named Barack Obama was on the rise, and even the local billionaire mayor, Michael Bloomberg, was immensely popular. The economy had rebounded from the first dot-com crash and the shock of 9/11, and there was even a new tech boom. Adults on scooters returned to Manhattan streets.

But tabloids need to stir things up if they want to move product at the newsstand. So the gossip press seized on a triumvirate of attractive young celebrities—Paris Hilton, Britney Spears, and Lindsay Lohan—as objects of particular judgment and fascination.

Our readers obliged with an appetite for stories about the destruction of these young women. Accordingly, we roasted them like pullets on a spit.

Others, like Jessica Simpson and Jennifer Lopez, also took their turn in the rotisserie. But Hilton, Spears, and Lohan were the holy trinity of targets.

Even as they crisped under the spotlight, however, they were acutely aware of their worth and played with media attention like matadors taunting a bull. When all three bunched into the front of Paris's SUV to stage their first photograph as a triumvirate—it was a contrived meeting, because they bitterly disliked each other—the *New York Post* ran it on the front page under the headline "Bimbo summit."

Lindsay's divorcing parents, Dina and Michael, used to call me separately to spin what they hoped would be the next day's news. At Fashion Week one season, W Hotels promoted its new Aloft brand by placing a vintage aluminum trailer inside its backstage VIP lounge as a kind of "VVIP" enclosure. I was there one afternoon as Lindsay went inside and began inhaling very loudly through her nose, in short bursts, while Dina sat outside and they discussed their schedule for the day through the closed door. It was up to the W Hotels publicist to go in afterward with a damp cloth and wipe down the surfaces.

Paris used to keep the paparazzi on a chain by sliding out of limousines, long legs first, to reveal no underwear under the shortest of skirts. But it was all fun and gams until somebody lost her hair.

In February 2007, the *Daily News* devoted its entire front page to a photograph of Britney shaving her head with electric clippers, with the headline "Britney Shears" alongside the concern-trolling cover line, "Shocking pix as superstar teeters on edge of a breakdown."

Four days later the paper's front-page image was of a bald Britney hammering at a paparazzo's SUV with a green golf umbrella, and the headline read, "Britney's Fury."

It was rank hypocrisy from the tabloids. Public interest in Britney's unraveling mental health was selling newspapers and fueling ever-more-invasive coverage. Clearly, what she needed was rest and privacy—but no newspaper was going to give her that.

With Lindsay also in the headlines for erratic behavior, death by suicide or misadventure for at least one of these young women seemed like it could be a distinct possibility. And we in the gossip media were there, goading them on—waiting for a Princess Diana moment, when we could step back and feign shock while profiting from the tragedy.

These women were controversial because the media treated their prominence as a referendum on female power. No editor ever raised an eyebrow at the fact that a man could become famous for masculine things, like being good at sports. But women whose appeal was rooted in more feminine fields, like fashion or celebrity—those frivolous wastes of time—were begrudged their success.

In the tabloids, we treated them as cultural products rather than cultural agents. Surely they must have been the symptom of something else that was going on, something more important? They couldn't possibly have been in charge of their own destinies—because, as the *Post* said, they were only bimbos.

The tabloids, which only obsessed about young women who embodied a narrow sexual ideal, treated them like dolls in a sideshow ball toss, set up to be knocked down. There was always an edge of male anger in the way women like Paris Hilton were portrayed. And for a few years in the '00s, Paris could plausibly claim to be the most famous person in the world.

She and her almost-three-years-younger sister, Nicky, first started showing up in the gossip columns in the late 1990s. Then billed as "the Hilton sisters," they were the third set of photogenic blond siblings to come out of New York's wealthy Upper East Side in a decade.

Before them came Samantha and Serena Boardman—wallflowers by comparison to the Hiltons—whose father's hedge fund controlled a reported six billion dollars.

There were also the storied Miller sisters, heiresses to an empire of duty-free stores worth over four billion dollars: Marie-Chantal (who married Crown Prince Pavlos of Greece), Pia (who bagged a Getty oil heir), and Alexandra (who wed Alexander von Fürstenberg, son of designer Diane and Prince Egon, a German aristocrat).

But the Hilton sisters embodied a more aggressive time. They personified the same strain of consumerism-as-feminism that was also running through popular culture courtesy of television hits like *Sex and the City*.

The mainstream media took notice almost immediately. The *New Yorker* magazine (of all places) gave the teens a double-page photograph, along with a slender two hundred words of copy, in an October 1999 issue. *Vanity Fair* dedicated a feature-length profile to the pair in September of the following year.

In 2003, the Fox network offered the sisters a reality show, *The Simple Life*, modeled on the 1960s sitcom *Green Acres*. Nicky, already sensing that she would prefer a future away from the spotlight, declined to participate.

Paris found a new sidekick in Nicole Richie, a daughter of the R & B star Lionel Richie, but it was apparent when the program aired across America that she was the star of the show.

A year later, a sex tape she had filmed in 2001 with her then-partner, Rick Salomon, was commercially released by Red Light District Video under the title *1 Night in Paris*. Many expected the shame to bury her, but she surfed it to only greater success.

The New York gossip columns sometimes claim to have invented Paris, but we didn't—she invented herself.

Paris's combination of beauty, privilege, and personality tapped into the yearnings of the time. She aligned with a cultural shift toward wealth, rather than just the traditional route of show business, as a path to celebrity.

But the reflexive hostility toward her, especially after she survived the sex tape scandal, was both immediate and inchoate. When pressed to articulate exactly what was so wrong with her, however, critics were reduced to muttering.

She did not deserve the attention, some said. By being "famous for nothing," she was guilty of doing something wrong—robbing us, somehow.

And she wasn't merely criticized—there was a hot rage directed at her from both men and women. Part of what made Paris such a phenomenon was that she was capable of rousing in some quarters a deeply felt anger.

It's true that she wasn't a role model—my own column recorded a number of her nasty, racist remarks. Nor was she much of a pet parent, overfeeding and then discarding her trademark handbag Chihuahuas, like the poor, doomed Tinkerbell.

But in her own way, with her antics, she was raising a middle finger to the patriarchy. The fact that she controlled and obviously enjoyed her own sex life was a big part of what pushed people's buttons. Because, how dare she?

Paris may have used sex to catch people's attention, but she retained it by performing a Grand Guignol of race, gender, and class. In this, she had an assist from other currents in the culture. She emerged as a stereotype of white privilege at a time when the most influential commentary on materialism was coming from hip-hop, the dominant artistic movement of the age.

Hip-hop didn't so much critique wealth culture as embrace it in a bear hug. Despite the recurring homophobia and misogyny of its content, rap's hypermasculine avatars appropriated surprisingly feminine signifiers of high-status fashion, including gold necklaces, fur coats, and conspicuous diamonds. They took care that their bodies were beautiful.

By drenching themselves in consumer luxury, the artists were making a statement about access to money and power by historically disenfranchised communities of color. But the imagery also operated on a literal level, defining for a large audience what it looked like to be rich. Designers picked up on the shift. After decades as a fashion taboo, fur staged a comeback; watches got bigger; and suddenly Swarovski crystals were on everything. "Bling" became pervasive to the point of ubiquity.

Paris, an actual rich person who possessed inherited wealth from a famous old-guard family, leaned hard into this aesthetic.

Her great-uncle Conrad had been the first husband of Elizabeth Taylor, who knew a thing or two about wearing diamonds. But Paris's bedazzled sunglasses and crystal-encrusted flip phone owed more to hip-hop's appropriation of WASP status symbols than they did to any real jewels hanging on her own family tree. As a rich person performing being wealthy for the purpose of gaining celebrity, she appropriated it right back.

Paris may have been a natural, but she wasn't doing it alone. In 2005, she dumped her Los Angeles publicity firm, run by powerhouse Pat Kingsley, and switched to Dan Klores Communications, a smaller operation based in New York that handled rising stars, musicians, and rappers.

There she was represented by a talented young publicist named Rob Shuter, who had a knack for placing his clients at the center of the biggest gossip stories of the moment. Another of his clients was Sean Combs, the rapper who regularly confounded journalists by changing his nom de guerre from Puff Daddy to Puffy to P. Diddy to Diddy. Rob would often say Combs's instinctive grasp of the forces that shape publicity taught him everything he knew about the business.

Under new guidance, Paris scored a key PR coup. A 2005 article in the Arts section of the *New York Times*, titled "Paris, Inc.," framed her not as some feckless waif who didn't realize the world was laughing at her but as a strategic opportunist in charge of a multinational business.

"Obviously I know what I'm doing," she told the journalist Lola Ogunnaike.

Inevitably, the story contained multiple comparisons to Donald Trump. And while it hardly inoculated her from tabloid snickering, the article perceptibly changed the narrative around who Paris was and what she was doing.

After all, those multimillion-dollar revenues spoke for themselves. Maybe she was a canny businesswoman after all?

It was into this cultural context that Kim Kardashian confidently marched—courtesy of my "Gatecrasher" column—in January 2007.

The two slowest weeks of the year for gossip are at the end of August and between Christmas and New Year's Day. In August we filled the space with pictures of celebrities in their bathing suits in the Hamptons; in December we filled the space with pictures of celebrities in their bathing suits in Mustique. We also ran "packages"— prewritten set pieces like "Ten celebrities on what they're buying for holiday presents this year" or end-of-year awards for bad behavior.

Covering this graveyard gossip shift in the last week of 2006, I was passing the time reading the website of the *Sydney Morning Herald*. Paris Hilton was visiting the city, where it was the hot, wet Australian summer. She was then at the pinnacle of her fame and had a friend-cum-assistant from America along with her.

Seeing pictures of them posted together on Bondi Beach, I was struck by the star quality of the other young woman—an unknown Los Angeles resident named Kim Kardashian.

Popular culture imagery at the time was dominated by a fantasy of youth and wealth rooted in Southern California. Breezy television shows like *Laguna Beach*, *The O.C.*, and *The Hills*, which introduced words like "Kitson" and "Speidi" into the vernacular, defined the zeitgeist.

Paris was a queen bee of that scene, anchoring a posse of equally photogenic girlfriends that included her sister, Nicole Richie, and *The O.C.* star Mischa Barton. Their various feuds, friendships, and romantic liaisons were charted by celebrity magazines the way British royal historians obsess over the Tudors and the Stuarts.

Mischa dated Paris's buddy Brandon Davis, grandson of a billionaire oil mogul turned Hollywood studio chief. In turn, he feuded picturesquely with Lindsay Lohan, calling her "fire crotch" on the sidewalk outside Hyde nightclub one spring evening. The gossip columns, including mine, covered the remark as if it were Martin Luther nailing his Ninety-Five Theses to the door of Wittenberg's Castle Church.

It all seemed like the acme of young adult glamour. Magazines were full of pictures of fresh-faced celebrities shopping on Robertson

Boulevard, like the tiny Olsen twins, clutching huge cups of Starbucks coffee while being shepherded by hulking bodyguards into gigantic SUVs, bathed in the flattering Los Angeles sunshine. Their friends all had Von Dutch caps and Ed Hardy shirts and @tmail addresses for their Sidekicks, and everyone was dating Wilmer Valderrama.

And then, all of a sudden, there was Kim.

With her sultry looks, framed by saucer-sized obsidian glasses and an almost architectural blowout, she exemplified everything that was fun and attractive about that moment in pop culture. I was sure that she would crop up again and made a mental note to look for her.

In fact, her curtain-raising moment arrived just two weeks later.

The first journalist to write about her sex tape may have been Jawn Murray, in a blind item for AOL Black Voices at the end of 2006. Without mentioning names, he suggested that "a certain R&B singer, who has never really caught a major break," was poised to release a steamy private video in order to embarrass his ex-girlfriend, who had since moved on with another man.

Separately, I got wind that Vivid Entertainment, an adult film company that had a sideline in celebrity sex tapes, was shopping a video featuring the minor hip-hop star Ray J. The woman in the tape was Kim, who was then working odd jobs around Hollywood as a stylist for Ray's sister, the better-known singer Brandy Norwood, as well as being Paris's assistant.

It was common practice for anyone looking to sell a celebrity sex tape to talk to the New York gossip columns. First, the free publicity was important to stimulate demand for the product. But even more important, it was a strategy to talk up the value of the tape in order to make it more lucrative for its subjects to sign over the rights.

To be clear, it is illegal to sell or broadcast a video of two people having sex without their consent. Celebrities often like to muddy this point, because they don't want the public to understand that if a sex tape of theirs is being sold by a third party, it almost certainly means they have authorized its release and are benefiting from the proceeds.

Paris Hilton received a reported $400,000 from her video, although her camp initially spun the payment as punitive damages extracted from Salomon and Red Light District Video, rather than a revenue share. In the 2005 *Times* article, however, her lawyer admitted that she was, in fact, profiting from the tape.

The legal consequences of not getting consent can be significant. Just ask the gossip website *Gawker*, which published a brief clip of a sex tape featuring the wrestler Hulk Hogan without his permission. When he sued, a Florida court awarded him $115 million in damages, a sum that forced *Gawker* to close.

For these reasons, I believe Vivid's willingness to talk about the tape was their way of getting Kim and Ray to sign on the dotted line. The item ran in my column on January 11, 2007.

Kim initially denied the existence of the video, saying: "There is no tape. It is false."

But my source told me: "She and her camp want to decide exactly what gets released and what doesn't. She is actively involved in its sale, but wishes to do it through a third party."

The tape was being brokered for a million dollars.

"It's your typical graphic sex tape," the source said. "There's a golden shower at the end."

The tipster also allowed that edit approval was on the table in return for securing release rights. The final video did not contain a golden shower, which Kim always denied participating in, and she later cited that detail as the reason why she initially disavowed the tape's existence.

Nonetheless, a few weeks later, she came clean. It was also not lost on anyone that a sex tape is what launched the career of her mentor and soon-to-be-former best friend, Paris Hilton. It wasn't a catastrophe; it was a business model.

Still, Kim did not want to be seen as benefiting from the video. She told me for my February 4 column: "I'm not poor; I'm not desperate. I would never attempt to sell a tape. It would humiliate me and ruin my family. I have two successful businesses, and I don't need the money."

After some further maneuvering—Kim filed a lawsuit against Vivid, then negotiated—she came to an agreement with the video company, which put the tape out under the title *Kim Kardashian, Superstar*.

Ten years later, the *New York Post* would report the video had "been viewed online more than 150 million times and ha[d] made over $50 million." Despite her discomfort over its content, the tape proved to be rocket fuel for Kim's career.

An early indicator of her new position in popular culture was that status-sensitive Paris Hilton immediately stopped being seen with her.

In another twist of the knife, the E! network canceled Paris's star vehicle, *The Simple Life*, in August 2007—the same month it announced it would begin developing a new, unscripted series that debuted later that year, called *Keeping Up with the Kardashians*.

A few months later, some sweaty tipster sent me a series of consensually taken topless photographs of Kim's older sister, Kourtney Kardashian. Was it an egregious violation of her privacy or just the next phase in the rollout of the family business plan?

Who knows. Exhausted, I deleted them.


K im Kardashian grew up around Hollywood and knew exactly what to do with her nascent fame. The empress had no clothes, on purpose.

But Paris Hilton inspired more people than just her star protégé. Her conspicuous success brought on a wave of other imitators, in what came to be known as "the heiress trend."

Suddenly young women, and the occasional man, from wealthy families were hiring publicists to keep the press abreast of their lifestyle, social calendar, and various brand extensions.

The most successful of these were Gillian and Lydia Hearst, two stylish, beautiful, and couture-loving sisters in their early twenties. Along with their equally mediagenic cousin, Amanda, the three were great-granddaughters of the publishing baron William Randolph Hearst, model for the title character in *Citizen Kane*.

The media empire he founded, headquartered in a handsome tower on Eighth Avenue, is still in his family's hands. Today, Hearst Communications makes most of its money as a business data provider. But among consumers it was still best-known for its newspaper and television holdings, including part of the sports broadcaster ESPN, as well as a stable of popular magazines like *Harper's Bazaar*, *Esquire*, and *Town & Country* (where I am a contributor).

With her fine-boned features, Lydia was the sister who most resembled her mother, Patty Hearst. Patty made international headlines when, as a teenage undergraduate at Berkeley in the 1970s, she was kidnapped by a left-wing domestic terrorist group that called itself the Symbionese Liberation Army. She was not only brainwashed into committing crimes with the group—and later jailed for them—but she also spoke of being raped and tortured by its members.

Despite her traumatic experiences, in later life Patty came across as a warm and well-adjusted woman with an unusually sly sense of humor. She used to unnerve me, whenever we spoke at charity events, by making jokes about her own notorious past. Although she always had a twinkle in her eye, meant to put people at ease, I never quite found it possible to laugh.

Patty's niece and daughters represented the second wave of the heiress trend. It was a glitzier update on the fusty notion of New York debutantes—young women from wealthy families who would be formally presented to society at a ball held in the last week of every year at the Pierre Hotel.

The implied difference was that debutantes behaved, and heiresses didn't. Fortunately for their immortal souls, however, the Hearsts never managed to match the hell raised by their immediate predecessors, the sisters Hilton.

While Gillian and Amanda seemed to only modestly enjoy the spotlight, Lydia thrived in it. Her career as a working model received considerable buoyancy from the wave of interest in heiresses—she landed the cover of *Vogue Italia* and walked in shows for Chanel and Fendi, among other high-profile jobs.

Lydia was likable and ran with a fun downtown crowd. At the same time, however, another well-born young lady trying to make it as a model was having less success.

From her late teens, Ivanka Trump had walked in shows for established houses, including Vivienne Westwood, Thierry Mugler, and Paco Rabanne, as well as more avant-garde designers like Marc Bouwer and Zang Toi. While she was never taken seriously within the fashion industry, she was among the first to use the personal-branding template that became the standard for those who followed.

One important element was to hire a publicist fluent in the methods of New York high society. Both Lydia and Ivanka worked with R. Couri Hay, a veteran whose experience dated to the 1980s. Back then he worked with Cornelia Guest, the daughter of old-school society hostess and original Capote swan C. Z. Guest, to whom he attached the tabloid-friendly sobriquet "Debutante of the Decade."

His knack for packaging socialites as a cultural commodity artfully exploited a growing niche demand for society publicists. Their exclusive ranks included Catherine Saxton, who was closely associated with the Trumps and the Hiltons, and Norah Lawlor—who had become a friend, despite being the same Canadian gatekeeper who had denied Horacio and me entry to Idlewild that frigid February night years before.

Suddenly there was a large market in representing the daughters of wealthy families, who, even if they lacked a famous name to monetize, each hoped that they could parlay party pictures into lasting fame.

The culture's momentary obsession with heiresses like the Hearsts, the Hiltons, and their doomed friend Casey Johnson, scion of the Johnson & Johnson billions, even spawned its own media. These included the *Gossip Girl* books and television adaptation, as well as snarky, anonymously written blogs like *Park Avenue Peerage* and *Socialite Rank*, which addressed the field of players in the tone of judges at a dog show.

*Socialite Rank* captivated the competitive uptown set with its numerical listing each week of which girls were gaining and losing popularity—and, most important, who was on top. The women who shuttled up and down the list each week had names like Arden Wohl, Bettina Zilkha, Lauren Davis, and Fabiola Beracasa—while the also-rans ended up in a section cruelly titled "Don't Kill Yourself, You Almost Made It."

The table stakes required to play this game were photographs from society events. For this it was necessary to get in front of Patrick McMullan, a onetime media acolyte of Andy Warhol who built a career as the city's leading nightlife photographer. Among the social crowd, the word "Patrick," as in "to Patrick someone"—meaning to search for their name on his website of party pictures—was just a more specific form of the verb "Google."

All this created a frenzy of jealousy and ambition among those who went out each night longing to be photographed. For these women, it was anathema to be seen in the same outfit at different events, even if they were held consecutively on the same day.

During Fashion Week, some women would change five times a day, often in the backseats of cars between events, so they could maximize the number of different looks they offered to photographers at different shows and after-parties.

It got to the point where they wouldn't even bother going inside the event they were nominally attending. I stood outside many parties and observed an aspiring socialite enter the red carpet and stroll smiling in front of the flashbulbs, only to get back into her waiting car and drive off when she was out of sight of the photographers.

Most of the hopefuls trying to leverage their money into fame were women. But there was also the occasional male socialite, like Fabian

Basabe, a gorgeous eel who made the cover of the *New York Post* in 2004 by dirty dancing in front of photographers with the First Daughter Barbara Bush. After his initial brush with fame, he employed Couri Hay at a fee he said was $10,000 a month to keep him in the gossip columns as an "It boy."

Another was Eric Villency, a former model turned industrial designer who was promoting himself as the face of his family's furniture business. Eric attended events with his equally attractive girlfriend, Kimberly Guilfoyle, a Fox News anchor and former wife of San Francisco's Democratic mayor Gavin Newsom. At openings, the pair would plant themselves in front of photographers and not budge, until I started referring to them in my column as "red carpet roadblocks."

But nobody who ventured onto the society circuit in the early 2000s was more ambitious than a gust of humid Southern air named Tinsley Mortimer.

Tinsley was the prettiest girl in Prettytown. Preternaturally photogenic, she had blond, ringleted hair that looked like it was spun fresh every morning in a cotton candy machine.

Summer styles suited her, and she liked sleeveless, flirty sundresses cut tight in the bodice and flared to a skirt that ended midthigh, paired with strappy high heels.

The Tinz—as the social blogs christened her—owned Chihuahuas named BeBe, Bella, and Bambi. She didn't carry them in public, but their fussy presence seemed to invisibly surround her, like a fragrance. Her favorite color was pink.

Tinsley was a Virginia-raised debutante who married her high school beau, Topper Mortimer. His money derived from an ancestor who had been president of Standard Oil. She went out almost every night, and her strenuously cultivated social profile kept her in the number one spot on *Socialite Rank* for over a year.

The Tinz was a spectacle to behold, dutifully passing through all the Stations of the Cross on her road to socialite fame—right up to crucifixion and burial.

Following the Hilton playbook, her first move was to debut with an equally blond sister, Dabney Mercer. Next, she positioned herself in front of Patrick McMullan's lens, beginning a collection of what would grow to become thousands of pictures on his website.

Then came a major coup. Dior made her a "beauty ambassador" and even named a shade of lip gloss after her: Tinsley Pink. It was only a logical next step that Tinsley should design a handbag line, which, she would gush to reporters, was hugely popular in Japan.

And she anchored a short-lived reality series called *High Society*, presented on the CW network in 2010 as a real-life version of its hit social soap, *Gossip Girl*. The show bombed quickly, but the hothouse atmosphere of social rivalry it created spilled over into the real world with comic results.

When Olivia Palermo—a younger socialite who appeared on *The City*, a competing reality show—began to gain a following on the fashion-and-beauty turf that Tinz had staked out as her own, the pair squared off in the gossip columns.

There used to be an annual charity fashion show called Dressed to Kilt—an overlong event with a Scottish theme that invited a seemingly endless parade of local socials to do a turn on the catwalk. Eric Villency used it as an excuse to take his shirt off; Donald Trump was a regular in the audience.

One year, the Palermo camp claimed that Tinsley elbowed their girl backstage, as they passed each other en route to the runway.

"She checked her so hard that Olivia fell into the railing," claimed one of two witnesses who called the alleged incident into "Gatecrasher."

Tinsley denied it, telling me: "I never came within an arm's length of her."

But it gave Olivia's publicist, Kelly Cutrone—star of her own one-season Bravo reality show, *Kell on Earth*, where her catchphrase to her staff was "If you have to cry, go outside"—the chance to drop one of the great on-the-record comments of the claws-out socialite era.

She told me: "The only thing Olivia Palermo is guilty of is being beautiful, smart, and a size two. If there are people in the community that get jealous, then we're going to pray for them."

By this stage, the public was beginning to tire of all the Paris Hilton clones clopping around New York in their high-heeled wedges. But the real postscript to the heiress era was provided by Casey Johnson, one of Paris's closest friends.

Casey was five foot two, with a Kewpie doll face and a fondness for flaunting her family's multibillion-dollar fortune by wearing enormous diamond jewelry to accessorize her Chanel suits.

But she also had a large appetite for drama, which could sometimes have a malevolent edge. She was known for getting into public, screaming fights with friends she'd fallen out with—and harassing them afterward.

For a while, she was adept at keeping her fingerprints off any incriminating evidence. Like a luckless innocent who was perpetually in the wrong place at the wrong time, she often found herself in nightclubs seated at tables that deteriorated into brawls around her.

These included Bungalow 8 in New York, where Nicole Richie cut the face of Casey's former boyfriend with broken glass, and Xes in Los Angeles, when her pal Bijou Phillips got into a fistfight with one of Casey's female rivals.

Later, her methods became more direct. In 2009, she was arrested by Los Angeles police after breaking into the home of yet another nemesis—stealing that woman's jewelry and clothes and leaving a used vibrator in her bed as a calling card.

Casey's family distanced themselves from her after an unseemly feud over a boyfriend—the other woman being her even more wealthy and connected aunt, Libet Johnson—played out in the pages of the *New York Post* and *Vanity Fair*.

After becoming estranged from her father, Woody Johnson—the owner of the New York Jets NFL team, who would later become President Trump's ambassador to the Court of St. James's—Casey moved permanently to Los Angeles, where she hoped to pursue a career in front of the cameras.

Aspiring to be a serious actress, she turned down the costarring role in Paris Hilton's career-making reality show, *The Simple Life*, feeling that the format was beneath her.

Later, unable to find work in the movies, it was a decision she vocally regretted. In an effort to find another point of entry into that world, she embarked on a high-profile relationship with the bisexual reality star Tila Tequila.

Even in Los Angeles, the world capital of exhibitionists, Tila was a standout talent. She and Casey would sloppily make out on red carpets and pose for photographers with matching raised middle fingers.

After their relationship ended, Tila went through a period when she contemplated suicide each night on Ustream, a short-lived social-streaming platform that was like a live version of YouTube. Dressed in lingerie, she lounged in front of the camera during West Coast prime-time hours, pressing a handgun to her temple and sometimes sticking it in her mouth, exhorting fans to weigh in as to whether she should live or die.

In addition to Tila, Casey dated Courtenay Semel, the daughter of a former Yahoo! CEO. Courtenay, who had her own designs on fame, liked to call herself "the lesbian Don Juan." Just to complete the circle, she also appeared with Fabian Basabe in *Filthy Rich: Cattle Drive*, a reality show devoted to the idle children of wealthy parents.

The heiress moment was all about celebrating the learned incompetence of tremendous privilege—with the glib reassurance that parental money would buy off any consequences. Casey reveled in the line-skipping, plebeian-avoiding power she believed this brought. But along the way, she became addicted to drugs and alcohol, which exacerbated her existing diabetes and borderline personality disorder.

In 2007, she adopted a newborn baby from Kazakhstan, naming her Ava-Monroe, after her idol, Marilyn Monroe. The following year, hoping to jolt her stalled show-business career, Casey invited me to a party she threw during Oscars week at her Los Angeles mansion.

It was a tall white house on an odd-shaped block, with a steep canyon wall rising immediately behind it. The unkept pool was bright green with algae, and inside the home had a sense of being uncleaned and only partially unpacked.

A smattering of the city's celebrity set showed up to meet the newly arrived Ava-Monroe: Joan Collins, Tara Reid, Nicky Hilton, and Donald Trump's second ex-wife, Marla Maples. I remember Nicky's mother, Kathy Hilton, sitting on a straight-backed chair in the white foyer, delightedly bouncing the baby on her knee and cooing like it was her own grandchild.

And when Casey's family staged an intervention, it was Kathy—not her own mother, Sale Johnson—who took temporary custody of the baby.

Trying to pressure her into rehab, Casey's parents stopped paying the bills, and she lost the house and her car. She briefly checked into residential treatment at Cliffside Malibu but soon walked out and moved into a West Hollywood guesthouse owned by a family friend.

It wasn't the drugs that killed Casey, but they prevented her from managing her diabetes, which was the cause of her death at age thirty.

Around one a.m. on December 29, 2009, she tweeted: "Sweet dreams everyone . . . I'm getting a new car . . . Any ideas? Cant b a two seater cause we have a daughter . . . sedan, sports car, suv??"

She likely died a few hours afterward; her body was discovered by a maid six days later. After that, nobody wanted to be an heiress anymore.

**H**arvey Weinstein only telephoned when he wanted to yell.

Early in my career at the *News*, I was walking along a street in midtown one evening when he called from the Miramax jet, heading back to Los Angeles from New York, screaming bloody murder.

Harvey was the producer of a stage version of director Baz Luhrmann's *La Bohème*, which had just had its Broadway opening night, attracting an unusually large brace of Hollywood stars.

He was an enormous man who wore his appetites on his sleeve— and sometimes his shirtfront, where food stains would accumulate like a list of sins. Because he was so large, I discovered that a good tactic for covering his events was to follow along behind him, like a remora on a whale, and take note of whoever he was speaking with.

On this occasion I overheard him telling different guests, including Tom Hanks's wife, Rita Wilson, in two separate conversations that he was "fighting with Jeffrey." From the context, it seemed clear he was referring to his fellow Hollywood heavyweight Jeffrey Katzenberg. So, with the caveat that he had not mentioned a last name, I reported it that way.

And Harvey was not happy.

Mid-harangue, the pilot made him hang up because the jet was beginning its descent into the Los Angeles airport. Fifteen minutes later, after the plane was safely on the tarmac, he called me back to resume yelling.

His publicist, Matt Hiltzik, arranged another call after Harvey had calmed down. That same week, the *New Yorker* had run a profile of the mogul that focused on his volatile temper. Matt was on a damage-control mission that included the novel strategy of having Harvey blame his outbursts on a heightened blood-glucose level from eating too many M&M's.

So I ran a follow-up item that portrayed Harvey—albeit tongue in cheek—not as a screaming volcano of id but as a mellow new age guy who was working on himself.

The squib concluded: "Asked if this was the dawn of a kinder, gentler Harvey, he replied mildly: 'It's always been this way.'"

That item hasn't aged well. It was intended as winking sarcasm, but still, it was flattering coverage in exchange for access.

Matt was always cleaning up Harvey's messes, and he made an effort to keep cordial relations with the columns. Once Harvey had him call to ask the identities of the personalities in a blind item of mine:

"Which New York bigwig, visiting his ex-wife and young daughter in Los Angeles, tried to score points with the child by telling her he was in town for a meeting with Harvey Weinstein? The ex later sniped: 'She's eight years old, like she's going to be impressed by Harvey Weinstein!'"

I was happy to tell him the item referred to Donald and Tiffany Trump, and Marla Maples.

Unlike the *Post* gossip writers, nobody at the *Daily News*, as far as I'm aware, received money from Harvey while they were on staff. It's possible that, since we were the second-ranked gossip outlet in the city, he just didn't think it was worth the investment.

Still, there was always the scent of cash, like cheese in a trap. In 2001, Talk Miramax Books published a memoir by a former *News* gossip columnist, A. J. Benza, who had done a deal on his way out the door four years earlier.

In its review, *Variety* noted that Miramax also planned to develop the book into a film. (While that film never materialized, A. J. would later feature as a supporting player in Harvey's efforts to silence his sexual assault accusers as a freelance gossip investigator digging up dirt on his behalf.)

And that was just what was going on in plain sight. Harvey also wielded influence in other, more clandestine ways.

One of the morning rituals in the newspaper gossip business was to review the celebrity photographs that had come in overnight on the wire services. They ranged from tame, posed pictures on the red carpet to intrusive, long-lens paparazzi shots of stars sunbathing nude on vacation.

One day, around the time of the Cannes Film Festival, a series of images came in of Harvey cavorting in the sea with a buxom, unidentified young woman in an undersize bikini. At the time, he was still married to his first wife, Eve.

Swimming with a person of the opposite sex may not have been grounds for divorce, but as the photo series progressed, the couple retired to a hotel pool, where Harvey reclined on a severely taxed lounge chair and his companion . . . lay on top of him.

It looked about as comfortable for the woman as installing a fridge while eight months pregnant, but there it was in color.

Later in the day, the pictures were bought by an unknown party. Although the purchaser remained anonymous, whoever it was certainly wasn't a publisher, because the photos never appeared.

Although the *Daily News* did not buy rights to print the images, we could report on the fact that we had seen them. One of the other gossip columns—there were at least four at different times during my tenure—claimed the story and made the call to Harvey.

But just like the vanishing pictures, the written version of that story never appeared, either. The producer negotiated a deal to kill it in exchange for dirt on other Hollywood power players.

Harvey didn't get it all his own way in the gossip pages—he was often portrayed as a vicious bully and a womanizer. But we certainly didn't treat him like the rapist that he was later convicted of being.

Harvey exactly fulfilled the archetype of the bellowing, overbearing old-time studio head, and we knew he was sleeping with many of the actresses whose careers he could influence. But we treated it all with gallows humor: it was suggested in the newsroom that a cocktail could be named after one of his Oscar-winning leading ladies, called the Harvey Weinbanger.

In our complicity in the bigger network of favor trading—and at other newspapers, actual payola—we imagined that if it was not pleasant for these women to have sex with Harvey, then at least it was a consensual, career-minded decision on their parts. That was wrong, and we failed in our duty to hold Harvey Weinstein accountable.


Newsrooms are stressful places. And if you're not under stress as a journalist at a daily tabloid, you're probably not doing your job.

Nonetheless, the *Daily News* was a pretty good place to work. Our publisher, Mort Zuckerman, left us alone—his main reason for buying the paper was so that he could go on the Sunday morning political shows and expound his opinions. I saw him less often in the newsroom than I had seen Murdoch visiting the *Post*, even though the latter owned newspapers throughout the English-speaking world.

Things started to change around 2007, however, when a new editor was hired to oversee the features section. Bronagh Cailleach was a tabloid veteran with a sketchy reputation. It was whispered that at her previous job, an underling had been suspended after growing so enraged that he cleared her desk with a sweep of his arm. But she was good friends with some of the other journalists whom I greatly respected, so how bad could it be?

When Bronagh arrived, she was smart and beautiful and pure, unalloyed evil. A wimple of lustrous red hair framed her pale, freckled complexion. She had a great figure and dressed flatteringly in pencil skirts paired with sweaters in a palette of Benetton-y scarlets and greens. She smoked and drank and had once lived in Los Angeles, where she had been the girlfriend of a famous Irish actor.

She seemed like a buddy with whom you could belly up to the bar and have a really good gossip. And, having once been on the movie-star-boyfriend circuit, she had some great stories.

Immediately upon moving to the *Daily News*, Bronagh had blinds installed inside the glass walls of her office so that her meetings would be private. She also replaced her standard-issue swivel chair with a Louis XIV–style, gold-painted straight-back, its round seat upholstered in leopard print. A small pile of acrid-smelling pumps in her signature red and green began to accumulate under the desk.

In the early days, she made it clear to the columnists that it was us against the world. We were a team that was going clear the cobwebs out of the *Daily News* together.

Being in favor meant being invited into her office for endless blinds-down secret meetings, during which Bronagh would craft plots against the rest of the newsroom.

After blocking all outside light, she would set a match to one of the endlessly available Diptyque scented candles—which were the favor-currying gift of choice to send editors at the time—as a strategy for masking the smell from the Kool cigarettes she was about to smoke.

If the meeting took place after six p.m., she would send an intern out to get wine—usually something cloyingly sweet and cheap, like Cupcake Butterkissed Chardonnay or Barefoot Riesling. It was awful even being on her good side—but that didn't last long.

Bronagh targeted the other women in the office first, reducing the gentle books editor to tears. That editor's office, which was tucked around a corner from the features newsroom, became a trauma center for those recovering from their latest run-in with the boss.

She was also big on public humiliations, which she performed with great élan during the weekly staff meeting. Woe betide the intern who made an insufficient number of photocopied handouts, because she would stop a meeting of thirty seasoned journalists in order to berate a twenty-year-old until she cried.

One day, a door to one of the stalls in the ladies' room was found hanging off its hinges.

"I know that's about me," Bronagh said of the apparent act of vandalism. "And if that's how they want it, fine. I told facilities *not* to fix it."

At the time Bronagh was dating a dignified, silver-haired man named Niall. The ups and downs of that relationship directly impacted the experience of those of us who worked for her, and any time they spent the night together it made the following day in the office much more bearable.

It was one of her quirks that even as she was cruel to the staff, she would overshare details of her personal life. So, we all knew that there was a particular weekend away coming up on which she had pinned her hope that he might propose.

Instead, he dumped her, and we started updating our résumés.

Everything about Bronagh set me on edge, from her conspicuous cruelty to having to breathe in her mentholated cigarette smoke. And she clearly washed those sweaters when they should have been dry-cleaned; the pilling drove me nuts.

An early casualty of her behavior was her decades-long friendship with the other journalists, which burned into cigarette ash over a period of six months. Then it was my turn to fall from grace.

Standard practice at the paper was that if a big story on your beat broke over the weekend, a news desk editor would call and you'd get to work. If you didn't get a call, then congratulations—you got to have a weekend.

But Bronagh instructed me to monitor breaking celebrity news over the weekend and proactively report out stories, independent of getting an assignment from the desk. That meant I was never off duty and constantly watching the wire for fear of missing something.

But without an editor's deciding what warranted an assignment, anything that happened—a minor television actor getting married or having a baby, for example—could potentially be the subject of a story. It turned me into a nervous wreck.

Bronagh—just saying her name felt like having a dog's tongue in your mouth—also had a talent for assigning fruitless, demeaning assignments. One memorable weekend she assigned me to stand outside a Hamptons estate to watch Angelina Jolie drive in to attend a fundraiser and, four hours later, drive out again.

But this was not gee-oh-ell-eff. And I enjoyed the job, so I kept my head down—until the final twist.

When celebrity stories were especially good, they were taken out of the gossip columns, in the middle of the paper, and put in the news section, which filled the first several pages. This was known as getting stories in "the front."

Bronagh told me that I needed to get more of my stories in the front. To that end, I should make them flashier, "and worry if they're true later."

There is a proud tradition in tabloid media of the "beat-up," meaning to blow a minor incident out of proportion in order to create the impression of a major scandal.

This felt like going further, and I had no intention of doing that. But editors can do whatever they like to stories between the time they are filed and when they appear in print.

And the damage that an editor's last-minute changes can do to a journalist's reputation lasts longer than any individual job. So, much as I loved the *Daily News,* in the spring of 2008, I quit.

One of my last bittersweet stories was breaking that, after twenty-three years in business, Florent Morellet would be closing his diner. In that time, his rent had gone from $1,350 to $30,000 a month.

With Florent's shuttering, the remaking of the Meatpacking District was complete. An Apple store now stood on the corner that had once overlooked the neighborhood's sex clubs, and one street away in Chelsea, Google would pay $1.9 billion for the same block-sized building across from the apartment I had shared with Horacio that had once disturbed us all day with jackhammering.

Before I left "Gatecrasher," however, there was one more assignment to cover. I had been invited to attend Ivana Trump's fourth wedding, to a slick-haired Italian of no apparent profession named Rossano Rubicondi.

At the time, she was fifty-nine years old and he was thirty-six. The event was to be hosted by her most famous ex-husband, Donald Trump, at his Palm Beach club, Mar-a-Lago. The invitation specified white suits for men and pastel colors for ladies—but no pink or yellow.

The wedding seemed like it would be fun. And besides, I had already bought the suit.

# 11

## Mar-a-Lago

nly a meager mind could find the relationship between the Trump and Hilton families as fascinating as I do. But to a gawping foreigner, they're the same kind of American.

The families have been friends for generations and share a number of superficial similarities, including the same social circles, development-related wealth, and a fondness for naming their heirs Barron. Even their origin myths are alike.

The Hilton founding patriarch, Augustus, was a nineteenth-century Norwegian immigrant who married a German American. Donald's grandfather Friedrich was an exact contemporary who emigrated to the United States from Germany.

Both families got into the hotel business early. Friedrich Trump ran a cathouse called the Arctic Restaurant and Hotel during the Yukon gold rush, while Augustus profitably added rooms to his general store in New Mexico. His son, Conrad, launched the Hilton empire proper when he bought the Mobley Hotel in Cisco, Texas, in 1919.

Around the same time, after Friedrich's death in 1918, his son, Fred, went into partnership with his widowed mother. They founded a home construction business in Queens, New York, that would later be known as the Trump Organization.

While the Trump fortune accumulated slowly, the Hiltons more quickly hit it rich. Seduced by Hollywood, the wealthy Hilton men embodied a new archetype of martini-swilling, nightclub-going twentieth-century playboy. They became staples of an emerging media form, gossip magazines, which chronicled the explosion in celebrity created by the American film industry.

In 1941, Conrad married the Hungarian-born screen siren Zsa Zsa Gabor, becoming the second of her nine husbands. The marriage lasted a year.

In 1950, his son Conrad Jr. (known as Nicky) wed the actress Elizabeth Taylor, who was then just eighteen years old. He became the first of her seven husbands—or eight, if you count her two marriages to Richard Burton separately.

That marriage lasted less than a year, after which he cycled through many of the Hollywood beauties of the day, including Natalie Wood and Joan Collins. He even bedded his former stepmother, Zsa Zsa—or so she would later claim.

While all this boudoir-hopping was taking place in Los Angeles, Fred Trump was keeping his head down in Queens, building houses. He could not have been less like the Hiltons, who were drawn to show-business glitz and defined in the tabloids by their excesses of money and libido.

But such inherited glamour must have been attractive to Fred's ambitious son, Donald, who was desperate to move the family operation out of marginal Queens and into the center of power. With his equally flamboyant young wife, Ivana, by his side, he befriended Rick and Kathy Hilton after making the jump to Manhattan in the 1980s.

The Hilton family had managed to slip in an extra generation since Augustus and Friedrich got their start on different sides of the new continent. Rick's father, Barron—who was worth $2.3 billion when he died in 2019—was the son of Conrad Sr. and younger brother to Nicky.

(Rick and Donald both have sons called Barron—the maiden name of a Hilton matriarch—which will always remind me of the fake Sydney aristocrat and his bogus credit cards. Such ersatz nobility may also have resonated with the president, who in the 1980s used the alias "John Barron" with journalists when he was pretending to be his own spokesman.)

Both the Hilton and Trump families also experienced a history-diverting shake-up in the order of succession after losing an eldest son to alcoholism. Barron became the Hilton heir after Nicky suffered a fatal, alcohol-related heart attack at age forty-two. Donald's older brother, Freddy, died from alcoholism at forty-three.

In some ways, the Donald Trump and Rick Hilton generation of the dynasties would prove to be mirror images of each other, even as the same cultural tide that was turning the rich into celebrities was lifting the profiles of both families.

Donald was constantly having affairs and getting divorced but had children who seemed relatively well-adjusted. Rick and Kathy, by contrast, enjoyed a placid marriage while presiding over a brood who ran riot.

But the families' outrageous behavior created beneficial synergies, and their escalating antics provided a cultural context and platform for each other's increasing fame. The Hiltons were the Trumps before the Trumps became the Hiltons.

The Hiltons were playboy celebrities first. Then Donald won the eighties, rocketing to tabloid fame with his divorces and showy lifestyle. By the 1990s, a teenage Paris Hilton was taking the game to the next level, eclipsing everyone who had come before.

Donald did not fail to notice Paris's sex tape, nor the remarkable brand platform it provided. *New York* magazine later reported he went as far as "encouraging" his own daughter, Ivanka, "to follow Paris's lead." (A White House spokeswoman called that suggestion "untrue and . . . disgusting.")

And then, for his next act, he scored the political coup that outdid them all. The louche, moneyed Hiltons anticipated Donald Trump, who set the stage for Paris Hilton, who created the conditions for President Trump.

To a close student of the tabloids, such seemingly disparate events are in fact highly connected. A gossip culturalist understands how the trashy stuff connects to the bigger picture, and that we ignore it at our peril.

A t different times I have spoken with each of Donald's three wives. Most often it has been Ivana, the mother of his three oldest children, who is an endearing oddball.

In 2017 she jokingly called herself Trump's "first lady"—earning an official rebuke from the East Wing of the White House, which issued a tart press release reminding the world that Melania was the true First Lady of the United States. In Trumpland, uneasy is the finger that wears the wedding ring.

In fact, the Slovenian-born Melania and the Czech-born Ivana have a lot in common. A New York City resident since 1976, Ivana never shed her almost-impenetrable accent, which turns every sentence she utters into thick alphabet borscht.

But that didn't stop her from talking. She learned the art of publicity from her ex-husband and spoke to me often over the years for articles on subjects ranging from gossip to fashion.

I once visited her town house in the East Sixties for a squib on

one of her vintage frocks—a heavily beaded Bob Mackie fantasy from
the 1980s. Behind its sober façade, Ivana's home was decorated in a
mix of patterns and fabrics not seen outside Chaka Khan's underwear
drawer.

There were acres of leopard print and pale green silk and gold
tassels, paired with flocked wallpaper and ormolu and gold-accented
tortoiseshell picture frames. A mural behind the curving staircase depicted a lush European garden with Roman statuary, with a trompe
l'oeil wrought-iron railing painted to match its real-life counterpart.

Her assistant presented the dress in a plastic dry cleaner's sheath,
which weighed a good twenty pounds.

"Yes, it's very heavy, but nothing ever stops me from having a
great time," Ivana cooed, staying on brand for her image as a nightlife-
loving femme fatale. "In fact, that's my slimming tip of the day: wear
a heavy beaded dress and go dancing every night."

Separately, I had become close with Ivana's best friend, Nikki
Haskell, who ran with an elderly girl gang that also included Joan
Collins and Beverly Johnson, the trailblazing black model. Nikki had
been one of the first women stockbrokers on Wall Street, married
and divorced the same man twice, and created a seminal 1980s cable-
access show about New York nightlife called *The Nikki Haskell Show*.

Nikki thrived around celebrity of any kind and through her show
formed friendships with stars like Liza Minnelli, Jeremy Irons, and
even Imelda Marcos, the Philippines' dictator's wife against whom she
would not hear a word.

She was also the indefatigable pitchwoman for StarCaps, her own
brand of diet pills, which were formulated with a proprietary blend of
miraculous ingredients in Peru. Nikki credited them for her never having budged a dress size and frequently appeared in sequined cocktail
dresses that she had worn for the first time at Studio 54, thirty years
earlier. Like Angelyne before her, she rented billboards on Sunset
Boulevard and plastered them with images of herself, wearing those
same spangled frocks, to keep StarCaps moving.

Nikki was my Virgil in the Trump Inferno. She adored all the family, particularly Donald, whom she recalled as being just another colorful rich guy until the mid-1990s.

What changed him, she believed, was the publication of an autobiography by the former chief executive of the Chrysler Corporation Lee Iacocca, which became an unexpected business phenomenon. *Iacocca: An Autobiography* was a bestseller for two years after its 1984 publication.

According to Nikki, Donald saw that and wanted the same credibility—as well as the fame that came with it—for himself. So, he hired a ghostwriter, and in 1987 published *Trump: The Art of the Deal*, a memoir–cum–advice guide for would-be captains of industry.

Something that may not have been obvious to those who observed the saga of Donald and Ivana from a distance—particularly after the fireworks of their divorce—is how fond of each other they remained. Their children cemented a bond between them, and Donald's divorce from his second wife, Marla Maples, who broke up his marriage to Ivana, probably also made relations easier.

So, when Ivana announced her intention to marry for a fourth time—to a ribbed and lubricated sheath of Italian manhood named Rossano Rubicondi—Donald made his Palm Beach club available as the venue.

Ivana's divorce from Donald had been tabloid performance art, and she applied everything she learned from that spectacle into optimizing her wedding for the media. From product-placing brands— most prominently her daughter's jewelry line, but also strategic speculation over which designer's dress she might wear—to selling the wedding photographs, nothing was left to chance.

Two weeks before the ceremony, the *New York Post* published a story that laid bare all the calculation that had gone into putting the event together.

Richard Johnson landed a scoop that on March 17, less than a month before the wedding, Palm Beach police had gone to Ivana's mansion on Jungle Road, responding to a 911 call for a domestic disturbance. The cops cuffed Rossano but unshackled him after speaking with Ivana—a liberal "catch and release" policy that is certainly not shared by their counterparts in the NYPD.

"Page Six" went on to allege that the fight was over the groom's dragging his feet about signing the prenuptial agreement, which had been drafted by Donald's legal team. Nobody quite knew what Rossano did for a living—the couple had met in Saint-Tropez, where the wealthy and the attractive are known to go fishing for each other—but he seemed not to have much money of his own.

Finally, the column said that *OK!* magazine had paid one million dollars for exclusive rights to the wedding photos, in addition to whatever income may have been generated from inviting two nationally syndicated television programs that were known to pay for access.

As a gossip item, it was a masterpiece, containing everything a reader could possibly want to know about the hidden lives and moneymaking motives of the super-wealthy. It also got the *Post*, my chief competition, disinvited from the wedding—leaving me with the exclusive.

Mar-a-Lago, built in the late 1920s by Marjorie Merriweather Post, a cereal heiress, is a mishmash of ersatz Venetian, Spanish, and Portuguese styles. It looks like a hacienda that would belong to the villain in a period telenovela.

Most of the wedding events took place on the terrace overlooking the pool and surrounding gardens. At the rehearsal party on Friday, champagne stations dotted the lawn, and waiters carrying trays circulated among the hundreds of sharply dressed guests.

The hors d'oeuvres were pigs in blankets and caviar, both available in large supply. Its abundance impressed even this well-heeled group, most of whom were not used to lining up for food. But soon, small trails of people formed in front of the great silver urns filled with crushed ice to chill the kilogram tins of sturgeon eggs.

In the caviar line, I chatted with Lisa Gastineau, the former wife of a professional football player and costar—along with Brittny, her daughter from that marriage—of an E! network reality series called *The Gastineau Girls*. (Although it ran for only two seasons, the show is interesting for being an early iteration of the female-driven, glamourous-family formula that the network got right with its next attempt, *Keeping Up with the Kardashians*.)

Lisa stiffened when Brigitte Nielsen, a muscular Danish actress, appeared at the top of the stairs. Brigitte was also having a moment as a reality star but, worse, had stolen Lisa's footballer husband back in 1986.

She turned away and remarked disapprovingly that the caviar was being served with metal spoons, which would taint its flavor.

Dotted around the lawn were familiar faces like Neil Sedaka; Robin Leach; Rick and Kathy Hilton; Dr. Ruth Westheimer; George Hamilton; Janice Combs, mother of the rapper Diddy; and South African billionaire Sol Kerzner.

I spotted Nikki Haskell chatting with Catherine Saxton, the plummy British woman who worked as a longtime publicist for individuals in the Trump and Hilton families, as well as many of the Trump properties. They were with Ivanka, who was reliably smart and funny, so I went over to get a quote for the column.

"I don't know what to get her for the wedding," Ivanka said about her mother. "It's not like she needs a microwave."

A few hours before the ceremony the next day, Donald Trump flew in on his private jet. We were not at that moment on the best of terms.

One of the quirkier characters around New York was Baird Jones, a freelance gossip stringer who went to parties every night and had an encyclopedic memory for celebrity trivia.

Baird ran into Donald just before a gala for the Save the Music Foundation, which raised money for music education in public schools. He remembered an anecdote about Donald once clobbering his music teacher and asked him about it.

"Not true," Donald replied. "I had altercations with everyone, but

I never punched him. I did not like him and he was not a very good instructor. He had a major mental deficiency."

After Baird called the item into "Gatecrasher," I set about tracking down the source of the original story. It turned out to be Donald's own book, *The Art of the Deal*.

"In the second grade, I actually gave a teacher a black eye," he wrote. "I punched my music teacher because I didn't think he knew anything about music, and I almost got expelled."

I contrasted the two statements in my item, and concluded with a fairly tame kicker: "Isn't it crazy how these rumors get started?" But Donald preferred his press to be fawning and did not appreciate being called out.

He arrived at the wedding from Las Vegas, where he had attended the previous night's final of the Miss USA pageant, which he owned. I had heard he was mad at me, so when I saw him standing on the terrace of his club, I approached gently and tossed a softball question: "Do you have a message of support for Ivana on her wedding day?"

When Donald saw me, his face changed color from orange to red like the highway signs in Australia that warn of the risk of bushfires. He let loose with a stream of bluster, his spittle making rainbows in the Florida sun. Perhaps if I had known that one day he would be president, I would have paid more attention to what he said before he turned on his heel and stomped off. As it was, I recorded his response in my column as: "Of course I do. Why wouldn't I?"

Donald did not sit with the guests on the lawn for the ceremony but could be glimpsed with his arms crossed on the terrace above. Melania was upstairs in the family's private quarters with their toddler son, Barron, sequestered like the new Mrs. Maximilian de Winter in the west wing of Manderley.

The wedding was something to see. There were twenty-four bridesmaids, plus Nikki as the matron of honor, and twenty-four groomsmen. Each group filed down a different side of the twin staircase in the garden, like two columns of ants headed to the same picnic.

Ivanka was the maid of honor, in a column of yellow, while Ivana wore crystal-studded pink chiffon, hence the ban on guests' wearing those colors. The bride walked down the stairs to "Unchained Melody," accompanied by her sons, Donald Jr. and Eric, who gave her away. The groom jogged in, smirking, to the theme from *Rocky*.

Maryanne Trump Barry, Donald's sister and a federal judge, conducted the ceremony under a twenty-foot garlanded trellis. Her Honor was solemn to the point of being severe, which was in contrast to the groom, who made constant wisecracks and generally behaved like an adolescent throughout the ceremony.

This behavior was not lost on Ivana's sons, who had no doubt also read with great interest the report on the domestic disturbance that had led to their new stepfather's being handcuffed by the police. At the reception that evening, Don Jr. delivered the toast customarily made by the father of the bride.

"We are a construction company and we have job sites, we lose people," he said from the microphone in front of the three hundred guests. "You better treat her right, because I have a forty-five and a shovel."

Like a true Trump male, he also managed to comment on his mother's "great boobs," while his father watched from the sidelines. Then Neil Sedaka sang and the couple cut into a twelve-foot-tall wedding cake, which weighed 770 pounds and had been sent from Germany.

Notebook in hand, I buttonholed the bride to get a quote for the column.

"What have I learned about love?" she asked rhetorically. "That it's more about trust and friendship and support. And love. But it's a combination, you know?"

The couple split four months later. But the wedding was bonkers and absolutely everything I had wanted it to be.

Most of the guests had left the reception by midnight. Around that time, I came across Kathy Hilton, alone in a corridor. She was standing in front of a full-length mirror, holding the hem of her dress in an outstretched arm, and dancing with her own reflection like a happy teenager in her room.

The image was so sweet and uncynical that it was almost jarring. And I felt that it said something about the strange, intertwined relationship between the Trumps and the Hiltons, how differently the two families experienced their money, and where they found their pleasures.

I thought, At least all this silliness is making somebody happy.

After the "Gatecrasher" column ended, I returned to the News Corp building on Sixth Avenue for a brief and highly inglorious career as a personality on, of all things, Fox television.

For a live breakfast program called *The Morning Show with Mike and Juliet*, I appeared on a Wednesday-morning segment called "The Male Room." With the comedian Chuck Nice; a radio host, Patrick Meagher; and a celebrity-guest panelist, we were meant to deliver straight talk on "guy stuff."

Like most programming Fox produced, *The Morning Show* needed additional male perspective about as much as the Catholic church. One "Male Room" segment, for example—nominally on "self-image and confidence"—involved women in the studio audience standing up to discuss their bodies and having the panel comment.

Except, the producers had cast me without realizing I was gay. I had thought that was the reason I was on the panel—Fox does diversity! But, nope. They just didn't know.

In retrospect, I'm not sure how a thirty-eight-year-old white man could possibly have believed he was on Fox television as a diversity hire. Perhaps clueless conservatism really is in the water at that studio.

One week the "Male Room" guest was Joe Francis, the creator of the *Girls Gone Wild* video series—a man who had spent nearly a year in jail after pleading no contest to child abuse and prostitution charges—who was treated like any other anodyne celebrity. And the creepy host

Mike Jerrick would often throw me innuendo-laden questions about women on live television, which I parried as best I could.

So, I outed myself to the producer, Marvin Daye, in an awkwardly worded email: "Has it been apparent to you that I'm gay?"

The result was: Marvin, Chuck, and Patrick shrugged; Mike stopped talking to me on the air; and the cohost, Juliet Huddy, adopted me as her new gay best friend—at least for the twenty minutes each week that I was in the building.

During our brief best-friendship, Juliet was married for the third time. Over furry cantaloupe slices in the green room one morning, she mentioned the groom's grandmother had lent a prized vintage fur coat as her "something old" for the wedding, which she lost two hours later at the reception.

The union lasted four months, with "Page Six" reporting that the groom asked for his rings back. But *The Morning Show with Mike and Juliet* ended even before her marriage; it was canceled just a few months after our panel began.

Marvin moved on to CNN, Chuck continued his successful television career, and Patrick resurfaced years later as the love interest of a character on a Hollywood reality series.

Mike ended up on local television in Pennsylvania, where his leering sexism attracted comment both from late-night comedians and *Philadelphia* magazine, which dubbed him the station's "resident perv." Juliet married a fourth husband and, in 2017, settled a sexual harassment lawsuit against Fox News's star anchor, Bill O'Reilly, for an undisclosed sum.

But even if *Mike and Juliet* was over, my career as Fox talent had not yet reached its nadir.

In 2009, I was also appearing as an entertainment commentator in a web-only talk show on FoxNews.com called *The Strategy Room*. It was anchored by Jill Dobson, a bright and empathetic host whose talent nobody had any idea what to do with. Being Fox News, their only plan was to put her in a short skirt and keep her blond highlights touched up.

Jill was smart and funny, and I loved working with her. *The Strategy Room* had a tiny audience, and one that apparently didn't include any actual Fox News executives, since, during my time as a *Daily News* columnist, I used to delight in taking shots at their network. (Although they shared a building, the money-minting cable network Fox News was separate from the broadcast operation, Fox television, which had produced *Mike and Juliet*.)

One of them finally tuned in on a day when I was on the air. Jill, who had a laptop on which she would read emails from viewers and get prompts from producers, suddenly announced, "We have to excuse Ben."

I was told by the host—live, in the middle of the show—to escort myself off the set. So, I did.

On my way out, the flabbergasted producer told me the network public relations chief, Irena Briganti—an old sparring partner from my time at the *Daily News*—had turned on the show and given the order to throw me out, immediately.

The reason, the producer said, was that she believed I was writing an unflattering book about Fox News and wasn't to be allowed in the building.

That wasn't true, at the time. But I made a mental note that one day I should get around to it.

So being a television star for the Murdochs didn't work out, again. But I found a regular spot as a commentator on *Showbiz Tonight*, the entertainment program produced for CNN's sister network, HLN, and was able to freelance on fashion and celebrity stories for my former *Daily News* boss Colleen Curtis, who had moved on to the web giant AOL.

And I still enjoyed spending time with many of the characters I had met on the gossip beat, like Catherine Saxton.

Then almost seventy, Catherine spoke in a cut-glass British accent that I suspect had been polished for the benefit of her American clientele. She had a helmet of "done" blond hair and mischievous blue eyes, and lived directly across the street from Elaine's, which at that point was the *Star Wars* cantina of faded literati.

There were writers at the bar who seemed to be made out of parts of other writers, and long-retired publishing executives looking to reminisce about past hits like tweedy disco stars. Elaine would greet them, from behind her enormous round glasses, in a raspy voice that chiseled hieroglyphs into the air.

Catherine and I would sometimes meet at a front table for dinner. She was the only person I ever met whose drink order was a vodka martini with a vodka chaser, served at the same time.

Born in Britain during the Second World War, Catherine had enjoyed every moment of the swinging sixties. As she refilled her half-full martini glass with the chaser, she would recount being a frisky mod who hung out with the Beatles in Germany.

She also survived a life-threatening car accident that knocked her off the party circuit. Back in London, she worked on a film event attended by Her Majesty the queen, which opened her eyes to the lucrative possibilities of working with fancy people.

In New York, she represented the Plaza Hotel after Donald Trump bought it in the 1980s, when Ivana's gilt-and-marble interior design choices for the restoration of the midtown landmark were making daily news. She delighted in detecting and ejecting uninvited guests from the hotel's many events and shared my mother's incredulity that anyone would voluntarily brand themselves "gatecrasher."

Catherine survived the heavy weather of the Trump divorce, staying on good terms with both parties. She also did ad hoc personal publicity for Rick and Kathy Hilton, as well as their increasingly public teenage daughters, Paris and Nicky.

As the in-house PR for both the Trump and Hilton families, Catherine understood the emerging cultural trend for wealthy people to present themselves as celebrities. And just as she had worked out how to sell her royal experience to moneyed Americans, she also recognized there was an even larger market of people in the next tier down who aspired to be just like the Trumps and Hiltons.

One warm night I ran into Catherine on the terrace of Denise

Rich's Upper East Side penthouse, which looked over the Plaza from the other side of Fifth Avenue.

Denise was a songwriter, close friends with show-business figures like Natalie Cole and Nile Rodgers, and a major donor to the various Clinton campaigns. She was also the ex-wife of Marc Rich, an oil financier who fled abroad after being indicted by the US government on charges of fraud, racketeering, and tax evasion. Marc was pardoned by President Clinton on his last day in office, igniting one tiny last scandal on Clinton's way out the door.

Denise threw great parties, and lots of them. So many, in fact, that her fancy co-op building wouldn't let her guests walk through the front door—we always had to use the tradesmen's side entrance, a long corridor that would be decorated with balloons and streamers for the evening, and have a headset stationed out front. Her triplex party pad also contained a full recording studio, and when she made the decision to sell, David Geffen bought it for $54 million.

On this particular night, Catherine wanted to introduce me to a couple she had just taken on as clients.

Ken Starr (not to be confused with the Javert of President Clinton, with whom he shared a name) was an accountant and money manager who worked with a long list of celebrities, including Sylvester Stallone, Uma Thurman, Al Pacino, Natalie Portman, and Martin Scorsese. Diane, his fourth wife, had been Ken's favorite dancer at Scores, a popular gentlemen's club near the West Side Highway.

The couple turned heads wherever they went. He was sixty-four, with a bald pate and rounded shoulders, and always wore black. Diane was thirty-two and had a figure like tomatoes on the vine. She favored Cesare Paciotti high heels, pendants worn low into her cleavage, and figure-hugging eveningwear with lots of cutouts.

Ken was an engaging storyteller. A self-made kid from the Bronx, he got his break with the banking heir Paul Mellon, who introduced him to the people who would become his celebrity and society clientele. He enjoyed talking up the deals he was making to multiply

his clients' money, like an investment in South American voting machines, which he promised was poised to make billions.

Diane's guiding ambition, meanwhile, was to get pole dancing
recognized as an Olympic sport. To this end she founded Pole Superstar, an organization that held local competitions that in turn, she
hoped, might be spun off into a reality show.

Ken hired Catherine to raise Diane's profile and introduce them
to people who might be able to help. His wife may have had a later
start than those other girls, but who knew? Maybe she, too, could be
the next Ivanka Trump or Paris Hilton.

Apparently, people who might be able to help included journalists
like me. AOL and *Showbiz Tonight* weren't keeping me that busy,
frankly, and we started dining together once a week.

The Starrs enjoyed having me around enough that I started accompanying them on jaunts, including their second-wedding-anniversary
weekend in Las Vegas. I think the fact that Ken could safely leave me
alone with his knockout wife was a big part of my appeal as a traveling
companion. We flew on a chartered jet and stayed in separate suites at
the Wynn hotel, and the three of us enjoyed their anniversary dinner
at a ludicrously expensive Las Vegas restaurant.

Then, in the summer of 2009, I was invited to join the couple on
a week's vacation in Spain. We flew commercial, which Diane seemed
mildly put out about, with them in the front and me in the back.

In Spain, we split our time between Ibiza and a long weekend in
Barcelona.

Diane liked to go topless, which attracted considerable notice on
the beach and by the pool. When we chartered a boat to visit an island known for its natural mud pools, she disembarked barefoot and
wearing only a bikini bottom. But the sand was so hot that I had to
carry her on my shoulders up the shore, like a child holding two large
helium balloons.

Ken was thrilled by the attention this attracted, and Diane was
very happy with our sun-filled itinerary.

"I'm so glad we're not in Europe," she said one day, lying on a lounge at our resort, when it was just the two of us. "Ken *always* wants to go to Europe."

A few days after returning from the Spanish trip, I started to feel a little flu-y. When my breathing became shallow, I attributed it to asthma. And I blamed muscle strain from the gym for the tugging, lateral ache that developed in my chest shortly afterward.

All of this I managed to ignore for a few more days, until I found myself at dinner with my friend Karen Peterson, unable to take more than quick sips of breath, each one accompanied by a sharp pain.

The next morning in the shower I coughed up a handful of mucus-thickened blood, the color and texture of a decent homemade red sauce.

The urgent care facility I walked into called an ambulance, which felt excessive. When the EMT came to collect me from the treatment room, he brought a collapsible-frame wheelchair.

"I can walk," I told him.

The guy shrugged. "We're supposed to," he replied.

So I got in and we trundled out to the street, across from Union Square Park on a glorious summer day. It felt kind of good, being pushed. And frankly, there is no better way to ride through the streets of Manhattan than in an ambulance.

The sheer population of New York can make its citizens feel perpetually second-class, as if all the good stuff is set aside for someone else. The restaurant where you want to eat doesn't have a reservation available anywhere near dinnertime, but there's a table at five p.m. or ten thirty. The Broadway show or the concert or the movie you want to see is always sold out. No, you can't bring a guest to the party, and anyway, there aren't any taxis to get there because they're full of other people.

But riding in an ambulance finally feels like first-class service. It comes complete with lights and music and, although you can't see it from the back, the satisfying sense that this once, the human sea is parting just for you. Arriving at the hospital is a crushing anticlimax.

At Beth Israel—a hospital a disappointingly short ride from Union Square—they told me I had developed a blood clot on the flight back from Spain. It had moved from my leg, where it is known as deep vein thrombosis, to the lungs, where it became a pulmonary embolism. Treatment involved a blood thinner with a morphine chaser.

"You have fat blood?" asked a concerned fashion friend in a tone that made me think it wasn't a joke. But bobbing along on the ripples of morphine was such a pleasant experience, I didn't care.

I'm so glad we're not in Europe, I thought to myself dreamily as I enjoyed the view of a brick wall outside the window of my hospital room.

After four days, the hospital cut off the morphine cruise and told me to go home. I got back on my feet, unshowered and minimally deloused, with a few books and other necessities that friends had brought hanging limp by my side in a white plastic supermarket bag. I had dark rings under my eyes, sallow cheeks, a patchy beard, and small pieces of god knows what hospital detritus stuck in my sweaty hair. Karen came to pick me up.

I had forgotten that about a month before the trip to Spain, I had received a letter from a film production company. It offered me two hundred dollars for access to my apartment in case they needed to hang equipment from my windows to light a scene they planned to shoot in front of the building.

As the taxi dropped us off at the end of the block, a full movie crew was gathered outside my little green-and-white town house on East Fifth Street. I got my pathetic plastic bag out of the cab and staggered toward them.

Later I would learn they were shooting *Eat Pray Love*, which came out the following year. Julia Roberts's character had moved in with James Franco's character, and they were using my address as the exterior of his bohemian East Village pad.

Both actors were waiting on their marks between takes, sitting patiently on my front steps as the crew busied themselves with other tasks. With a set of house keys protruding through my knuckles like spikes, I approached. Nobody stopped me.

Julia was the first to register mild alarm at this interloper on the set. James just looked stoner bemused.

But as I threaded in between the crew, making my way like an assassin through a crowd, I bumped up against the director, Ryan Murphy.

After meeting through mutual friends, Ryan and I had been on a memorably awkward date about a year before. I sometimes wonder if that date became the inspiration for his later series *American Horror Story*.

After our dinner, the evening had concluded on the entirely unsuitable two-seater sofa that stood near the foot of the bed in his suite at the Soho Grand Hotel. Frankly, I'm surprised he's still gay after the experience.

"Ryan," I said. "Hey!"

As I stood there, waiting for Ryan to reply, a small piece of hospital food fell from my chin onto my shirtfront. I considered breaking the ice by saying: "Don't worry, it's not AIDS. HA! HA!"

But instead I filled the silence by reminding him of my name.

Then I told him I'd go upstairs and leave him to finish directing his movie. I trudged up the front steps, knocking James and Julia in the shoulders with my plastic bag of belongings.

The scene they were shooting that day made it into the trailer for the film: Julia with her duffel bag at the end of the affair, waiting for her buddy Viola Davis to drive up and collect her. Although it looks like the production team tried to sweep them up, lining the street are bright seams of fallen yellow blossoms. That fixes the date of the scene to a particular week each August when summer reaches some invisible zenith and the East Village trees drop their flowers in a thick blanket on the sidewalk.

I always loved that week, which felt like a neighborhood secret to be cherished. Other private urban pleasures, like the inflation of the Thanksgiving Day Parade balloons outside the Museum of Natural History on the Upper West Side, or Manhattan-henge, when sunset aligns perfectly with the midtown street grid, had long been subsumed into the tourist guidebooks.

But there was no calendar listing for when the downtown trees, in a collective coital shudder, dropped their summer rain of yellow blooms. It almost felt like a personal gesture the city extended to close friends, a small act of kindness in the otherwise incomprehensible blur of illness, recovery, weird dates, and bizarre celebrity encounters that makes up New York life.

# Sunset Boulevard

In the weeks I spent recovering at home from the pulmonary embolism, two seemingly unconnected things happened that would turn out to be different halves of the same event.

One afternoon, I was surprised to find a check in the mail from Aetna, my insurance company. It was a return of one month's premium.

Thinking myself conscientious, I had prepaid months in advance, before switching over to a new provider. Except, in that time, the premium had gone up very slightly, meaning I still owed them twenty dollars, out of many thousands paid, at the end of the policy.

For that twenty dollars, Aetna canceled the last month's coverage on the grounds of nonpayment—when I had been in the hospital. So, the bill for that free trip to Spain would end up being north of fifteen thousand dollars.

As usual, hanging with rich people just turned out to be stressful and expensive.

Separately I was contacted by TMZ, the hugely popular gossip website that also produced a nationally syndicated half-hour television show every day from its newsroom. They were looking for a managing editor; was I interested?

TMZ was known for its attention-deficit-disorder prose style, aggressive video paparazzi units, and focus on the seamier side of celebrity. There was none of the rakish swagger of an old-time tabloid columnist in its tone—it covered Hollywood with the panting snicker of an aroused eighth grader.

But I had a paper storm of incoming hospital bills on one side and a decently paid job prospect on the other. There was nothing to lose by flying out to Los Angeles for an interview.

I met TMZ's founder, Harvey Levin, at the BOA steakhouse on Sunset Boulevard. We had an early dinner reservation, in accordance with TMZ's daily schedule: staffers were at their desk every morning by six a.m., ready to start shooting the show within the hour, as it would be broadcast in some Eastern markets as early as two p.m. Pacific time. A fitness fanatic, the boss was almost always in the office before six, having begun his day at the gym at four a.m.

Harvey has the vigor of an entire professional basketball team bottled in his five-foot-five frame. He is a human guarana shot. When he speaks, he has a habit of looking past you into the rafters above, as if his focus is on something much larger, just about to drop onto your head.

I detected in Harvey a worldview that is also apparent in some other highly successful individuals, like Donald Trump and Jeff Bezos: that other people's time and money should rightly belong to them. By this way of thinking, which after all is only rational under late capitalism, any dollar in someone else's pocket is in the wrong place. Likewise, each minute an employee spends away from work is waste bordering on theft.

While we were speaking, a double-decker tour bus drove by on the boulevard, plastered from headlights to tailpipe with TMZ branding. Harvey scowled. He resented paying the tour company for advertising and felt the TMZ logo was worth more than the bus it was on.

"I don't know why we're giving them money," he said.

Against the feeling in the pit of my stomach, I took the job.

Moving to Los Angeles without knowing how to drive wouldn't be a big deal, I figured. Surely there would be time to learn.

My starter home for the new job was in La Brea, the neighborhood of the famous dinosaur-devouring tar pits, and opposite the Grove, a large mall. It was in a complex of short-stay professional apartments that served the entertainment industry, attracting a transient mix of young show-business hopefuls. Any time you stepped into the hallway you might pass a reality-show cast, a nascent boy band, or a telegenic magician with a British accent.

The main laboratory in this Frankenstein's castle of celebrity creation was the gym. There, the would-be famous worked to assemble themselves out of component parts.

There were several distinct tribes in the gym. One crew did free weights and floor exercises in full-body Lycra suits, as if training for a superhero film. Others were young women who seemed to have recently undergone cosmetic surgeries and wanted to keep working out while they healed.

One strikingly good-looking young man used the treadmills for half an hour every day. These faced a window, but there was a wall-length mirror to the right. He ran with his head cocked at an uncomfortable ninety-degree swivel, so that he never had to take his eyes off himself for a moment.

My apartment was on the ground floor of the four-story complex. It was a wedge-shaped unit whose only exterior window was behind a thickly planted stand of banana palms that blocked out any sun from the courtyard. But that lack of light only bothered me on weekends, since on weekdays I would leave well before dawn and not get home until after sunset.

Each morning, I woke in time to take the 5:25 a.m. bus—the first one out of the depot—from the Farmers Market stop, up Fairfax Avenue, to the TMZ newsroom on Sunset Boulevard.

Abutting the Grove on the east side of Fairfax was CBS Television City, a studio campus where the network filmed many of its game shows. The most enduringly popular of these was *The Price Is Right*, which selects audience members as competitors, nominally based on who exhibits the most enthusiasm as its camera pans the bleachers full of cheering faces.

There is a lot of competition to get into that studio taping. Some days, aspiring contestants would already be lining up by the chain-link fence outside the gate when my bus went past, braving the early morning chill. Many of them were couples or groups wearing the outlandish matching getups they hoped would allow them to "come on down" for a chance to play the game.

In the bleary predawn, the line of shivering hopefuls faintly resembled the red-carpet processionals that precede televised awards shows. But instead of couture gowns and fitted tuxedos, these were adults dressed up like hot dogs and pineapples in search of their Hollywood moment.

Very occasionally I'd see the contestants a second time, at the end of the day, as I was picking up dinner from the nearby Farmers Market: exhausted game show tourists with name tags still stuck to their Halloween-store costumes, sitting around beers on outdoor tables, reliving the day's adventure.

Their evident satisfaction seemed to derive not from the consumer goods and Florida vacations they may or may not have won from the game show, but from something purer—the chance to touch the god-head of daytime network television. Something Quentin Crisp had told me ten years earlier, at the Cooper Square Diner, returned to my mind.

"American life is not divided between the haves and the have-nots," he had said. "It is divided between the people on television and the people who are not on television. And the envy is just the same."

Using Los Angeles public transport initiates you into a subculture that remains invisible to many lifelong residents. Riding the bus at strange hours on a regular schedule feels a lot like sitting on the jury of a lengthy trial.

There are about a dozen of you, give or take a few alternates, and you see the same people in the same confined space every day. Also, your fellow commuters feel strangely vetted, as if they have passed some kind of test for good citizenship, since there aren't many ne'er-do-wells who arrange their lives around leaving for work every morning at five thirty a.m.

The bus also had a television screen, on which it played a strange loop of custom-made programing. Called Transit TV, it was a bizarre mix of the kind of local tidbits that a small-town newspaper might run in a column called "Potpourri" or "Village Voices," crossed with a sanitized version of public access cable television.

Among the weather reports and trivia quizzes, Transit TV also solicited content from riders, including original artwork and jokes.

"Why does Miss Piggy gargle with sugar and vinegar?" one riddle posed. "Because Kermit likes sweet-and-sour pork."

I don't know what it is about that particular joke, but it has haunted me ever since.

I would arrive every day at TMZ, faintly rattled by Transit TV's sense of humor, just before six a.m. And the first thing I had to do after sitting down was to get up again, since Harvey stood in my cubicle to film the daily television show, which usually began shooting before seven.

Like Quentin's take on American life, the newsroom was divided between those who were on television and those who were not on television. Fortunately, there was so much competition for screen time among the other staffers that I was usually able to skulk in a corner and not worry about being called upon by the cameras.

As soon as the show wrapped, my first duty was to lead the actual morning news meeting—in the back office on a whiteboard—that Harvey's schtick, with his Day-Glo markers and illuminated, transparent slate, was the television version of.

It was the season of the Tiger Woods infidelity scandal, and with its impeccable sources, the site was breaking scoop after scoop. In New York, tipsters still called "Page Six," but outside those five boroughs, the rest of the country thought of TMZ first.

But that machine required workdays that were often fourteen or sixteen hours long. And the buses stopped running for the day at eight p.m., as I discovered one chilly evening as I waited and waited like a jilted bride at the altar.

It wasn't the most dignified look, sitting on a bench backed by an advertisement for a cut-rate traffic injury attorney as my colleagues steered their BMWs out of the parking garage. Eventually I found an alcove in a nearby apartment building where I could cower and call a cab on late nights, out of sight of the street.

Life was becoming more pathetic by degrees.


You never quite knew how people were going to respond to learning that you worked at TMZ.

Younger stars mostly loved it and went out of their way to court its attention. Older stars, inasmuch as they understood TMZ's blend of aggressive street photography and reporting, mostly hated it.

"Careful, Percy!" Joan Collins said to her husband one evening as they were leaving a restaurant, in a video clip that never aired but amused the newsroom no end. "Cameras have microphones now!"

One Saturday I went to lunch with Nikki Haskell and her friend Barbara Davis, a Los Angeles philanthropist and socialite. Barbara was famous for throwing the Carousel Ball, a charity gala that mixed crowned heads of state with Hollywood movie stars and had raised over seventy million dollars to fight juvenile diabetes.

She was also the widow of billionaire Rocky Mountains oilman turned 20th Century Fox studio owner Marvin Davis—and grandmother to Jason and Brandon "fire crotch" Davis, the Hilton-sisters pals who often featured in the gossip coverage of the day.

The three of us lunched in the garden of the Polo Lounge of the Beverly Hills Hotel, one of the great, divinely silly old-school pleasures of Los Angeles. Inside, the restaurant's masculine décor is a relic of the seventies three-martini lunch, with Sherwood-green walls, enormous fluted banquettes, and a bar with a reputation for attracting working women in Jacqueline Susann–esque long-sleeved evening dresses after five o'clock.

Outside, however, the patio looks like a playset for the original 1959 Barbie doll, complete with rhododendrons tumbling over pink walls and tables set with white cloths and old-fashioned wrought-iron garden chairs.

The Polo Lounge is also fun for the random celebrities who are bound to be scattered around the other tables: that day it was Alex Trebek, host of the game show *Jeopardy!*, and Nikki's friend Beverly Johnson, who became, in 1974, the first African-American model to appear on the cover of American *Vogue*.

Barbara, who was then seventy-nine, was the image of Nancy Reagan–era feminine power. Which was fitting, considering her family, whose oil wealth had allowed them to buy much of Denver, was said to be the inspiration for the feuding Colorado plutocrats depicted in *Dynasty*.

Her late husband, Marvin—who had stood six foot four and weighed well over three hundred pounds—could not have looked less like his on-screen avatar, played by the dapper John Forsythe. But he promoted the connection by reproducing the desk used by Forsythe's character, Blake Carrington, for his own office at 20th Century Fox.

Later, after Marvin sold the studio to Rupert Murdoch, his family followed the *Dynasty* script even more closely. Following his death, the children discovered his reputed six-billion-dollar family fortune was largely a mirage and began suing each other, and their mother, for scraps in the mere tens of millions.

In public, however, Barbara maintained a façade of diamonds and chinchilla—she was once robbed of ten million dollars' worth of jewelry in a single holdup—that shamed her small-screen simulacrum, Krystle Carrington. And she had hair the way Arnold Schwarzenegger had muscles. Her strawberry-blond coiffure was like one of those dust storms on Mars that envelop three-quarters of the planet. It wrapped around the back of her head and came at you from three directions at once—over the top and around the sides—suspended in its own unbreathable hydrocarbon atmosphere.

Despite the big-budget production number that was her appearance, however, Barbara exuded warmth and had a knack for flattering her tablemates with attention. That day at the Polo Lounge, she was curious and alert and made amusing conversation—traits not common among the billionaire class, who tend to prefer that the effort flows the other way.

I was dreading the moment, which I knew would come, when she asked me what I did for a living.

"I'm, um, I'm the managing editor of TMZ," I stammered over a chopped salad with shrimp.

Barbara clasped her hands together as if this were simply marvelous news.

"Oh, I love TMZ," she gushed. "I look at it to see where my grandchildren are."

Working at TMZ is vampire heaven. In winter, employees arrive before dawn and leave after dusk, and because the newsroom is also a studio set, heavy blackout curtains line the windows, permanently blocking the sun.

By a typical Friday night, I would be hallucinating with fatigue after a week of long workdays. All I wanted to do was go home to my equally sunless apartment and sleep through the weekend until work started again at six a.m. Monday.

One particular Friday, however, Horacio was in town for a visit. It was his birthday, and he invited me to go with him to a dinner event at the Chateau Marmont—the old-school Hollywood hotel and infamous movie star party den.

Although I was practically vibrating with tiredness, I hadn't seen him—or any other friend—for the several months that I had been in LA. And the hotel was a three-minute walk from TMZ's offices, so I agreed.

Loosely modeled on a castle in the Loire Valley, the Chateau is a brooding Hollywood-gothic pile with baronial furniture and heavy drapes in its public rooms, and peaked windows looking out onto shady colonnades.

All sorts of fabulously bad behavior happens at the hotel. John Belushi died of a drug overdose in one of its bungalows, Jean Harlow and Clark Gable had an affair there, every rock star you've ever heard of has smashed up a room, and James Dean once jumped out a window.

It even has a Sunset Boulevard address. All that's missing is the body of Joe Gillis—the ill-fated screenwriter who gets shot by Norma Desmond—floating facedown in the pool.

So, off I went to the Chateau. And I remember exactly what I was wearing, because it turned out to be a black-tie dinner and I was dressed for casual Friday at an LA gossip website: sneakers, jeans, and a blue polo shirt that may have been in need of laundering.

The event's organizer didn't look thrilled to see me. Cort was a very good-looking blond-haired, blue-eyed publicist from New York with whom I had a tepid relationship. His handsome face instinctively contorted into a sneer, which he had to realign in midair into an expression that said, "Great to see you!"

I could hardly blame him. I was neither invited nor welcome, didn't especially want to be there, and was mortified at being so underdressed. But Cort couldn't afford to offend the managing editor of TMZ, so we were stuck with each other.

In retrospect, the look of disgust on his face would turn out to be the least terrible thing to happen that evening.

Cort put Horacio and me at a table of tuxedo-wearing men whom we didn't know, right at the back of the room, near the constantly flapping doors to the kitchen. I can't remember the reason for the event—some corporate celebration—but the entertainment was Joan Rivers.

That was at least interesting, because although I had interviewed Joan several times, I had never seen her perform. I had once done a blind item about a cocktail party she threw, whose covert purpose was to gauge interest from potential buyers for her Upper East Side penthouse. Joan had flashy taste, which she described as "Louis XIV meets Fred and Ginger," with lots of gilded moldings, drapes with tassels, and uncomfortable, straight-backed wooden armchairs.

Before the party, she had assistants go around and touch up all the gilt. Except, she didn't leave enough time for the paint to dry, so any guest who brushed against the furniture came away with a gold smear on their clothes. A Saudi prince eventually bought the 5,100-square-foot apartment, nine months after her death, for $28 million.

Joan worked blue, even by the standards of other foul-mouthed comics, and her material that night was filthy. The minute she got going, the room was roaring with laughter; then my phone rang. It was work.

Late Friday evening, after the TMZ newsroom had cleared out, a tip had come in that the singer Morrissey had died. It was a plausible lead: just the month before, he had collapsed onstage, suffering from chest pains and shortness of breath, during a performance in southern England.

So now I had a potential scoop that I needed to report out, quickly and accurately, over the phone from a hotel ballroom. The tipster had provided no further information, and there were no other sources. The only thing I had to go on was a home phone number, from the TMZ database, for Morrissey's manager, Irving Azoff.

A famously fierce music executive who served as CEO of Ticketmaster and chairman of Live Nation Entertainment, he was ranked number one on *Billboard* magazine's list of the most powerful people in the music industry.

When I called, the phone was answered by his wife, Shelli. Although it may have been only around ten p.m., I got the impression that the phone was in the bedroom and that I had woken the couple.

The Azoffs had not heard anything about Morrissey, and it was a brief conversation.

From an internet search, I discovered the singer was scheduled for a number of spread-out European appearances around that time. Although it was hardly conclusive, it seemed possible that he might be in Germany, where it would have been around six o'clock on Saturday morning.

With nothing else to go on, and frantically pacing the Chateau's columned arcade, I started calling closed music venues and getting answering machine messages in German. The scoop was slipping through my fingers.

I returned to the table with nothing. Horacio told me he had read a recent article that said the music of Morrissey's former band, the Smiths, was increasingly popular with Hispanic audiences, who responded to its melancholia. So he started asking the middle-aged Mexican waiters if they had heard anything.

This did not prove to be productive.

My panic about messing up the story was rising. If the news was true, and I squandered the tip by not being able to verify it, then it would cost me my job come first thing Monday morning. And it was unlikely to be a discreet exit.

After about thirty minutes, I called the Azoffs back, reasoning that they may have made some inquiries in the meantime. I woke them up again, and Shelli started yelling.

"Who are you?" she demanded. "What's your name?"

I hung up.

I can't remember what else I tried that night, but I recall feeling sick that I had fumbled a major scoop. Eventually I went back to the ballroom, having missed all of Joan's performance, to feel sorry for myself.

And then the evening took its next turn.

Cort was in Los Angeles with his model fiancé, James. In every way that Cort was already handsome, his partner was a better-looking version: buffer, blonder, bluer in the eyes. They made an absurdly attractive couple.

Once the event was over and Cort had stopped working, a group of about eight of us ended up in his room at the hotel. By this time I had given up on being able to do anything with the Morrissey tip and was just hoping to enjoy my weekend on the way to a quick professional death.

But James was trouble. He was being highly flirtatious, seemingly just to annoy his betrothed. Once again, poor Cort could only watch and pretend to be amused, when in fact he was appalled.

The room had a seemingly endless supply of champagne, and we drank it. James kept flirting.

As the small gathering started to clear out, James made it clear that I and another young fellow were welcome to stay. I could sense Cort's blood pressure rising like a thermostat.

James was not unknown to me. He had appeared on an eye-catching cover of a gay news magazine with his previous boyfriend, also a male model, who would become a minor television personality. This former boyfriend also used to serve drinks at the East Village gay bars I visited, where he was obliged by the management to wear nothing but humiliatingly tiny underwear and never once smiled at me.

Obviously, sleeping with his ex would be amazing revenge for such a slight. And I felt up for anything, having been worn down by months of illness, stress, and light deprivation—especially with my career scheduled to blow up the following Monday.

Also, come on. I was being propositioned for a fourgy by a male model whom I had mooned over in a magazine, in Hollywood's most glamorous, louche hotel. Sorry, Cort.

In addition to the couple, there was a nice young guy called Cullen, whom I wanted to later ask out on a date, or at least make my first LA friend, but would never see again. In the bedroom, the king-size bed stretched out like the plain of Marathon, awaiting battle.

The awkward few hours that followed might have qualified as comedy if Cort hadn't been trying to kill me. It was like a naked Tom and Jerry cartoon, with slapstick pursuits and evasions and nothing going right.

Also, like a dog chasing a car, it turned out I didn't know what to do with a model once I'd caught one. He was so pretty and smooth and muscular, but ultimately it was like trying to mate with a really nice chest of drawers. So, I cowered at the foot of the bed and went back to worrying about Morrissey.

In the morning, I climbed back into my clothes, feeling like a surgeon who had just lost a patient. Horacio was also staying in the hotel, so I met him downstairs for breakfast.

In the sun-dappled courtyard, waiters in white shirts and dark ties were pouring coffee and serving muffin baskets. It was a gorgeous day and we settled into a table next to Warren Beatty, who looked like a textbook old Hollywood star, with his tan and his grin and the round tortoiseshell frames of his Persol sunglasses.

Then I checked my phone for the first time that day.

And freaked out.

Apparently, while I had been pacing outside the night before, waking up the Azoffs and calling empty German box offices, Horacio had sent a tweet. He'd posted that he had heard Morrissey had died.

Some New York media people, including the rival gossip website *Gawker*, had picked up on it. They were floating the rumor—in order to claim the scoop, if it proved to be accurate—and asking for more information.

A filter of rage passed in front of my eyes, and I caused a scene in front of Warren Beatty.

How could you be so stupid, I said. I am going to lose my goddamn job, I said. I may have used the word "betrayal."

I must have been hysterical because Horacio seemed very mildly chastened, which is the most contrite I had ever seen him. Fortunately, however, Morrissey hadn't died. And I didn't get fired come Monday morning.

TMZ got random tips all the time from people who didn't know what they were talking about. But we had to check each and every one of them out, because sometimes the craziest ones turned out to be true. Like the one that would soon come in about Tiger Woods's arriving by ambulance at a Florida hospital, having just crashed his car in his own front yard.

Luckily the worst thing about that weekend turned out to be the sex. Even so, I didn't last much longer in the job. I hated working there and consequently wasn't very good at it. After less than six months, just as TMZ was finalizing plans to launch its own fleet of sightseeing buses on which Harvey would not have to pay for ad space, I was back in New York.

I never did learn how to drive.

# PART 3

## Fortune

# Trump Tower

ossip culturalists understand that celebrity and democracy have a lot in common. Both are popularity con-
tests. Seen this way, nothing that has happened at the
highest levels of American politics is a surprise.

Gossip culture is popular culture is mainstream culture. And in a
democracy, mainstream culture dictates political outcomes.

Gossip culture ushered in the Trump presidency, complete with a
supporting cast that includes Kim Kardashian and Kanye West pro-
viding policy advice, and Harvey Levin as a welcome guest in the Oval
Office.

But Trump could not have moved into Pennsylvania Avenue without a figure who might be one of the few people more disparaged by

serious minds than the forty-fifth president himself. A figure as ubiquitous as she is derided, who nonetheless created the cultural context
that made the Trump administration possible.

That achievement alone is an argument to call her the most culturally influential person in twenty-first-century America: Paris Hilton.

This opinion is not widespread, of course. And the reason for that is
fairly obvious: it sounds like a really dumb thing to say. But Jerry Lewis
never got the Pulitzer Prize he deserved either, so let's just go for it.

After all, consider the fall of the Roman Empire.

A military historian may say its primary cause was pressure from
the north by barbarian tribes. Economists might counter that a sus-
tained financial crisis is what tipped the empire toward collapse.

Even plumbers have an opinion: the Romans all went mad from
poisoning because their water came through lead pipes. Each different profession understands events from its own point of view.

Gossip culturalists have one such perspective on modern times. It
is possible to draw a direct line from Brandon Davis's calling Lindsay
Lohan "fire crotch" outside a Los Angeles nightclub in 2007 to the
Trump administration's trade war with China twelve years later. The
butterfly flaps its wings.

The vehicle for Paris's first rush of (G-rated) national fame, *The
Simple Life*, began airing in 2003. The program could be compared
to *The Velvet Underground & Nico*, a seminal album released by Lou
Reed's band in 1967, in that it was more influential than it was successful. Brian Eno famously told *Musician* magazine in 1982 that although Reed's album sold poorly, "everyone who bought one of those
30,000 copies started a band."

So it was with *The Simple Life*, which puttered on for five seasons
over two different networks. It was finally canceled in 2007 amid
squabbling between the two stars, as well as distracting side dramas,
including DUI-related jail time for Paris and rehab for Nicole Richie.

But everyone who watched it started a band. Its most famous ac-
olytes were Kim Kardashian and Donald Trump, whose pincer attack

on America would capture both low culture and high office within
ten years.

In broad terms, reality television was priming the audience to think
of themselves as performers in the production of their own lives. More
specifically, wealth-porn shows like *The Simple Life* sent the message
that personal influence could be gained by inflating the appearance of
having money. That particular keg of gunpowder would meet its match
just a few years later, with the release of Instagram in 2010.

By then, rich people (both real and manqué) were undoubtedly
the new celebrities. Upon returning to New York after toiling in the
Los Angeles gossip mines, it was apparent to me that "ultra-high-net-
worth individuals" were in the ascendance as media subjects.

The rich have always been with us, of course. And it's always been
fun to gawp.

Mansa Musa, the sultan of Mali, was the Jeff Bezos of 1324, em-
barking on a pilgrimage to Mecca with a retinue of sixty thousand
people and distributing so much gold that he destabilized the economy of North Africa for a generation to follow. Elizabeth I conducted
a "royal progress" every summer of her forty-four-year reign, using
the soft power of pageantry to consolidate support among the nobility
(although not the commoners, who, unlike with royal tours of the
modern era, were often barred from her route on threat of arrest). It
was in the context of such historical pomp that I understood the moneyed exhibitionism on display in contemporary New York.

The bigger picture nationally was income inequality, which was
polarizing a large group of people in poverty on one side, and reward-
ing a vastly smaller group with great affluence on the other. But better
minds than mine—people who wouldn't try to convince you that Paris
Hilton was the most influential figure in twenty-first-century culture,
probably—were already on that.

In my niche, the friction was between the wealthy and the ultrawealthy. Because no matter how much these people amassed, there
was always someone who had more, and that drove them nuts.

Nothing annoys a millionaire more than a billionaire. And the class war that I observed was between not rich and poor but between the top 1 percent of income earners and the top 0.1 percent.

New York has around a hundred resident billionaires and more people worth over thirty million dollars than any other city on earth. A wealthy friend who has lived in both London and New York once put it to me this way: "In London, if you're a billionaire, that makes you a celebrity. But in New York, you're just another billionaire on the block."

In 2010 I was back freelancing for AOL, as well as blogging for *T*, the weekend style magazine of the *New York Times*, where Horacio had been the online director for a decade. And I enjoyed the weird distinction of being the only journalist to have both TMZ and the *New York Times* on his résumé.

I also wrote for the *New York Observer*, a weekly newspaper serving the city's upper echelon. Dubbed by media critics "the salmon sheet," on account of its being printed on distinctive pink paper, the *Observer* was a witty, high-level muckraker that Graydon Carter had briefly edited on the way to his perch atop *Vanity Fair*.

Like most newspapers, it was completely untenable as a business. But high-profile media properties are popular purchases for wealthy arrivistes because of the respectability they confer, so despite the unsound economics, a buyer can usually be found.

Its founder, a banker named Arthur Carter, sold it in 2006 after nineteen years of ownership to Jared Kushner, who was then twenty-five and in need of an image rehab.

His billionaire father, Charles Kushner, had served federal prison time after a particularly lurid scandal involving family infighting, hookers, and a sex tape. And Jared, a mediocre student, had been pilloried in the New York media for being accepted by Harvard University on the heels of his father's $2.5 million donation to the institution. Having "*New York Observer* publisher" appended to his name seemed preferable to what he had been called up until then.

For some years I wrote the article that accompanied the *Observer*'s annual "Rich List" of wealthiest New Yorkers. From that research, I learned the 1 percent had seen their annual wealth increase by around 4 percent a year since 2000, while the 0.01 percent had enjoyed double that growth.

The difference between the two groups could be stark. The 1 percent own private jets to ferry them between Aspen, New York, and Maui. The 0.01 percent, however, own not only bigger jets but also offshore airfields on which to land them, should the FBI or a populist mob come calling at short notice.

The most visible manifestation of the vast uptick in wealth was the boom in super-luxury apartments for the new overclass. West Fifty-Seventh Street, an aggressively charmless stretch of midtown Manhattan, become known as Billionaire's Row after a change in zoning laws spurred a surge in development of exceptionally tall apartment buildings.

In addition to altering the law around air rights—which caps the height of new construction—city authorities also stopped worrying about the shadows these buildings cast on public spaces like Central Park.

In the late 1980s, Jacqueline Kennedy Onassis led a public protest that successfully curtailed the height of a new development in the area that would have darkened playgrounds in the park for much of the year.

But by the early twenty-first century, the increased influence of the billionaire class and a waning of civic resistance combined to create a sense of inevitability that the rich would simply get what they wanted. Today, shadows from the towers of Billionaire's Row creep into Central Park like cold, ghoulish fingers reaching for live flesh.

The appeal of West Fifty-Seventh Street, as a neighborhood, is not easy to understand. True, it's nearby Saks, Bergdorf Goodman, and other establishments along the retail red-light district of Fifth Avenue. But it is not an area where you buy if you want to be close to a grocery store or good schools—or are ever likely to need local conveniences like a bookshop.

Nonetheless, as I discovered by reporting for the *Observer*, the most expensive apartments on the strip sold for over one hundred million dollars—a city record for individual homes.

But there was still a way to spend more if you wanted. Nearby, on Central Park South, one hedge fund billionaire bought a multifloor complex of different units for two hundred million dollars in a single transaction. His wife dryly noted that, since he makes one hundred million dollars a month, the purchase wasn't really that big a deal.

Another hedge fund billionaire bought a ninety-million-dollar apartment on the Row simply as a place to throw parties. And among the superrich, the parties are often pretty good. Some of the most notorious were thrown by the private equity chief Stephen Schwarzman, who is worth about thirteen billion.

In 2007, for his sixtieth birthday, he staged a party in New York City that was so lavish—re-creating a giant version of his own living room in the cavernous Park Avenue Armory for five hundred guests, with Rod Stewart performing in addition to Patti LaBelle singing "Happy Birthday"—it prompted *New York* magazine to christen him "the poster child for greed and self-indulgence of the new gilded age."

Stung by the criticism, he almost apologized. "Obviously, I wouldn't have wanted to do that and become, you know, some kind of symbol of sorts of that period of time," Schwarzman said at a conference the following year. "Who would ever wish that on themselves? No one."

But the next few years were so outrageously profitable that he soon forgot his brush with humility. In 2010, *Newsweek* reported a conversation in which he described President Obama's plan to close a personal income tax loophole enjoyed by private equity managers as "a war. It's like when Hitler invaded Poland in 1939."

Learning all this was my new homework, since I was now invited into these billionaires' parties and apartments on assignment. Gone were the days when "the Four Hundred"—an old nickname for the cream of New York society, held over from when nineteenth-century hostess Caroline Schermerhorn Astor could fit four hundred guests in her ballroom —kept journalists at arm's length. Now publicity was power.

Nobody understood this better than the Trumps. By 2010, Donald was in his tenth season as host of *The Apprentice*, his hit NBC reality show. Even as critics sniped that his wealth was a sham, and that in fact he was a serial bankrupt, every week he was successfully performing his role as a confident capitalist overlord in America's living rooms.

Just as a plumber will tell you Rome fell because of lead in the pipes, a reality-show producer will tell you governments are formed on network television.

One clear spring day in 2010, Melania Trump asked me to call at her gilded, marbled home in Trump Tower. She was inviting members of the press to discuss a new affordable jewelry range she was launching, to be sold through the home shopping network QVC.

At the appointed hour, accompanied by a video producer from AOL, we presented ourselves at the residential entrance on West Fifty-Sixth Street, across from the Armani store on Fifth Avenue. A mirrored elevator lofted us into Trump heaven.

The family's apartment, a triplex with views north and west, was a fantasy of czarist kitsch. If the Romanovs had bought off their murderers and escaped to Las Vegas to open a casino, it would have looked something like this. Whatever else Donald may have shared with Vladimir Putin, they seemed to use the same decorator.

The apartment had many sitting rooms, arranged in order by distance from the throne, like chambers for receiving visitors of differing ranks in a ducal palace. A *New York Times* writer who was assigned to the same story noted the "lunch of asparagus salad and salmon served by an omnipresent white-coated butler" in an upstairs dining room. But the parlor I was ushered into, I couldn't help noticing, was just inside the front door.

This made me nervous, as Donald worked in the building and

might come home at any moment. Our last encounter had been his screaming at me at Mar-a-Lago, after jetting in from the Miss USA show in Las Vegas.

Afterward, in my column, I had twisted the knife with word he had been annoyed that his preferred choice had not won the pageant. The tiara had gone to Miss Texas, an African-American contestant, while Donald had favored the very blond Miss Oklahoma.

Ironically, the item absolved him of a more serious rumor also floating around at the time, which is that he had the pageant fixed. But Donald didn't see it that way. He correctly sniffed out and ex-communicated my source for the story, who told me that I was in for another round of trouble the next time I saw him.

"Mrs. Trump will be down in a few minutes," said a handler, who offered me a seat on a remarkably soft, creamy-white couch.

While waiting for Melania, I had time to take in the Fabergé omelet of style that was the Trump abode.

The principal color scheme was eggshell white combined with gold leaf, a choice clearly intended to evoke the grand ceremonial halls found in European royal residences from Versailles to the Winter Palace in St. Petersburg. Washed with light from the plate-glass windows that oversaw Central Park, the colors blended into a vast vanilla-caramel swirl. It was like being inside the Beige Mahal.

The furniture was reproduction Louis XIV, paired with decorative objects that looked like they had been the most expensive things in a museum gift shop.

At the end of one corridor I glimpsed a large-format family photograph of a young-adult Donald with his father and three siblings, posed against a painted backdrop that made it look, from afar, like an oil portrait. Other paintings were on classical themes or copies of impressionist works, like the fake Renoir above the gilt sofa in Melania's office.

Although the floor space was generous, the ceilings were low and out of scale with the palatial aspirations of the furnishings. They were painted with faux frescoes bordered by reflective surfaces, which were meant to enhance a sense of height but just added to the impression that you were inside a really fancy elevator.

Donald also had a taste for risqué bronzes. On one table was a statue of Eros entwined with Psyche in a French Empire style, on another a Victorian pairing of two amorous young lovers. These brought a whiff of the bordello into the air-conditioned room—as if, at the touch of a hidden switch, the gold chandelier might retract into the ceiling, to be replaced by a disco ball, and the canvas reproduction of *Apollo in His Chariot Preceded by Aurora* over the white marble fireplace might fold down into a Murphy bed.

As I was absorbing all this, sinking ever deeper into the quicksand-cushioned couch, I noticed three oversize hardcover books on the round glass-top table in front of me. They were the only books visible in the apartment.

Although they were not really intended to be read—one was a *Vogue Living* coffee-table edition, the others big collections of photographs—I remember thinking, Well, at least there are books somewhere in this home. That was an encouraging sign, at least.

Eventually Melania appeared, beautiful and inscrutable. Her warmth had an icy quality to it, like a sports liniment. Her smile presented as two plump rows of teeth-on-the-cob, squashing her dark-rimmed eyes into slivered almonds over ripe-apple cheeks.

Donald had taken his first quixotic tilt at running for president two years earlier, and I asked how she would redecorate the White House, should she ever become First Lady.

I don't exactly remember her answer—it was an on-camera interview, without any notes taken—but she was too smart to say anything interesting. She seamlessly parried the question into talking points for the Melania Trump jewelry range, which were that she had created something special for busy women who were simultaneously moms, professionals, and wives . . . and so on.

Video of the interview has long since disappeared from the internet. But what I remember more than anything she said was her professionalism as a model.

Melania perched next to me on the sofa to be filmed. But before sitting down, she gathered up the three hardcover books from the coffee table and placed them on the over-soft cushions, creating a platform that would support a straight back for the camera.

I thought: So that's what books are for, in a house without any books. To sit on.

# The Hamptons

To be constantly popping in and out of the homes of the superrich felt like a clairvoyant power, as if I were able to glimpse some fabulous spirit realm that lay just behind the veneer of earthly reality. I had one friend who came from this world, and tagging along with her was an ongoing education into the strange habits and customs of its denizens.

Annabelle's ancestor had been so wealthy that it became a matter of national concern, prompting President Theodore Roosevelt to pursue antitrust laws. More than a hundred years later, money still flowed through her family's veins like a steroid, allowing them to raise not just grand houses but entire public institutions, as well as to move fleets of cars and stables of horses around the country with only a telephone call.

The family was so rich that it seemed like no laws applied to them, including biology and physics. Her mother's friends had faces that floated upward with age, as if filled with helium. It was like their Chanel suits had cryogenic properties, slowly freezing and compressing the preserved body inside, until the woman herself hardened into diamond.

Somehow Annabelle managed to remain clear-eyed and even cynical about her tremendous privilege. I marveled at stories from her building, a large apartment block on Fifth Avenue with commanding views of Central Park. The people in it clearly regarded themselves as too wealthy to conform to rules. One internal saga that I followed for months, begging her for regular updates, involved the building's many dogs.

Dogs were not allowed in this building—as decreed by the board of apartment owners who ran it as a co-operative—but the residents who owned them ignored the prohibition.

This infuriated the antidog faction, who were just as overprivileged as the canine-loving scofflaws. And what the rich do when they don't get what they want is blame it on the most vulnerable people available to them—their employees.

So as one set of billionaires sailed through the lobby every day with their pooches, another set informed the uniformed doormen that it was their responsibility to enforce the no-dogs rule. And if they didn't, they would be fired.

Naturally, the dog owners didn't take any more notice of the doormen's exhortations than they did of the building's bylaws, putting their employment in jeopardy. The situation continued to escalate over the course of a fraught summer.

Finally, after many months, a compromise was reached. The board decided that dogs would be permitted to live in the building only on the condition that they never touched any of the carpets in the common areas.

In practice, that meant all of the hallways and elevators and most of the lobby—requiring their owners to carry the animals from the front door of their apartment until they got out onto the street. Which they did not do.

Consequently, the doormen, in order to keep their jobs, had to transport the dogs themselves—either carried in their arms, or for animals larger than a cocker spaniel, on a rolling luggage trolley.

Every time I visited Annabelle in her grand building, the lobby looked like an animal shelter being evacuated in a flood.

Another Eleusinian mystery she initiated me into was the Hamptons, the beachside enclave of villages that serves as the summer playpen of New York's ultrawealthy.

Annabelle owned a Range Rover and liked to drive fast around the Hamptons' country lanes; for that crowd, speed limits were another law that did not apply.

Whenever Annabelle got a speeding ticket, she mentioned it to a particular friend and it would be withdrawn by the issuing town, like the sea retreating at low tide. It was like a natural phenomenon, awesome to behold.

For a lot of things like that, I could be very slow on the uptake about the privileges and behaviors of the seriously rich. It was during one of these high-speed jaunts around the Hamptons' narrow laneways that Annabelle was discussing, with another friend in the car, a recent divorce in their circle.

"It's such a pity we don't see her anymore," she said of the newly ex wife. "Everybody liked her a lot more than they like him."

Like a child strapped into a car seat, I piped up from the back: "So if that's the case, why didn't the couple's friends go with her instead of him after the split?"

The Range Rover turned a corner at speed, shredding a low-hanging branch with its roof rack. Inside the car was an awkward silence.

"Well, that's not really how it works out here," Annabelle said patiently. "Out here, the friends go with the money."

Oh.

In retrospect, that was one of the more obvious customs of the rich, and I was embarrassed that it needed to be explained to me. But others were just plain weird.

Our destination that day was a visit to Annabelle's friend Cristina Cuomo, who was nine months pregnant. We found her reclining on a lounge chair by the pool at her summer house, her enormous brown abdomen feasting on the sun.

After chatting for a while, her husband, Chris Cuomo, returned from a jog. A rock-jawed television journalist, he is the son of Mario Cuomo and the brother of Andrew Cuomo, both New York state governors.

Chris is very fit, and he was wearing nothing but running shoes, sunglasses, and a very small pair of nylon shorts. All of him was drenched in sweat that looked like it had been applied by a stylist with a spritzer.

Chris stood there glistening and said between pants: "I was just stopped on the road by a car. They wanted to know the way to the beach club. So, I said, 'What religion are you?'"

He was referring to something that rich New Yorkers seem to grow up knowing but is completely opaque to outsiders: the enduring separation between parallel institutions that serve wealthy Jewish and Christian families.

Even today—although their co-op boards would never admit it—there are Upper East Side residential buildings closed to Jews. The most sneering, anti-Semitic man I ever encountered among this wealthy set used to brag about keeping Jews out of his own building—although he preferred to keep secret that his private tastes ran to meeting younger African-American men in the gay sex clubs downtown.

The prestigious Maidstone Club in East Hampton, a hulking faux–English manor that rises out of the dunes, has a long and ignominious history of mistreating people based on their race. The Norwegian shipping billionaire Arne Naess Jr. was welcome in the 1980s—but not his wife, when he was married to Diana Ross.

Groucho Marx was said to have likewise been denied membership after playing a round of golf there as a guest in the 1950s. His retort: "My kids are only half-Jewish—can they at least play nine holes?"

My first visit to a Hamptons beach club came one weekend when I was the houseguest of a magazine publisher known for his voracious socializing. Our cadre of guests, which also included a minor television star, was loaded into a van each morning and kept to a strict schedule of parties and events.

Lunch was at the Bathing Corporation of Southampton, an old-fashioned beach club with a "particular" membership. The social thoroughbred Samantha Boardman was accepted as a member, for example, but not her husband, Aby Rosen—a real estate mogul worth several hundred million dollars, who is also the son of Holocaust survivors—when he applied at the same time.

The Bathing Corp. is quaint to the point of being an anachronism. For a thirty-thousand-dollar initiation fee, plus annual dues of up to five thousand dollars, members enjoy a small compound with a pool, frontage onto a beach (which is public property), and access to a clubhouse that has been unfavorably compared to a Holiday Inn.

But that is its bizarre appeal. Many of its members likely have summer homes in the area that are exponentially nicer than the facilities available at the Bathing Corp. But the "Beach Club," as its members call it, offers hamburgers off the grill and a place for kids to run around with other kids—even if they have been rather obnoxiously vetted before being allowed through the front gate.

When my publisher host took me there, we were meeting Brooke Shields and her family for lunch. It was an unusual gathering, because in addition to Brooke's two children, her mother, Teri Shields, was also present.

Teri didn't get out much, and her relationship with Brooke was strained. Her lifelong alcoholism and erratic treatment of her daughter—commissioning nude pictures of her at age ten and guiding the child actress into sexualized film roles and modeling from the age

of eleven—had cemented her image in popular culture as the archetypal pushy stage mother.

But this lunch with her grandchildren was a special treat for Teri's
birthday. And perhaps it wasn't coincidental that a bunch of people
they didn't know had also been invited to join the table, to act as
sandbags.

The hosts sat me next to Teri at the opposite end of the lunch table
from the rest of her family. She was a wicked, gossipy, bitter old crone:
in other words, the best company one could possibly hope for.

I probably enjoyed the lunch more than Brooke, whom Teri criticized constantly. The actress was centered, gracious, and clearly a
great mother—which was maybe why Teri didn't let up about her alleged parental failings.

At one point, when Teri complained that the children were doing
something that she thought they shouldn't be, Brooke said in exasper-
ation: "Mom, please. I watch them twenty-four/seven."

Teri struck at the phrase like a snake.

"Oh, twenty-four/seven?" she said patronizingly. "What a trendy
thing to say."

After the dozen-or-so lunch guests had finished eating, the rest of
the group decided to go to the beach with the kids. When I offered
to stay and keeping talking with Teri, Brooke mouthed a silent thank-
you.

Teri had not been drinking throughout lunch. But the moment we
were by ourselves, she got up from her chair, walked from place to
place, and drained every drop of leftover wine or beer from the glass
at each setting.

There was most of a bottle of white wine still chilling in the ice
bucket. Teri picked up an oversize plastic water glass, threw its contents into the bushes, and thrust it at my chest.

"Fill 'er up," she said.

A veteran nightclub promoter I knew in the East Village once
described the experience of doing cocaine with Liza Minnelli, decades

ago. He recalled preparing five lines on a mirrored tray, one for each person at the table, but passed it to her first since she was the ranking celebrity in the group.

Liza lowered her head and snorted all five lines, in quick succession.

Imitating the enthusiasm in her voice— and throwing in a pair of splayed jazz hands, like Judy Garland on the poster for *A Star Is Born*—he continued: "She looked up and said, 'Mama's here!'"

I thought of that line as Teri got her tankard of wine. The booze brought something elemental out of her, like wildflowers blooming in the desert. Whatever damage the drink had done to her health and her relationships, she was not herself without it.

When Teri had drained all the available alcohol, we repaired to the beach and joined the others. Shrouded in a collection of cotton sun wraps, with big dark glasses and a broad-brimmed hat, she pretended to read through a tote full of fashion magazines when in fact she was peering over the pages and passing judgment on every man who walked by.

"I'd give that one a seven," she said as her grandchildren scooped sand into a bucket nearby. "He needs to stop slacking off at the gym."

M eadow Lane in the Hamptons is a paved spine that runs the length of a five-mile spit of sand separating placid Shinnecock Bay on one side from the Atlantic Ocean on the other. The connecting inlet at the end of the road was punched through the barrier dunes during the Great New England Hurricane, which killed fifty Long Islanders after making landfall in 1938.

Despite its history of getting flattened by storms, this beachside strip is the most expensive and prestigious address in all of the Hamptons. Houses here, on lots ranging from a couple to several acres, sell in the twenty-to-thirty-million range. Even by the inflated standards of the area, the street has earned its nickname of Billionaire Lane.

Approaching from the village of Southampton, a visitor would pass ocean-facing houses owned by the designer Calvin Klein—a modern steel-and-glass box said to have cost seventy-five million dollars—and the Studio 54 nightclub founder turned hotelier Ian Schrager. Aby Rosen nurses any wounds inflicted by the Bathing Corporation membership committee in his house on the bay side. The other residents are mostly the founders of Wall Street hedge funds.

About halfway down the lane, which boasts its own heliport at the end, is the estate belonging to the family of the petrochemical baron, philanthropist, and libertarian David Koch.

With an estimated net worth of just over fifty billion dollars, David was the richest person in New York City. Along with his brother Charles, he had prevailed in the years-long lawsuit over the family fortune that was filed by his estranged twin, Bill, in concert with their eldest sibling, Fred.

With their position secure, David and Charles became the two most influential donors to right-leaning causes in the country. The *New York Times* reported that the brothers' political network—known inside the Washington beltway as the Kochtopus—gave just a shade under nine hundred million dollars to conservative causes during the 2016 presidential election.

He also personally contributed an amount likely in the billions to nonprofits benefiting a range of good causes, including medical research, arts, and education. The former New York State Theater at Lincoln Center was renamed in his honor following a one-hundred-million-dollar pledge. Likewise, the plaza outside New York's Metropolitan Museum of Art bears his name, in recognition of the sixty-five million dollars he donated for its restoration.

And despite his right-wing political views, he was also a major advocate for prison reform, allying with leftist groups to criticize the current system for its disproportionately high incarceration rates of low-income and nonwhite Americans.

David was not the Koch brother who once asked me out. But one summer weekend I accompanied a friend of his wife, Julia, to have dinner with their family at the Hamptons house.

The Koch estate— snapped up for a mere twenty-three million dollars before the area became quite as grand as it is now—sat on the Atlantic Ocean side of Meadow Lane. The main house was twelve thousand square feet, with seven bedrooms. The grounds featured a pool, a tennis court, and what looked very much like a sand trap on the manicured lawn, presumably so David could practice his gee-oh-ell-eff.

One of the big differences between East Coast and West Coast rich people is the approach they take to decorating. If you're in show business or technology, there's no limit to what you can spend money on in your house—everything is a set designed to show yourself off.

But for a certain kind of old-line conservative billionaire out east, after putting a chintz sofa in every room and a helicopter in the yard, there's nothing left to spend money on.

In the city, the Kochs had lived in Jacqueline Kennedy Onassis's old apartment at 1040 Park Avenue. They bought it for nine and half million in 1995 and sold it in 2006 for thirty-two million, before moving down to 740 Park, considered by many in the plutocrat caste to be the best address in town.

"Mrs. Onassis was very conservative financially, and she didn't spend much on it," David told the *Observer*. "We gutted the apartment and redid everything."

Julia added to *W* magazine that she wouldn't permit any photographs of the redecorating to be published, saying, "I don't want people judging our taste."

That taste was tame. Here in their home by the sea, there was a vaguely nautical theme; gestures toward beachside bonhomie may have included a faux-weathered inn placard featuring the profile of a salty dog. But she was from Iowa by way of Arkansas, and he was from Kansas, and they weren't trying to make a decorating statement like Donald Trump's vajazzled Versailles.

In fact, all the money in the Koch house seemed to be spent on buying vastly more expensive replicas of affordable, homey furniture. The overall sense was of a billionaire's unlimited resources thwarted by the finite options of what to buy.

It did cross my mind that if I had made different decisions, Julia and I might have been in-laws. Clearly, she was more prepared to make it through the night before breakfast at Tiffany's.

A former fashion assistant to Adolfo, an uptown couturier favored by Nancy Reagan, Julia met David on a 1991 blind date when he was fifty years old and she was twenty-seven. It did not go well.

"I was a little too, how should I say it, forward with my humor," David later told *New York* magazine of their first dinner together.

"Afterward we shook hands and I said, 'I'm glad I met that man because now I know I never want to go out with him,'" Julia told the *Times*.

A month later, David survived a plane crash on the runway of a Los Angeles airport. Five seconds after landing on a flight from Columbus, Ohio, his USAir Boeing 737-300 collided with a SkyWest twin-engine turboprop taxiing across its runway. The impact killed thirty-five people, including the only other couple sitting with David in first class.

That brush with death seems to have fueled his bacchanalian instincts. He became known for throwing what the *Times* described as "lavish parties, which attracted the kind of women that men don't often bring home to mother," with their "Hugh Hefner–esque decoration."

But it may also have reminded him that it was finally time to get married. After the accident, David and Julia re-encountered each other at a party. She told him that she was glad he didn't die.

David didn't remember that they had met. But, when corrected, he invited her to accompany him to the US Open. And in 1996, after five years of dating, the couple wed in a ceremony at his house on Meadow Lane.

Immediately upon her debut as Mrs. Koch, Julia leapt to the top of international best-dressed lists. Lithe and athletic, she favored light-weight designer gowns, often with a single strap that left her right shoulder bare. Everything looked right on her. And the moment Julia had her wedding ring, Anna Wintour tapped her to cochair the annual fund-raiser for the Costume Institute of the Metropolitan Museum of Art, commonly known as the Met Gala.

An annual ball organized by the *Vogue* editor, it is the most exclusive event in the New York social calendar. Tickets, at $25,000 each, are not available to the public—each purchaser must be personally vetted by Anna.

But the trouble with starting at the top is that it leaves you only one place to go. And her debut at the Met Gala, while generally favorably received, did not come off without a hitch.

A gimlet-eyed *New York Times Magazine* profile tied to the event mildly roughed her up, noting Julia's nervousness and her "defensive crouch" about letting magazines photograph her apartment.

The journalist dryly concluded, "How she handles the spotlight over the next months will determine whether anyone will be paying attention to her a year from now."

The knocks seemed to have left their mark. At home in Southampton that day, Julia was attentive and sincere but seemed to be consciously balancing her naturally upbeat personality with the gravitas required of a billionaire's wife.

The evening meal was served upstairs on a long dining room table made out of whitewashed planks. It might have passed for "shabby chic," which was in fashion at the time, had it not been accessorized by stiff-backed, white-jacketed staff pouring water out of pewter pitchers.

Separating the kitchen from the dining room was a restaurant-style door that pushed open both ways and took a long time to flap shut. It was endlessly distracting—I don't know how they lived with it during dinner parties—and every time it gaped, I couldn't help but look into the kitchen and observe even more white-jacketed staff inside.

Unease with household servants is a middle-class inhibition I will never be able to shake—like my mother, I will always clean up before the cleaner visits. In the homes of the rich, they are constantly present yet abnegated as human company. To me it feels like watching ghosts watch us back.

After we had spent the afternoon at his house, David, then in his midsixties, made his first appearance for dinner. A former student basketball star who now had two artificial knees, he was very tall and a little bit stooped. He made pleasant but subdued conversation—I got the impression that we were merely that night's cast in the endless variety show of his wife's visiting friends, which he preferred to watch on mute.

He laughed just once—it was the sound of a clown car backfiring—and then went back to his plate. Like the maximally optimized plain brown cushions downstairs, he seemed immutable and long past the point where the addition of another ten billion dollars would make the slightest bit of difference to anything about his life.

David's muscular support of conservative causes had made his name, like the Trumps', a byword for evil in some parts of his home city. But sharing a dinner table with him, he was an affable man in an expensive sweater—whose palatable views on prison reform and same-sex marriage coexisted with an agenda of removing pollution and all other environmental regulation from industry, and eliminating any kind of state assistance for the poorest citizens.

As a reporter, I felt pressure to glean some deep insight from being in proximity to this figure who was pulling the country's strings with his titanic wealth. But it was hard to connect the potentially devastating consequences of his policies with the personable, kind of checked-out guy who was sitting at the other end of the table, chewing.

If he seemed like a gentle soul, that was an illusion. Gentle souls don't become billionaires.

This, I realized, was a danger of covering the rich in close quarters, where social instincts and critical faculties are pitted against each other. It was so easy to be influenced by a warm interaction, rather than what I knew to be true: this man was actively campaigning to scrap the minimum wage, public health care, and even the postal service.

Franklin Roosevelt met "Uncle Joe" Stalin and declared him to be a teddy bear. I met Rupert Murdoch, whose media empire would install right-wing populist governments around the world, and came away marveling at his soft hands. Maybe it was time to be a little more skeptical about these people who controlled our lives.

David had returned to the house that morning after a week attending to business in Boston and had spent the day in seclusion. Midway through the meal, a nanny entered the dining room to present his two older children—they were both under ten years old, but there was also a toddler son elsewhere in the house—to say good night.

The children were dressed in clean pajamas, stood with straight backs, and spoke very formally. I couldn't be certain, but I got the impression they hadn't seen their father not only for the previous week but also during the several hours that day in which they had been in the same house.

As the children exited the room in orderly single file, the kitchen door flapped open to admit a steward carrying dessert—half a dozen white bowls lined up his arm with a single scoop of ice cream for each guest.

Once again, I couldn't help but turn my head and meet the watching eyes inside.

# 15

# The Ponzi Palace

**N**ew York in 2010 was an optimistic place. A popular mayor and a popular president were in office, and the recession brought about by the finance sector's shady dealings in the housing market had mostly ended.

Even if none of the architects of that crisis had been held accountable, the spectacular fall of financial adviser Bernie Madoff made a satisfying proxy. His unrelated $64 billion Ponzi scheme, which gratifyingly gouged only the very rich, went some way toward appeasing the national demand to string somebody up from a Wall Street lamppost.

The city snapped back to its old self like Silly Bandz, the colorful silicone bracelets that were all the rage that year and suggested the culture was ready for another round of whimsy. As always, there were parties. And while I promised myself I would stop getting snowed by oligarchs, being in the mix was still a lot of fun.

On assignment for AOL, I went to a book signing the designer Ralph Lauren was holding on the second floor of the Madison Avenue mansion that he had turned into his flagship store.

There, I chatted with the comedian Kathy Griffin, who said it was her fiftieth birthday. She was there with Gloria Vanderbilt, mother of her best friend at the time, Anderson Cooper, and the three of them were planning to go out to dinner to celebrate.

Gloria, who was born into great wealth and a theatrically dysfunctional family in 1924, was one of the most famous women of the twentieth century. I asked the then-eighty-six-year-old, who had been a prominent fashion designer in the 1970s, how she would describe her personal style, which is one of the ridiculous things that fashion reporters ask celebrities when they're likely to have only one question.

She fixed me with the warmest, most generous smile and said, in a voice cracking with age: "Trying to define yourself is like trying to bite your own teeth."

Likewise, I only had one shot with the laconic Karl Lagerfeld, who was visiting New York for the opening of a Chanel store in SoHo.

"Mr. Lagerfeld! What is your favorite website?" I yelled from the packed press line—which was still a reasonable question in in 2010.

The designer walked by without responding, then stopped, turned, and said with the utmost gravity: "I do not *do* the website."

Later I went with Nikki Haskell to a dinner thrown by Dennis Basso, the city's top society furrier. He does the classics—mink, sable, chinchilla—as well as exotics like ostrich and alligator. Individual coats can cost several hundred thousand dollars.

That year he hosted a benefit for Silver Hill Hospital, a mental health and addiction rehab facility he credited with saving his husband. I sat next to Nikki's friend Joan Collins, the guest of honor, who has a reputation for being frosty.

Aware that she had probably been bored by every known conversational gambit since beginning her film career in 1950, I tried what I hoped would be an original angle.

"You were a Bat-villain," I chirped, referring to her 1967 role as the Siren in the *Batman* television series. "That must have been fun! What was that like?"

Joan, who was then in her late seventies, fixed me with a look that caused my testicles to retract into my throat.

"*Why?*" she purred. "Was that *terribly influential* for you?"

I shut up and didn't try to speak to her again.

Joan was in town to perform cabaret at Feinstein's, a piano room at the Regency hotel. At the table, she complained that the musical director had not left her enough time between numbers to execute the required costume change, between two highly embellished, tight-fitting evening gowns.

"Who are you kidding, Joan?" said Nikki. "You could be overdressed in thirty seconds."

That struck me as a pretty good line. I walked to the bathroom through a cold marble hall and considered tweeting it. She'll never know, I thought.

But still, wounded as I was that she didn't want to be best friends, it seemed an ungallant thing to do. So I returned the phone to my pocket and went back to the table.

As I approached, I noticed that Joan and her husband, Percy, were filling in the idle moments by . . . scrolling through Twitter, searching for mentions of her name. Had I tweeted the crack, they would have seen it immediately.

It was a narrow escape, and a reminder that in the new world, surveillance cut both ways. As Joan herself might have put it: "Careful— the cameras have microphones now."

But it wasn't just movie stars who were adjusting to newly ubiquitous technologies. Social media was making a cultivated personal image more important to celebrities and civilians alike. Maybe not everyone was famous, but anyone could be a hipster, and they were.

Suddenly, the world was twenty-three years old and had a mustache. Hipsters cruised the block on their fixed-gear bicycles, messenger bags full of vinyl records slung crosswise on their backs, radiating attitude like vegan Hells Angels.

Overnight, chefs became the new rock stars. Everyone had tattoos— so many tattoos. Kale was a thing.

One silver lining was that as hipster culture took over, with its samurai topknots and ironic bowling shirts, the world seemed to lose interest in the ersatz heiresses who had been reality-television staples for the better part of a decade.

Finally, the little dogs could get out of those handbags. The heiress trend was declared dead when *Park Avenue Peerage*, once a must-read for desperate, status-conscious aspirants to high society, stopped updating. It was revealed to have been founded by James Kurisunkal, an eighteen-year-old college freshman from the suburbs of Chicago, working out of his dorm room at the University of Illinois.

*Socialite Rank*, uncovered as the work of two young Russians who may have been either siblings or lovers—nobody was ever quite sure—vanished from the internet entirely. Elsewhere, other stars also rose and fell.

Paz de la Huerta, the stylish downtown teenager who had caught the eye of Lee Tulloch so many years before, grew up into a head-turning actress who was often in the gossip columns. At that moment she was in a Manhattan criminal court, pleading guilty to harassment over an incident in which an MTV reality-show personality had been slashed with a broken champagne glass during an altercation at a nightclub. (The reality star allegedly started the fight by yelling, "Triple axel!" as Paz fell over a drinks table.)

Bill Clegg, my old landlord, published a bestselling memoir about crack addiction. Apparently, he sold the lopsided apartment we once rented to fund his own literary agency but spent the money on drugs instead.

When his girlfriend was away, he would meet guys from phone-sex lines, one of whom he moved in with at the fancy co-op on Fifth Avenue where I used to take our rent checks. Then he lost that relationship, as well as his new business, in a haze of crack smoke and hook-ups, he wrote.

"I hope you like it here. My girlfriend wrote her novel in this apartment," Bill had told us. Dude—talk about burying the lede.

In early 2010, Ken and Diane Starr bought a $7.5 million triplex on a quiet stretch of East Seventy-Fourth Street, which they showed off at a housewarming party in the spring.

The newly built seven-story condominium was all brushed steel, glass, and abrupt right angles. Most of the apartment's five bedrooms overlooked the paved garden—a princely luxury in New York City—from balconies on the second floor. The basement contained a screening room and indoor swimming pool, complete with an incongruous row of sun loungers lined up beneath the recessed ceiling lights.

It was a stunning rise for Diane, who was always trying to share her good fortune. But I could sense her frustration with dullards like me, who she thought weren't seizing the opportunities in front of them.

After the housewarming party, she set me up on a date with her hairdresser, Javi, a stunningly beautiful former actor in his midtwenties. Incubated as a potential Disney television star, Javi had dropped out after growing tired of the constant grind of singing, dancing, and acting lessons. But he still socialized with that group and, with some of them finding success, wanted to get back into the business.

Over dinner, I got the impression I had been sold to him as a celebrity-whisperer who could help reignite his career. His eyes shone with expectation, and his face was nothing but camera-ready angles. Since he'd friended me on Facebook a few hours before the date, I also knew exactly how good he looked in a bathing suit, which was displayed in every picture.

Javi was like a sports car that I had no idea how to drive. Aware that time is money, he cottoned onto this fairly quickly. After dinner, he suggested we join some of his actor friends at a bar for a drink, where he ditched me.

But I didn't care. I met a woman his age who was a series regular on a Disney show, who told me how the young cast had decided, as a group, to join Scientology for the networking benefit it could provide their careers. She was completely sanguine about their motives and believed getting out would be no problem if it no longer suited their needs. She and her friends viewed the religion as a kind of Hollywood LinkedIn.

Fascinated, I hung on every word. Javi had unfriended me on Facebook by the time I got home.

I was a little embarrassed to face Diane after this debacle, knowing how disappointed she'd be in my lack of hustle. But the next time I saw her, she was on the front page of the newspapers.

In April of that year, around the same time Ken was closing on the new apartment, his client Uma Thurman requested a meeting. She had noticed a million dollars missing from her account, and she wanted the money back.

Ken explained the money had been withdrawn for investments made on her behalf, but nonetheless the million dollars reappeared the next day. But that money had been illegally taken, according to prosecutors, from the account of another of Ken's clients—the lawbook definition of a Ponzi scheme.

It later emerged that, using his clients' power of attorney, he had also made a number of investments in businesses in which he had a financial interest. The world would soon be hearing a lot more about those South American voting machines.

Uma became one of the first client departures in what quickly became a rush for the exits. The children of another elderly client had also grown suspicious about the investments Ken had been making with their mother's money. They went to their local district attorney, who filed a criminal case.

The FBI came calling on the triplex at six thirty one morning, barely a month after they had moved in. The doorman asked if they were there for Andrew Madoff, a younger son of the convicted Ponzi schemer Bernie Madoff, who also happened to live in the building.

But no, they were coming for Ken.

Diane stalled them for an hour by saying he wasn't home, but they came back with a warrant, and he was discovered hiding behind the coats in an upstairs bedroom closet.

Prosecutors charged Ken in a fifty-nine-million-dollar fraud. He had gotten sloppy, they contended, because of his expensive young wife and sudden need to come up with money for a new apartment.

Reporters staked out the condominium for weeks, and the newspapers delighted in running front-page party pictures of Ken with Diane in her racier outfits. The details were tabloid catnip: a celebrity financial adviser brought low by his stripper fourth wife, the champion of pole dancing as a future Olympic sport.

And the names were enough to fill a newspaper column all by themselves. Ken's celebrity clients, some of whom had left before the scandal broke, included television eminences Tom Brokaw, Matt Lauer, Diane Sawyer, Walter Cronkite, Barbara Walters, Frank and Kathie Lee Gifford, and the executive Jeff Zucker; film directors Ron Howard, Jonathan Demme, Sam Mendes, and Michael Moore; actors Liam Neeson, Warren Beatty, and Candice Bergen; musicians Paul Simon and Carly Simon; writer Nora Ephron; fashion designer Isaac Mizrahi; and photographers Annie Leibovitz and Richard Avedon. There was no shortage of pictures of Ken and Diane posing with these stars, and many more.

Diane and her teenage son stayed on at the cavernous apartment for several more weeks. But with the family's accounts frozen—and being under order from the Feds not to liquidate her jewelry or other items of value—she had no access to money.

With nowhere else to go, they camped in their gilded cage as the gas and electricity, whose bills went unpaid, ticked toward being shut off. When I visited, I would buy a hot pizza from the corner, so they could eat.

At least Diane had a friend on the inside. Catherine Hooper, who had also recently moved in upstairs, was engaged to Andrew

Madoff. At sixty-five billion dollars, the Madoff fraud dwarfed Ken's, but Catherine supported Diane as she was pilloried daily by tabloids as the gold-digging wife of a crook. Between themselves, they called their building "the Ponzi Palace."

Ken, meanwhile, was adamant that it was all a misunderstanding. He told Diane to sit tight while he worked it out.

In contrast to his brief residence in the luxury of the Ponzi Palace, Ken was awaiting trial in the Metropolitan Correctional Center, a brown-brick tower of a jail in lower Manhattan. The MCC is a warehouse for all manner of local criminals, from aging Mafia dons to young punks and white-collar fraudsters, both those awaiting trial and those already convicted. After he had been in lockup a few weeks, I accompanied Diane on a visit.

Despite being located in one of the country's most densely populated urban areas, the MCC is strangely isolated inside a labyrinth of municipal buildings, devoid of street life. Getting into the place involves as much arcane knowledge as performing a Masonic ritual.

There are two things I wish I'd known before going. The first is to take a pen, because the first stop in the process is at an exterior guard station the size of a tollbooth, where you will be handed a form to fill out. If you don't have a pen, there is no place to buy one, and the guard makes it very clear it is not his job to provide writing instruments.

The second is to scout the nearest public restroom (it's in the courthouse next door, on the third floor), because it takes a couple of hours from filling out that first form before you arrive in the visiting room upstairs. Submitting to the process is like attending the ball-drop in Times Square on New Year's Eve—you're penned into one place, and if you need to leave, there's no going back to your place in the line.

Most visitors to the MCC have been there before, however, and once you enter the intake system, a sense of bonhomie develops. They are mainly women, and the ordeal takes so long that you have a chance to bond.

Immodest clothing, including open-toed shoes, is forbidden; cognoscenti also know to come wearing a sports bra, because no metal is allowed into the building. Underwire bras—which set off the screeching, airport-style metal detector—are a common bar to entry.

Once you clear the metal detectors, there is a long wait to get upstairs, in lines that snake back and forth in front of two decrepit elevators. Old hands amuse themselves by yelling, "It's ya bra, honey!" whenever a first-timer sets off the alarm. Then the embarrassed would-be visitor has to either turn around and go home, or struggle out of it underneath her shirt (because, no restrooms) and store it in the lockers that are provided for other contraband, like cell phones and keys. The people in charge seem to relish these small humiliations.

The other important piece of intelligence to know before going to the MCC is to take a stack of uncrumpled one-dollar bills.

When you finally get up to the fifth floor, there is another waiting pen before you enter the visiting room, and between the two, vending machines for soda, dry snacks, and microwavable sandwiches. However pleased the inmates may be to see their families, they equally look forward to the food from those machines, which only visitors can buy.

After another wait, Diane and I were called to begin our one-hour allotted visit. There was no glass partition; visitors sat on plastic chairs lined up with their backs to the wall, and families were allowed a very brief hug. Using my stack of dollars, I took in a Diet Coke and a couple of microwaved White Castle sliders.

Ken seemed to be in robust spirits as he devoured the miniburgers. The Madoff case had given Ponzi schemers an aura of celebrity inside the prison, and he said he was much sought-after by the other inmates for financial advice. He was also optimistic about being exonerated in court and getting back to both professional and married life.

A bail hearing was set for summer, he said, which was when his friends would spring him. After all, didn't his clients include financial titans like Pete Peterson, billionaire founder of the private equity powerhouse the Blackstone Group?

Diane looked at him nervously. Ken was so certain everything was going to be made right.

In July, bail was set at $10 million, which none of his former friends or clients stepped forward to post. After the lights were shut off at home, Diane moved out to stay with a friend, while her son went to live with his father in Brooklyn. In September, Ken pleaded guilty in federal court and returned to his cell at the MCC to await sentencing.

The iPhone 4 came out that summer, the first to feature a second camera for selfies, and at the beginning of October, somebody in San Francisco came up with a droll little time-waster called Instagram. By the end of the month, it was full of pictures of that year's hot Halloween group-costume theme, Chilean miners.

When Elaine Kaufman died in December of that year at the age of eighty-one, she got a full-page obituary in the *Economist*. Elaine's stayed open for only a few more months, before passing into New York City legend.

I met Catherine Saxton at the bar for one last martini with a vodka chaser, and we stared at the nicotine-tinged hole in the air where Elaine used to sit. She mentioned that she was looking to replace the Starrs on her client list.

When the time came, I accompanied Diane to Ken's sentencing, where he apologized to the court in a shaky voice. Judge Shira Scheindlin gave him seven and a half years in federal prison and ordered him to pay twenty-nine million dollars' restitution.

"He lost his moral compass, partly as a result of his infatuation with his young fourth wife," she said.

That afternoon, Diane changed her Twitter bio to read, "moral compass disabler." Divorce proceedings commenced a few months later.


On a February morning in 2011, AOL chief executive Tim Armstrong called a surprise all-hands meeting in the company's downtown Manhattan offices.

A former head of sales at Google, Tim was tall with broad shoulders. He looked like a cartoon handsome guy, with a face like a heavily moisturized cubist bust, under a dark beret of floppy schoolboy hair.

A friend who had previously worked with Tim once told me a story about stopping him in the corridor for a quick consultation. Tim was very busy and needed his colleague to come promptly to the point. He expressed this by saying, "I'm back-to-back-to-back, so let's get to the S-E-X."

Thereafter, I had never been able to see Tim without thinking of that phrase.

Standing next to him in the AOL staff kitchen that day was Arianna Huffington. Beaming, Tim got right to the S-E-X: he announced that AOL had just purchased her successful web publication, the *Huffington Post*, for $315 million. The two entities would be combining newsrooms immediately.

For many of us who were painfully familiar with the shrinking media landscape, it was obvious this merger would mean layoffs. Nonetheless, Tim tried to lead his employees in a rousing cheer.

The response he got was more of a tepid murmur.

I had known and liked Arianna for years, mainly because she loved to be interviewed and always gave great quotes. That morning, she had also brought along her sister, Agapi Stassinopoulos.

Arianna pushed her to the front and exhorted her, "Tell them!"

Agapi shuffled forward and said: "I'm just here to say, I've always used an AOL email address."

The room was silent. Arianna looked at her sister expectantly.

"And, and, I love it," Agapi added for emphasis.

There was another murmur-cheer. While the company was not a terrible place to work, staffers were deeply embarrassed by being forced to use AOL email addresses professionally. In the cutthroat world of online media, AOL's brand was a butter knife.

The appearance of the *Huffington Post* staff did nothing to reassure the AOLers, many of whom had come up through traditional print media. When they moved in, the HuffPost kids halved the average age of the newsroom overnight. It wasn't hard to see who was going to be on the losing side when that shook out.

The HuffPosters were very cute and mostly smart but painfully preadult. They certainly hadn't learned which fashion trends to ignore.

It was the summer when menswear blogs were telling the country's impressionable youth to wear enormous brown leather work boots, flared wide and unlaced, with the tongue teased out over the pant leg. It was up there with capri-length legs on suit trousers as a trend that it was possible to avoid from a great distance.

But not these boys. They tromped into work each morning with their huge boots unlaced and agape, like firefighters coming off a difficult shift. And just in case the old guard needed further help understanding how it was going to end, there was literal writing on the wall.

The newsroom men's bathroom was clean and modern, with white grout around white tiles. It had always been immaculate, but about ten days after the *Huffington Post* moved in, the first piece of graffiti appeared.

Written in black felt-tip pen on the grout at urinal eye level, it read, in small capital letters: "JIZZ."

A week later, I was sitting at a bris inside a gay synagogue in the West Village for the baby twins of friends, David and Patrick, one Orthodox Jewish and the other Roman Catholic. (New York, what a town.) My phone pinged with an email from work: effective immediately, all AOL freelancers had had their contracts canceled and were unemployed.

You had to hand it to *HuffPost*: they jizzed, they saw, and they conquered.

New York is nothing if not a city of options. But as jobs in journalism continued to vanish, it became clear that exchanging words for dollars made more sense as a hobby than it did as a way to earn a living.

Fortunately, the booming technology sector was employing people with editorial skills even as the media industry contracted. I landed a good job as editor in chief of a lifestyle brand under the online fashion retailer Gilt.

Compared to the stress of working in gossip media—where any mistake meant some combination of getting sued, getting humiliated, and being fired—corporate life was a pleasant revelation. I adored my colleagues and managed to refill coffers depleted by the diminishing returns of freelancing. For the next few years, writing was going to have to be on the side.

With the security of a dot-com paycheck, I began freelancing casually for the *New York Times*'s Style section.

I felt relieved to have avoided the various gossip traps (like taking envelopes of cash or writing flashier stories and "worrying if they were true later") that would have made me unemployable by the paper of record. And perhaps they were looking for a little tabloid flair in writing about garish rich people, which was the new growth area.

Just because the juice had gone out of the heiress trend didn't mean that wealthy, ambitious people didn't still want their faces in the paper. And on the Upper East Side of New York, the pages they wanted to be in most were the *Times*'s Style section.

Even for the rich, the shimmer of celebrity promised a fresh infusion of status, money, and power. Donald Trump and Paris Hilton were just then personally out of fashion, but they had normalized the use of publicity among New York's monied classes. And for that service they turned to a small band of society publicists, one of the city's more fascinating niche jobs.

For a steep fee, these professionals promised they could turn a nobody into a somebody. At the low end, this meant being placed at the kind of parties where they would be snapped by photographers like Patrick McMullan and join the de facto social register of searchable names on his fabled website.

The next step was sidling next to more famous people in photographs that might be published in the social pages. And they still
wanted to be mentioned in "Page Six," which retained its influence
even as the newspaper industry crumbled around it.

Many of the people who bought these services were frankly delu-
sional and harbored fantasies of making it onto the cover of *Vogue* magazine. In reality, the loftiest feasible coverage was a profile in the *Times*'s
Style section, which appears in the paper every Thursday and Sunday.

But just like celebrities checking the gossip columns for their
own paparazzi shots, these modern-day Becky Sharps were invariably
thinking about the pictures, not the words. The *Times* did not want
to appear impressed by such parvenus, and the accompanying profiles
were not always flattering.

Somehow, that never seemed to stop anybody. The rich are so
used to getting whatever they throw money at; why should fame be
any different?

Society publicists, although especially suited to the late-empire
moment we are currently experiencing, have a long pedigree in the
city. There have been social fixers in New York at least since Carry
Fisher, the consultant to ambitious nouveau riche women depicted in
Edith Wharton's *The House of Mirth*.

"It's rather clever of her to have made a specialty of devoting herself to dull people," one established socialite acidly observes of Mrs.
Fisher's work. "The field is such a large one, and she has it practically
to herself."

The mold for the modern society publicist was forged by George
Trescher, a San Franciscan deposited on the city's shores at the end
of his navy service in 1945. After working in promotions at Henry
Luce's mighty Time Inc., he left to found the fund-raising department
of the Metropolitan Museum of Art, ahead of its extended centenary
celebrations in 1970.

Not only were the festivities a great success, Trescher also mod-
ernized the fund-raising model for society events. No longer would
benefactors be stuffed into fusty Whartonian ballrooms. Now the

city's socialites attended galas in white big-top tents, with better catering, florists, lighting designers, and even the occasional marquee entertainer on the bill.

The cost of admission to these improved events was also much larger than they had been used to paying. But the social register proved willing to pay higher ticket prices for better parties that made their causes even more money. Everybody was very happy with the way George did things.

So happy, in fact, that he worked with not only the city's major philanthropic institutions but also its leading citizens. In his later career, he organized enormous dinners for Brooke Astor and orchestrated Kennedy-family weddings.

The author Christopher Mason, who apprenticed with George as a young college graduate in the 1980s, wrote in the *New York Times* about his "devastating shorthand" for deciding the seating arrangements at such grand events: "Self-important ladies and gents who lacked the crucial ingredient of charm were derided as 'heavy furniture,' doomed to be seated near the kitchen next to some thrifty plutocrat who 'wouldn't give you ice in winter.'"

Sometimes his job was in line with the old-school edict to preserve his clients' privacy, such as during Caroline Kennedy's 1986 wedding to Edwin Schlossberg at the family compound in Hyannis, Massachusetts. As staff were setting up the tents and tables, the bride's brother, John Kennedy Jr., stepped naked out of the sea following his morning swim and strode confidently past the staff wearing nothing but a towel around his neck. George was able to keep that little tidbit out of the wedding coverage.

Other times, however, a bit of press was seen as an advantageous thing. Mrs. Astor, for example, asked George to ensure that curious reporters were kept properly informed of her charitable works. If she gave a dollar, she wanted people to know about it.

Forty years later, the justification of every nonentity who hires a press agent to get them social coverage is still: "But Brooke Astor had a publicist!"

Gradually, just like private juice chefs, pet psychics, and yoga instructors before them, the position of personal publicist became part of the retinue of the New York rich. When he represented Tinsley Mortimer, the publicist R. Couri Hay instructed her to cite Tory Burch—the lissome blond socialite whose name became an aspirational fashion and lifestyle brand, and who accumulated a personal net worth estimated to be six hundred million dollars—as a role model in interviews.

"Everybody wanted to be Tory because Tory Burch had parlayed being attractive and going to parties and being on the [charity] committees and being in the right dress at the right time, in the right place with the right people, into what became a billion-dollar empire," he told *Town & Country* magazine.

Tory was the "right" name to emulate for respectable strivers. But if she was the Eve of social climbers, then Paris Hilton was their Lilith—the real originator, who had been written out of scripture for being shameless and ungovernable.

Six years after "Paris, Inc." appeared in the *New York Times*, millions of would-be influencers were following it like a road map, whether they knew it or not. Her publicist, Rob Shuter, had been able to sniff the breeze and understand the culture was ready to worship the Hollywood version of a business idol—a trend that would yield unforeseen political consequences.

Rob was the most notorious celebrity publicist of his day. Other press agents had bigger clients, but Rob loved intriguing with the gossip writers, making him a more influential presence in tabloid culture than the grander movie-star flacks who mostly kept their distance.

He was charming and roguish and knew how to stretch the truth as if it were chewing gum. His career, including the sudden and unexpected termination of his relationship with Paris Hilton, provides a window into that entire era of celebrity machination.

Rob got his start in the entertainment business through his partner, Bruce Sussman, a longtime collaborator with Barry Manilow, who cowrote hits including "Copacabana." They met in 1993, when Rob was a university student in Edinburgh, selling concessions at a stage musical based on the song.

A decade later, with the help of Sting's immigration lawyer, he was a big-deal publicist in New York. Barely two months after the triumph of "Paris, Inc.," however, Rob played a role in the first of three mini-scandals that combined to sink his career.

In July 2005, he supplied an item to "Page Six" about Paris's being assaulted in a London nightclub by Zeta Graff, a Greek socialite whose family was in the diamond trade. In a trademark Shuterian flourish, he told the column the deejay was playing "Copacabana" as Zeta attacked.

The only problem was that the incident never happened, and Zeta sued for defamation. Paris settled for a sum reported to be "north of $2 million."

In an attempt to recoup the loss, Paris then sicced her lawyers on Rob, accusing him of being responsible and demanding $10 million in damages. He responded that he was only passing on what she told him.

"Zeta went after her, and she came after me," he told me for a profile I wrote in the *Observer*. "Ultimately, I won; she had no evidence. We had all the evidence: texts and emails."

The next one wasn't his fault. In 2004, Rob had taken on the young singer Ashlee Simpson as a crisis client, after an infamous lip-synching incident that caused her to flee the stage during a broadcast of *Saturday Night Live*.

As soon as she signed, he set his sights on also landing her older sister, Jessica, who was a bigger star. "A member of Ashlee's entourage told me the most important person in the Jessica Simpson machine was her dog, Daisy," he said. "If I turned up at the Ritz-Carlton and Daisy liked me, I would get Jessica."

On the day of the meeting, Rob packed his pockets with pastrami. Daisy jumped all over him, and he got the business.

When Jessica began dating John Mayer in 2006, the *National Enquirer* and *Us Weekly* both got the tip independently. Knowing the story was about to break anyway, Rob offered the print exclusive to *People* magazine.

The following week, the attractive new couple were in supermarket checkout racks around the country. Then Jessica appeared on Rosie O'Donnell's talk show and forgot her lines. When asked by the host about her new boyfriend, she panicked and denied the relationship.

"We were all surprised by her answer," Rob said. "In her defense, Jess was not prepared for such a direct question."

The gossip blog *Gawker*, which had long painted Rob as a liar, reveled in the fallout. "In one masterstroke, Shuter had shattered his own credibility (ha), made his own client look like a desperate liar, pissed off fellow celebrity flacks and, perhaps worst of all, made enemies of some powerful celebrity magazines. He was then fired by [Jessica's manager father] Joe Simpson, for all of the above reasons," it wrote.

Rob often played loose with the facts, but this time, ironically, he got in trouble for telling the truth.

Looking to get right with his boss by replacing Jessica with an even bigger client, he heard Britney Spears was looking for new representation and made a pitch. But he didn't know that she had previously left his agency on bad terms and, in the ensuing stink, was sacked for violating an industry protocol against poaching.

After public relations, Rob switched sides and reinvented himself as a celebrity journalist. The *Observer* profile was pegged to a short-lived morning gossip program he hosted on VH1, and later, he wrote a column in the *National Enquirer*.

But his monument is that *Times* article. By positioning Paris as a businesswoman, Rob nudged the culture toward viewing wealth and celebrity as interchangeably monetizable. All anyone needed was the right personal publicist.

The Starrs turned to Catherine Saxton, the veteran Trump and

Hilton family operative, who didn't quite manage to pull it off. Others, like Andrew Borrok, the handsome scion of a real estate family worth hundreds of millions of dollars, went to Norah Lawlor.

A lawyer with vast resources to spend on his hobbies, Andrew wanted to position himself as a celebrity chef/restaurateur. He blitzed the Hamptons one summer, underwriting polo matches and promotional events for films, where he was photographed with celebrities such as Martha Stewart and Catherine Zeta-Jones.

He also threw lavish parties at his mansion in the tony hamlet of Water Mill. There, he produced trays of appetizers made from sushi-grade fish flown in from Tokyo, out of a kitchen fitted with expensive gadgets like a cryogenic freezer. I went to one such soirée where he served lobster by the pool, which had been dyed pink to match the wine.

Inevitably, he wanted a profile in the *New York Times* Style section. When it came, it sliced him into sashimi.

The story pointed out that he planned to open a restaurant despite never having worked in one. And it lingered on details like the subject's twenty-five-year-old *Playboy* model girlfriend, whom Andrew was at pains to point out was not attracted to him for his wealth, because she's "not like that."

The restaurant never opened. After he switched professions back to law, Andrew was next heard from in a *New York Post* article about how much of his fortune he was spending as a candidate in a Brooklyn judicial election.

"Essentially, this guy is buying a judgeship," an anonymous rival sniped. (It worked.)

Such are the personalities who are drawn to hire society publicists. But it isn't just nobodies who spend money to tell the world about themselves—sometimes the rich and famous need some shoring up, too.

In 2015, Wendi Deng was invited to cochair the annual Met Gala for what by then had been renamed the Anna Wintour Costume Center.

Two years after her split from Rupert Murdoch, she was ready to return to the spotlight.

The gala launches an annual exhibition of individual artworks from the museum's collection, paired with items of historical or contemporary fashion. Its 2015 theme was announced as *Chinese Whispers*, a tone-deaf title that was soon retracted and replaced with *China: Through the Looking Glass*.

Under the watchful eye of Ms. Wintour, Wendi's cochairs included the actresses Jennifer Lawrence and Gong Li, as well as Marissa Mayer, then the chief executive of Yahoo!. Silas Chou, a Hong Kong fashion and textiles billionaire whose companies had formerly controlled the Tommy Hilfiger and Michael Kors brands, was named as chair.

To cochair the Met Gala is one of the most prestigious honors in a status-obsessed city. So, when HL Strategic Solutions (a firm that, according to its website, "advises business leaders on how to best convey their message, [or] overcome a reputational challenge") offered an interview with their client Wendi Deng less than seven days before the event, the *Observer* dropped everything to put her on its next front page.

I got the assignment. Even a deposed Murdoch, it seemed, was not immune to the admixture of status, money, and power that a little celebrity could impart.

But, after I made calls to the museum seeking background information for the profile, something surprising happened. Wendi suddenly became unavailable.

This was especially mysterious, given that it was for a last-minute story her own publicist had pitched. Every day I tried to get an hour on her schedule, and every day her representative—the same person who had asked the *Observer* to write the article—said she was too busy to speak. The story had to be filed by Monday afternoon to be in print Wednesday morning, and yet even on Sunday she wasn't free.

I will never know for certain what happened to derail the profile.

But I strongly suspect Anna Wintour does not throw a party every year for the Anna Wintour Costume Center so that the newspapers can do a front-page story about Wendi Deng. Or perhaps it was mere happenstance that Wendi changed her mind just a few hours after the museum learned about the article.

Nonetheless, I kept calling and Wendi kept stalling. Over the weekend, the paper abandoned the idea that she would be its front-page feature. But none of us wanted to let go of the story entirely.

So, we contrived a compromise: I would attend the press preview of the exhibition on Monday morning, where many of the cochairs would be present. And there I would run into Wendi, entirely seren-dipitously. At that chance encounter, I would speak with her—then rush home and turn the story around in three hours.

It turned out to be a blisteringly hot morning. Henry Kissinger—still accepting credit, should anyone care to offer it, for Richard Nix-on's 1972 visit to China—sat in the front row for speeches held against the dramatic backdrop of the Temple of Dendur.

Several of the cochairs, including Anna and Wendi, addressed the room. Mayer, the Yahoo! high priestess, raised my hackles by praising the Met for its "beautifully curated content." For our internet over-lords, apparently, artwork of staggering beauty was just a fungible commodity like anything else beneath their jaundiced gaze.

When I spoke to Wendi as planned, she kept her remarks so col-orless that I didn't use anything from the interview and quoted instead from her speech. And I had just enough time to write five hundred of the most boring words ever committed to print on the subject.

As we were all streaming out of the museum that morning, I re-member that one person was crossing the David H. Koch Plaza against the flow of two hundred journalists and preview guests.

It was a woman who appeared to be in her midfifties, wearing a long gold evening gown, with a matching clutch and very heavy makeup, on a day that was sending heat shimmers up off the pave-ment.

She was very clearly dressed for the gala that evening and trying to crash the event by sneaking into the space as the preview emptied out. I turned and watched as she entered the building through the exit we were all using.

I have no idea how far she got, but I desperately hope she found a ladies' room, pulled out something to read from that small gold clutch, and remained undetected for all six hours until the party began. Maybe she even got to speak with Wendi Deng.

One unexpected convenience of aging is that you don't have to wonder when, exactly, you officially turn "old." The world is only too happy to let you know.

It happened to me March 19, 2016, at forty-five years and two months of age.

That morning, I drowsed through my normal Saturday routine of putting the red kettle on a blue gas flame to make coffee, commanding the voice robot to play National Public Radio, and thumbing through Twitter while the water boiled.

Through bleary eyes, I thought I must have accidentally selected my mentions rather than the main news feed, since most of it was about a story of mine that had just published on the *Times* website. But, not all of it? That was weird. Also, the tone was a tad spicier than usual.

Oh, god. It wasn't my mentions, it was the main feed: I had "gone viral," as people too young to remember the AIDS crisis liked to say. And the online mob, they were not happy.

A few months earlier I had been approached by a publicist for Mic.com, a news website for millennials. She wanted a Style section profile on Chris Altchek, the company's handsome young CEO.

Chris was twenty-eight and had every marker of privilege, having been educated at an elite New York private school and then Harvard. After college, he moved into a Wall Street job at Goldman Sachs, which he left to cofound Mic with a high school friend who had become a journalist.

Chris had a glamorous girlfriend and looked like a *Gossip Girl* heartthrob who had been extruded through a drinking straw—impossibly tall and thin with dusky, hooded eyes. The pitch from his publicist was: "He might be about to join the board of the American Ballet Theatre. You could break that exclusively."

Well, no thanks.

But Mic, with a staff and readership that were mostly under thirty, had the zeitgeist on its side, so the publicist and I went out for drinks to try to find an angle. And by the second martini, the stories about the antics that took place in its newsroom got pretty good.

There was the twenty-seven-year-old audience development manager who told his boss he needed a week off to attend a friend's funeral in his home state, when in fact he used the time to build a tree house, which he chronicled on social media.

"I said that I was leaving town for a funeral, but I lied," he wrote in a blog post that he then promoted on Twitter, to make sure everyone saw it back in the office.

If we could get more anecdotes like that, I told the flack, she'd get her *Times* story. And it turned out there were plenty more.

Later, when the dust settled, I learned Mic had been without a director of human resources at the time. Such a person might have advised against milking the staff's questionable behavior for a newspaper story, but without that check, everyone involved was more than happy to overshare.

The result was an article titled "What Happens When Millennials Run the Workplace?" As a framing device, my editor had dropped in at the top a quote from a CNBC article that summarized the millennial stereotype as "entitled, lazy, narcissistic and addicted to social media." What could anyone possibly find risible about that?

When the story hit the internet on the last day of winter, a great rattling could be heard across the land as an entire generation clutched its pearls in unison. The kids *hated* it.

I watched the mushroom cloud spread over Twitter as the kettle whistled to itself on the stove. Based on their profile pictures, the haters and those who enjoyed the story seemed to cleave pretty much at exactly forty years of age.

The first critic to target me by name was, of all people, a third-tier gay porn star. He tweeted: "@BenWiddicombe LOVED your piece about @micnews - better title though 'The undeniable evolution of news makes @nytimes write bullshit.'"

How did this pillow of the community manage to get in first? I wondered. Maybe he was filming a daddy scene and had to hold a newspaper for two minutes, flipping through the fashion pages concealed under the cover of the Business section.

He nailed the tone of the criticism, though. The first hot take—a short online essay in response to topics trending on social media—appeared just a few hours later on *Teen Vogue*. Its firebrand blogger Lauren Duca called me the exemplar of "almost-dead white men in armchairs"—which was actually pretty fabulous. Better to face critics than crickets, after all.

Being swarmed on Twitter felt like getting a full-body fish pedicure. The ticklish discomfort of being constantly nibbled turned out to be its whole tingling appeal.

Even the *New Yorker* weighed in. Having assigned the hot take to a blogger under the dividing age of forty, it took a position against me, which stung slightly. For anyone even mildly invested in the romance of being a writer in the city, getting called out by the *New Yorker* is like having the Statue of Liberty flip you the middle finger as you pass by on the Staten Island Ferry.

Over the following week, the response grew from online hot takes and chin-stroking think pieces to articles aggregating the social media responses and even an op-ed published in the *Los Angeles Times*. The circus lasted long enough for there to be a backlash to the backlash, with a couple of foolhardy souls (over forty, I suspect) defending the piece in their own publications.

Eventually the opining horde moved on, like locusts to the next field. After my first experience of being barraged by criticism on social media, my main takeaway was that in one short decade, the geniuses of Silicon Valley had managed to completely revolutionize the art of hate mail.

Only ten years had passed since the *Daily News* received those creamy white envelopes inscribed by an elegant hand in green ink, with no return address and a Connecticut postmark. It turned out the only thing stopping everyone else from also sending those letters was not a milder temperament but the inconvenience of having to locate stationery and a stamp. Hate mail had been broken, but the technocrats fixed it.

At least the fuss had been good for the story. All the hate reads made "What Happens When Millennials Run the Workplace?" one of the most-viewed *Times* stories of the year.

Amid the post-publication brouhaha, Chris Altchek, his publicist, and I met for a drink at the bar of a hotel in SoHo. He didn't mind the story, but with Mic's audience demographic and his own newsroom aligned in opposition, it behooved him to stay quiet.

A large picture of him had run to accompany the piece, those half-open eyes lending a come-hither quality that was perhaps more matinee idol than media visionary. His only feedback was, he didn't like the photo.

As the 2010s progressed, the desire among wealthy private citizens to be the subject of movie-star profiles in the fashion pages only increased. Business for the social publicists swelled accordingly. And in New York, the dean of the profession was R. Couri Hay.

Couri liked to tell the story of being a comely teenager, dining with his grandmother at the Ritz Hotel in Paris, when he caught the eye of Andy Warhol. The artist approached their table and sucked him into the turbine of 1970s society, setting him on the path to becoming an uptown queenmaker decades later. Inside the Upper West Side town house he bought with the proceeds from a successful career, the walls were hung thick with work by famous artists of the era, including portraits by Warhol and Peter Max.

Couri wrote for Andy's *Interview* magazine and had a gossip column in the *National Enquirer* in the 1970s and '80s. He claims credit for brokering one of the tabloid's biggest scoops, a picture of Elvis Presley, lying in his coffin, that ran on the front page. For this, he says, he became the first print journalist in America to have an annual salary and expenses package in excess of a million dollars a year.

He also did publicity for Studio 54 and studied at the sharp elbow of Aileen Mehle, a social arbiter who wrote the widely read society column "Suzy." In later life, he became the well-connected consigliere of New York society, always at the party, and always with two halves of a pair of reading glasses on a chain around his neck, ready to snap together with a magnet at the bridge.

His work with the younger female members of established society families like the Hearsts and the Guests also made him a sought-after Pygmalion for hungry debutantes who wanted their faces in the kinds of magazines that have letters rather than names: *T, V,* and *W.*

Couri recalls Tinsley Mortimer's approaching during a party at the Guggenheim Museum. "I had become well-known for helping guide the social girls that wanted to be models, or wanted to have products, or wanted to be designers," he told *Town & Country* magazine. "Tinsley said, 'Couri, all I want to do is be a little socialite.'"

She proved to be an excellent example of his formula in action. The first step in transforming a civilian into a society figure is to install her on the "right" charity committees—preferably something with a flashy annual gala, like the opera or the ballet, or one of the name-brand museums. The Crohn's & Colitis Foundation does great work too, but it's nobody's social launching pad.

In New York, members of the society set under the age of forty-five serve on junior committees, suitable for heirs with living parents who haven't yet inherited the full heft of the family fortune.

Once a socialite ages out of the junior committee, in order to stay competitive on the charity gala circuit, they are expected to make a substantial personal gift to an institution—at least in the hundreds of thousands, and often more—in order to be invited to join its board.

That transition is the great winnowing. You can borrow a dress and hire a publicist to get on a junior committee, but if you can't pony up to get on the board, your Patrick McMullan photos are likely to come to an abrupt end.

Another thing that separates authentic socialites from the pretenders is they hate being called socialites. It's only the arrivistes who aspire to be socialites—those born into it want to be called "philanthropists."

Couri was able to place Tinsley on event committees for the Central Park Zoo and the American Museum of Natural History—two highly suitable causes for a fresh-faced young climber. Her swift social success garnered a lot of attention, from Dior cosmetics to bloggers watching Park Avenue from their midwestern dorm rooms.

Many others aspired to tread a similar path. One of the most successful was an Upper East Side dervish named Jean Shafiroff, who spread her riches among the publicists of New York like Mansa Musa disbursing gold on the way to Mecca.

Jean was a middle-class girl from Hicksville, Long Island, who married a wealthy Wall Street financier. She raised two daughters and became involved with charity through fund-raising at their schools. After they left home, good works became her driving passion, and she raised several million dollars for causes ranging from animal hospitals to mental health services.

Jean was in her seventh decade but blessed with beauty and a figure that looked twenty years younger. And she loved the dressiest of evening fashion, keeping several hundred poufy, maximalist ball gowns between her apartment on Park Avenue and her mansion in the Hamptons.

She was also renowned as the most aggressive publicity seeker on the social circuit. Over the years, she used more than half a dozen different publicists—sometimes being on the books with up to four separate agencies at one time, including Norah Lawlor's and Couri's. As she liked to say in her own defense, "Brooke Astor had a publicist."

As a result, Jean was constantly being pitched to the gossip columns, and her representatives needed to find increasingly creative ways of inserting her into the news cycle. When the newspapers ran a story about a pack of coyotes that had been discovered living on the airfield at New York's LaGuardia Airport, for example, her publicists had her in the columns the next day, volunteering to organize a catch-and-release rescue mission.

I profiled Jean for the Style section, which ran a gorgeous photograph of her twirling the ample skirts of a lavender evening gown on the front of the section. The article, however, made gentle sport of her dual passions for publicity and philanthropy. It noted that she went out four nights a week during the fall gala season and appeared in an almost unprecedented eight thousand photographs on the Patrick McMullan website.

"There's a lot of people in society who snipe about Jean. They think that she could be out just to get attention," said Emily Smith, the editor of "Page Six." "What is ridiculous and sometimes quite annoying is that we will get pitched by every one of [her four press agents]. If we fail to mention her, her publicists will complain, and I get the impression that she probably complained heavily to them."

Jean was surprised anyone could be so cynical as to question her charitable motives. Especially when she had made clear her commitment to good works by reading aloud, at some length, from her own book on the subject during our interview.

But she forgave me enough to invite me to her annual holiday lunch, a gathering of wealthy uptown characters who seemed to leap from the pages of a comic novel.

These included Prince Dimitri of Yugoslavia, a jewelry designer and scion of a defunct European royal family; Sharon Bush, an ex-wife of one of the less famous brothers in the Texas political dynasty, who angered the clan by going very public with her disgruntlement on the way out the door; and Susan Gutfreund, a famous society hostess and widow of a man who had been nicknamed "the King of Wall Street."

That year, Susan had just listed her apartment for $120 million, making it the most expensive property in New York City. After lunch, she got trapped in the ladies' restroom for a period of about five minutes, which so traumatized her that she demanded a large tequila from the restaurant manager in restitution.

In fact the lunch was quite successful as an old-fashioned social event, which made it something of a throwback. Because the irony of people spending money on publicists to break into "society" was that there was no society to be found once they got there.

True, there are still galas in the city and garden parties in the Hamptons. But the social structure underpinning the bygone rituals of black-and-white balls and ladies' teas has vanished into the past.

What we think of as classic "New York society"—those golden afternoons of Truman Capote and his swans waiting at La Côte Basque for Babe Paley to walk in with an Hermès silk scarf knotted around the strap of her Chanel bag—was created as a response to the institutions of male authority from which women were excluded.

It was a shadow government of soft power that did its business not in flannel suits and boardrooms but in satin ball gowns over vodka stingers at the Plaza. But once women themselves could make partner in a law firm, instead of just their husbands, really, what was the point? Women with better things to do were only too happy to get out of that scene and make their own money.

Consequently, the gala circuit had increasingly become the purview of those who still considered themselves to be professional wives, who were sometimes not the most interesting set. For the new generation of strivers, celebrity had decisively replaced society as the goal.

Among those who noticed my article on Jean were two ambitious siblings who lived inside the Dakota apartment building on Central Park West. Toby Milstein, then twenty-four, and her brother,

Larry, then twenty-one, were heirs to a family real estate fortune valued in the billions. Even at that youthful age, their means had enabled them to become major philanthropists, contributing millions of dollars to the city's hospitals and cultural institutions.

They also loved expensive fashion and giving parties and thought that they, too, would like to be featured in the *New York Times*. So, they called each of the publicists listed in Jean's article and asked how they could arrange a similar profile in the Style section. Couri took them on as clients.

The siblings lived with their parents in the apartment formerly occupied by the great conductor and composer Leonard Bernstein. So, the Milsteins and their new publicist cooked up a plan to hold a séance by the piano in their living room to communicate with his ghost. As the hulking, Germanic-style apartment building is already a spooky place, the idea had some appeal.

After accepting the pitch, I called Leonard Bernstein's son, Alexander, for background. He told me stories about how as a child, he would listen to his father rehearse with Placido Domingo and Kiri Te Kanawa at the grand piano in the living room. Their upstairs neighbor, Betty (who was better known to the public as Lauren Bacall), would use the maids' stairs to come down and let herself into their kitchen when she was in the mood for a chat.

Property records indicated the Milsteins had paid $20.5 million for the apartment in 2008. The family money originated with a Russian immigrant ancestor, Morris Milstein, who had made it big in flooring. His descendants liked to tell the story that Morris had many different companies but didn't want to waste money on multiple letterheads. So, he just used one that read at the top: "Office of the Undersigned."

But there had been a schism between Morris's grandchildren, over a fortune that had grown to be worth $5 billion, and now the city had rival branches of Milstein cousins, all inordinately wealthy and many of them leading philanthropists. It behooved a reporter to keep straight which Milsteins he was visiting, and which other Milsteins he should not mention in their company.

Larry and his sister, both bright as new pennies, were thrilled to welcome a Style reporter into their home. Toby wore a gorgeous Fendi halter dress, and her brother was in fur-lined Gucci slippers. But in their youthful exuberance, they may have overstaged the party just a little.

The décor in the apartment was very heavy and keyed to the Dakota's 1884 German Renaissance–style architecture. There were thick drapes, lots of wooden furniture, and many Victorian allegorical oil paintings showing bow-lipped young women making moral choices. Subway trains rumbled audibly underneath.

To set the séance mood, various scented candles had been lit, and a silver candelabrum blazed extravagantly atop the piano. There were macarons, chilled mini champagne bottles, and a bottle of Jack Daniel's—a favorite of Leonard Bernstein's, apparently—that Toby kept in a cut-glass ice bucket. Then their friends started showing up.

There was a glamourous redhead in a tuxedo dress by the Kooples, who told me friends described her look as "Lindsay Lohan, but predrugs." There was a pretty descendant of the painter Camille Pissarro, an art historian who was in her early twenties, and the son of a former ambassador to France, who was dating Larry.

But nobody made an entrance to compare with Princess Noor Pahlavi of Iran, a granddaughter of the late shah and daughter to the country's exiled crown prince, who arrived with a cheese plate.

"Mama Noor! Literally!" Toby said, greeting her at the door.

The young princess, a stunning beauty, was dressed to kill in Saint Laurent heels and a short black Thierry Mugler leather dress. "I had to get really Persian. It's just, like, so controlling to bring food," she said, handing over the plate. Toby replied that Jews could relate.

Getting into the séance spirit, the princess brought up a television show on the E! network called *Hollywood Medium*, in which a fey twenty-year-old with aggressive blond highlights purported to contact the dead relatives of C-list celebrities. Even by the low bar of television psychics, this young man had not convinced many people he was gifted with second sight. But Princess Noor was a fan.

"I believe in this stuff," she said. "Not to be, like, really a downer, but there's a lot of tragic death in my family, after the revolution. So I have creepy stories like that, too."

The intersection of trash culture and momentous global events is my sweet spot, so I would have liked to ask a lot more. But I didn't get a chance, because it was time to start the séance.

Toby solemnly gathered her friends at the piano and poured measures from the bottle of Jack Daniel's before offering a toast to the shade of Leonard Bernstein. "To Lenny," she said, and we drank.

But she lost her footing slightly when she tried to link the composer's with-it seventies politics to her own generation of social justice warriors.

"He was also an activist. He brought a lot of activist figures in here," she said, indicating the apartment. "Right here, the Pink—oh my god, the Pink Panthers, LOL—[I meant] the Black Panthers. Like, he's organized a lot of major activist groups here."

(Although Bernstein did organize a controversial fund-raiser for the Black Panthers, it was held in the apartment he occupied before moving to the Dakota. Tom Wolfe skewered that evening in a *New York* magazine piece that coined the phrase "radical chic.")

After toasting the Pink Panthers with Jack Daniel's, a pianist and professional singer led the group in numbers by John Lennon and Leonard Bernstein, as well as something vaguely death-related by the contemporary artist Zayn Malik. It all felt more Beyoncé than séance-y.

Leaving the party in the fusty, wood-paneled elevator, I thought of Baron Perhapsburg, still dangling the use of his nonexistent family apartment in the Dakota as we circled above New York in an airplane, twenty years before. He probably would have quite fit in with this crowd.

Around the corner on Columbus Avenue, many of the storefronts were unchanged since that first summer I spent selling hot dogs and yogurt out of the Mellow Mouthful: the Swatch store on the opposite corner, the Betsey Johnson boutique across the street, even the old-style family pharmacy next door.

The narrow room that had once been my place of business had disappeared, however, knocked through by its cosmetics-store neighbor for an extra hundred square feet of floor space. Only the steel doors to the cellar, where I once chopped and bled into the raspberries, remained as a clue to what had been there before.

But the new façade might as well have been a mirage. Standing there on a chilly March afternoon, I realized I had reached another milestone of aging, where what had been on the street before was more real to me than what was there now.

# Rockefeller Central

I n 2016, Rupert with the soft hands married Jerry with the
feng shuied hair. Nobody saw that one coming.

That year, the city was stuffed with money. Everywhere,
new luxury towers that seemed to be made up entirely of penthouses,
from the second to the seventieth floor, were casting their shadows
on the groundlings below. Brooklyn and Queens, which two decades
before had seemed like pastures compared to the Manhattan skyline,
were newly forested with steel-and-glass residential skyscrapers.

In their megalomania, the rich thought they were saving us. But if
there was an upside to living in decadent late-empire New York, it was
that the parties were fabulous. And I discovered another tier higher

than clipboard, wristband, iPad, or headset: there was also one called helicopter.

In the spring of 2017, a trio of messianic tech investors, the eldest of whom was barely thirty, threw a dinner at the Rockefeller family estate in Westchester, just north of the city.

It was a kickoff event for something called the Kairos Society Global Summit, which had a tech-utopian vision of start-ups saving the world. Among the two hundred guests, there were only a handful of names that were not world-famous. Princess Beatrice of York, whom I was supposed to interview for a Style section squib, dropped out at the last minute. So instead I filed a report for *Vanity Fair*.

The evening started in the departure lounge of Blade, a charter helicopter service that flew from the West Side of Manhattan. I strapped in next to General Michael Hayden, a former director of the NSA and CIA.

His nose was out of joint because he'd just met Joseph Gordon-Levitt, an actor who had recently starred in Oliver Stone's film about Edward Snowden, the notorious leaker of classified information.

"The movie made him out to be a hero," the retired four-star US Air Force general grumbled during the twenty-minute flight. We were wearing heavy, noise-blocking ear guards, and he had to yell to be heard over the roar of the rotors. His wife nodded sympathetically.

Approaching by air, the Rockefeller estate looked like a vast and very expensive board game. It was a patchwork of timeworn mansions and follies. On one side was Kykuit, the famous country home; on another, an incongruous red barn, surrounded by livestock, like Marie Antoinette's hobby farm at Versailles. And everywhere were sand traps for golf.

We landed near a sagging pagoda, much in need of paint, next to a koi pond and a single cherry tree in gorgeous blossom. As we touched down, the general muttered approvingly: "Much more comfortable than a Black Hawk."

The estate's Playhouse—a Gatsby-era pleasure dome with a wood-paneled ballroom, two-lane bowling alley, and indoor swimming pool—had been made over into a magical nerd prom for the evening.

Our hosts included Ankur Jain, a twenty-seven-year-old executive at the dating app Tinder. He introduced me to his father, Naveen Jain, who had become famous in the first dot-com bust for presiding over a company that suffered one of the largest reversals of fortune in corporate history.

Naveen's latest quixotic venture was founding a mining operation on the moon, which he talked about at length. He seemed annoyed that I wasn't taking it more seriously.

A floor had been laid over the formal lawn, enclosed by a vast white marquee, to create the dining room. Guests included *Wall Street Journal* editor in chief Gerard Baker; hip-hop mogul Russell Simmons; AOL CEO Tim Armstrong; NBC News chairman Andy Lack; global financial crisis villain Dick Fuld; Dr. Mehmet Oz; Birchbox cofounder Hayley Barna; Periscope cofounder Kayvon Beykpour; Warby Parker cofounders Neil Blumenthal and Dave Gilboa; cosmetics legend Bobbi Brown; Dollar Shave Club cofounder and CEO Michael Dubin; Carl Icahn's son, Brett; Kairos cofounder and Tinder VP David Wyler; Richard Edelman, CEO of the eponymous PR empire; Verizon Wireless president Ronan Dunne; and restaurateur Eugene Remm.

Deep breath. Also: Rent the Runway cofounder Jennifer Fleiss; FUBU founder Daymond John; *Saturday Night Live* producer Marci Klein (daughter of Calvin); Barclays vice chairman Tim Luke; Factory PR CEO Mark Silver; filmmaker Casey Neistat; former prime minister of Greece George Papandreou; Amazon CTO Werner Vogels; SoulCycle CEO Melanie Whelan; JPMorgan Chase CEO of global investments Chris Willcox; and, just to make sure no one stole anything, the estate's senior heir, Mark Rockefeller.

At dinner, which was a big chunk of steak and another big chunk of tuna, served beside each other on each plate, I sat between Gordon-Levitt and the *New York Times* CEO Mark Thompson. Next to him was Vicente Fox, the former Mexican president, who was as handsome as a Roman bust and completely silent, and his glamorous wife, Marta, who twinkled like a star.

Between courses, we heard speeches about the start-ups and venture capital funds that were making the world a better place. Some of it was pure gibberish. One young fellow, purporting to have fixed the broken advertising model that was dooming so many legacy media outlets, confidently explained: "The problem is, content has been democratized, but editorial has not been democratized."

I stole a look around the room to see whether this made sense to other people. The moon miner was nodding enthusiastically.

After dinner Kimberly Guilfoyle, the Fox News anchor, sashayed by in a figure-hugging dress. She had split from her second husband and former red-carpet partner, Eric Villency, and seemed to be kicking the tires on potential replacements.

She handed Ankur a tall glass from the bar. "If you drink this, I'm not responsible," she said. "It's a double, maybe a triple, tequila with some soda water."

"I'm not drinking that," he said, and took a long sip.

I thought, so this is what replaced the old New York society. The setting would have been familiar to F. Scott Fitzgerald, but the characters had been radically updated. Now a Fox News anchor was playing the part of Daisy Buchanan and the twenty-seven-year-old director of product for a dating app was Gatsby.

I wondered whether these parties, where we stood around drinking George Clooney's tequila and talked about series financing for coworking spaces that promised they could solve the global refugee crisis, would exert the same pull on future generations as the grand balls described by Fitzgerald and Capote had on us. They probably would, I thought. After all, people will always be fascinated by money.

On the circular forecourt outside, stretch limousines were waiting to take us back to the city. They were the kind with one long, uncomfortable, L-shaped bench, and we squeezed in like an overlarge wedding party, bumping knees.

I sat next to the man who invented Siri. Nobody could work out the controls to lower the fabric blinds on the windows, so we drove back without a view, sequestered from the world like nuns.

# 17

# "No Regrets"

**T**wo years into the Trump administration, New York had the ominous mood of Europe in the 1930s. It was the feeling of a gin hangover—a thin, stringy pain in the frontal cortex, like the bill coming due from good times recently passed.

It had also been two years since Bill Cunningham, the legendary street fashion photographer for the *New York Times*, had died at the age of eighty-seven, and his absence was still being felt in the Style section. Ambitious women had been known to spend hours walking in circles around his favored corner of Fifth Avenue and Fifty-Seventh Street, just across from Bergdorf Goodman, hoping to have their picture appear in the Sunday paper.

In the reorganization that followed, I picked up a weekly social column in the Thursday edition. I quoted my old boss Joanna Molloy in my pitch for the job: someone had to go to these parties, where champagne flowed like blood from a guillotine, to represent the poor schmucks who weren't invited. It was positively altruistic on my part to volunteer.

Joanna would have fit right into the Style newsroom, whose politics were briskly woke. The stark differences between the winners and losers of the Trump era informed all aspects of the section, which was increasingly covering the culture of technology as much as fashion shows.

One of the designers came up with the column's name: "No Regrets," meaning to accept every invitation, and also signaling its purpose was not necessarily to play nice.

One of my first assignments was to cover the 2018 holiday party for the CBS network, whose chairman and CEO, Les Moonves, had recently been ousted amid allegations of sexual abuse. The party was normally held every year on the executive floor of the CBS building, but, as one employee joked grimly, that was now a crime scene. So they moved the event to a midtown restaurant.

CBS, which was sensitive about the negative press it was getting in the wake of their #MeToo scandal, turned down my request to cover the party. So, I threw on a suit and talked my way in. It had been years since I gatecrashed a party, but it was gratifying that the skills I had learned as a self-employed fashion gossip columnist were just as effective as an unwanted *Times* party reporter.

Jeff Bezos, the founder of Amazon who is sometimes called the richest person in history, was another reluctant subject. I cornered him at the Amazon Prime Video party in a penthouse of the Beverly Hilton hotel, right after the 2019 Golden Globe Awards.

Jeff had been pursuing an exercise regime, whose progress was admiringly documented by the tech media, and he was taut in his fitted tuxedo. But he was never a man of intimidating stature, and the pounds he'd shed from working out further reduced the amount of space he took up in a room. With his bald eraser of a head, he looked a bit like a sharpened pencil.

Despite an impressive slate of nominations, Amazon had a middling night at that year's Globes, picking up two trophies for acting but generally finishing second to its streaming rival Netflix. Not that I could detect any sense of disappointment from Jeff, who was grinning from ear to ear.

I put that down to his being surrounded by three attractive women who were dressed in long-sleeved, figure-hugging metallic and sequined gowns. They were striking not only for being tall and slender but also for their being appropriately middle-aged, which is unusual enough around billionaires to be notable. None of them was his wife.

Jeff made himself pleasant to the *Times* photographer, Elizabeth Lippman, who snapped some pictures. He proved more elusive to me, however, and his companions walled him off like the all-female bodyguards who used to run interference for Muammar Gaddafi. (Appropriately enough, Western media dubbed them "the Amazons.")

Finally I buttonholed him at the raw bar, where Alaskan king crab legs reached out of the ice like spiders in a scary movie. He didn't want to talk and fobbed me off by busying himself at the buffet.

But when he popped a mollusk into his mouth, he immediately spat it out into a napkin. "Bad oyster," he muttered.

It wasn't much, but when the richest man in history gags on an oyster at his own Golden Globes party, it's enough to add some color to the column.

In fact, we had more color than we knew. The next day, it would later emerge, the *National Enquirer* contacted him, threatening to expose details of an affair he was having with a woman who was also married. The tabloid even claimed to have incriminating, X-rated pictures lifted from his own phone.

Jeff stalled, and three days later tweeted the announcement that he was divorcing MacKenzie Bezos, his wife of twenty-five years.

The other woman turned out to be a minor Los Angeles media personality named Lauren Sanchez. And she had been one of his Amazonian companions at the Globes party.

It was a nice scoop for Elizabeth, who suddenly had the only pictures of the world's most famous new couple together. But my inner gossip columnist was twisted in knots at having been so close to the story and missed breaking it. All I got for my trouble was a fleck of oyster-tinged billionaire spittle.


N one of these antics came as a surprise to Carl Robinson. I was kvetching about rich people with him some months later, outside an event at the Plaza Hotel.

Carl has lived on the streets of that neighborhood for three decades and has a philosophical perspective on the wealthy.

"The truth about rich people is they are a nation, a culture unto themselves," he told me. "They are a cultural class unto themselves, and know not other cultures."

Carl spoke in the educated, cynical tones of a college professor who has been worn out by generations of students who never seem to learn anything. He once worked in a mail room, but these days, when he is aboveground, he gets by on panhandling. When he is operating in the subway system, where that is illegal, however, journalists must take care to say only that he "accepts donations."

That night, Carl was rattling a white plastic bucket on West Fifty-Eighth Street as a black-tie benefit emptied out.

"On a good night, this should be good for a couple of hundred dollars. But sometimes an event like this is zero, because everyone who attended, it was free for them. So when they go to a free event . . . ?" He shrugged. "Most wealthy people don't want to be bothered. They consider it to be a nuisance.

"And also, about seventy percent of wealthy people never handle cash anymore. They go digital with their money—the Venmo, PayPal," he said. "I've been trying to get them to lend me a credit card but it has never happened."

Having lived in the area for so long, Carl knows plenty of the neighbors.

"I met Donald Trump dozens of times. I spoke to him about a dozen times," he said. "The first time I met him was the early eighties; I met him on the subway. I asked him, 'What's a rich guy like you taking the train?' And he says, 'It's faster than the car.' He was coming back from the US Open in Queens."

Carl gestured down Fifth Avenue with his free hand. "He lives right there in Trump Tower. A lot of times when I used to meet him, he used to own here," he said, meaning the Plaza Hotel.

"Between the hours of one and three in the morning, he would walk from his office to the hotel all by himself, disguised in a white cap pulled over his hair and eyebrows. But I would always recognize him, because he was tall."

And did Donald ever give him money? Carl shook his head.

"He's not that kind of guy," he said. "His psychology is, 'Money comes to me, not from me.'"

Most of Trump's cronies were doing considerably better out of their association with him than Carl ever did. And now that he was in the White House, his old friends were all over.

Some in the New York billionaire class, which had formerly looked down on Trump as an arriviste clown, were now working in his cabinet and administration. Mingling with them at their lunch parties and Hamptons mansions was a constant reminder of the tension between the personal and the political.

Wilbur Ross, a gnomish octogenarian with a net worth of almost $3 billion, was a charming figure on the circuit with his fashionable and popular wife, Hilary Geary Ross. Trump made him commerce secretary. I chatted with them at the wake for a society designer, Mario Buatta, where they told many funny stories about his work on their various houses.

"I came home from a trip, very tired, and the entire living room was bubblegum pink," Wilbur recalled about an apartment the couple had occupied in the Sherry-Netherland, a prestigious building on the southeast corner of Central Park.

"So I called Hilary and said, 'What the hell is this?' She put Mario on and he said, 'After a year, you'll love it.'"

They both chuckled as the secretary paused before delivering the punch line. "He knew I had mistaken the primary coat for the final color. But he didn't say anything!"

At the time, the government was experiencing a prolonged shutdown that denied paychecks to around eight hundred thousand federal workers. The day after we spoke, Ross caused a furor by suggesting they could cover the deficiency by arranging personal loans.

He was also an ardent proponent of adding a question about citizenship status to the decennial US census. This was widely interpreted in liberal circles as an attempt to scare off immigrants from responding, which would in turn reduce the funding that flowed to their undercounted communities from the federal government.

But he's an ever-so-amusing chap at cocktail parties.

As time went on, and the bizarre conduct of the administration in Washington became normalized, the latent support for Trump among the city's wealthiest class became more visible.

In the summer of 2019, I covered a benefit for a Hamptons environmental center that was underwritten by Andrew Sabin, a precious-metals magnate. He explained that he was a fervent environmentalist, as well as being a strong supporter of President Trump, for whom he was hosting a fund-raiser the following week.

"I've never seen a crowd like this. It's not even a Trump rally, it's amazing," he told the gathering during his opening remarks. Half laughed, and half didn't.

The event was a surreal mishmash of ostentatious wealth and consciousness-raising for native marshland species. Above us were nesting houses for purple martins, each of which, Andrew explained, ate three thousand mosquitos a day.

Among the event's sponsors, meanwhile, was Rolls-Royce, the no-toriously fuel-inefficient automaker. Sitting on the lawn were three of its newest models, which guests could test-drive and retailed for just under half a million dollars each.

Kimberly Guilfoyle, who by then was dating the president's son, Don Jr., arrived in an eye-catching red dress. She also enthused about the Trump family's commitment to the environment.

When I asked about her boyfriend's widely circulated pictures of big-game hunting in Africa, she replied, "He hasn't shot anything since I've been around."

Andrew said he was expecting great things from the Trump ad-ministration on the environment. "I'm extremely politically active," he said. "I'm focusing on politics and the environment: clean air and clean water."

Scribbling in my reporter's notebook, I asked what environmental goals the president had achieved. Andrew said: "He's done an incred-ible job on ocean plastic. I think that with bipartisan help we're going to fix up all the national parks, and we have a save-the-wildlife bill we want to get."

A month later, Trump took an axe to the Endangered Species Act, making it easier for logging, mining, and fossil fuel drilling in at-risk habitats. The *New York Times* tallied eighty-five significant rollbacks of environmental regulations under his administration, including safe-guards against air and water pollution, greenhouse gas emissions, and toxic chemicals.

With billionaires wildly profiting from the policies of an admin-istration so at odds with their stated values, it was a good time to be a social writer. It almost made me nostalgic for David Koch, the anti-environmentalist and richest man in New York City, who died later that year aged seventy-nine. At least he had always been up-front about his agenda.

To be fair, the Trumpists were not the only billionaires living in a bubble of hypocrisy. There were plenty of left-leaning environmental-ists, especially in Hollywood and Silicon Valley, whose commitment to saving the planet did not extend to giving up their private jets. And I had a similarly bonkers conversation with Jerry Hall, at a party she hosted that summer in a Times Square nightclub.

Jerry was promoting the Equal Rights Amendment, which would enshrine gender equality into the Constitution. I had been warned by the event organizers not to ask about her husband, Rupert Murdoch.

But he was the first thing she brought up. "He's a big feminist," she said in her Texas twang.

I replied that seemed hard to believe, in light of the very public sexual harassment scandals that had plagued Fox News, the Murdoch cash cow that has been known to bank over $500 million in profit *per quarter*. More than a dozen women had settled with the network after detailing a pervasive culture of sexual abuse that existed for decades under its late chief executive Roger Ailes. Eighteen other employees had filed suit alleging racial and gender discrimination.

Jerry countered that Rupert had to be a feminist, because he employed so many women executives. She also said he supported passage of the ERA.

Press materials supplied by her own event, however, identified conservative opposition as the main reason the amendment had been stalled since 1923. Couldn't Rupert, as the owner of the most influential conservative news outlets in the world, at least do something about that?

Alas, no, Jerry explained. Rupert's hands were tied by a strict policy of not meddling with the independence of his journalists.

"I don't think he interferes," she said sweetly.

The most important person of the twenty-first century, Paris Hilton, was also there to lend her support. In a VIP room off the main floor, she was filming social media videos alongside two of Jerry's daughters with Mick Jagger, Lizzy and Georgia May.

With my notebook hanging open expectantly, I asked her to explain the process by which amendments to the Constitution are ratified.

Paris paused for long enough that I could sense the nib of my pen drying in the air.

"Is it . . . legislation?" I prompted.

She nodded. "Legislation," she repeated, crackling the word with vocal fry.

Look, I didn't say she was a mastermind; I said she was influential.

In the spring of 2019, Couri Hay called to offer me an exclusive interview with the scandal-tainted billionaire Jeffrey Epstein.

The source of Epstein's vast wealth was something of an enigma. Although he was generally described as a financier, nobody knew who his clients were. Some muttered that he supplemented his income as a blackmailer or was even on the payroll of some government intelligence agency—although for which country was anyone's guess.

Adding to the air of mystery were his large and opaquely financed properties around the world. In New York he owned what was reputed to be Manhattan's largest private home, a double-wide, limestone-faced town house on East Seventy-First Street, just down the block from the Frick Collection. Then there were a mansion in Palm Beach, Florida; a large survivalist compound outside Santa Fe in New Mexico; his private Caribbean island; and a tony Paris apartment, close to the Arc de Triomphe.

Epstein flitted between them, without attracting much attention, using his small fleet of private aviation, which included helicopters as well as Boeing and Gulfstream jets. He was Nosferatu in jeans and a chambray shirt.

Epstein was reclusive, but not by choice. In fact, he craved the glittering social connections to be made on the international party circuit, where he had once been welcome. By 2019, however, he had a serious reputational challenge to overcome.

The financier was seeking to restore his standing after serving jail time in Florida on charges of procuring underage prostitutes. It had been a sweetheart deal arranged by friendly authorities, and barely a slap on the wrist given the true extent of his crimes, which included decades of molesting young women and girls. Nonetheless, the light sentence was on record as time served, and Epstein felt he could put it behind him.

So he approached a society publicist about putting together a media strategy that might once again make him palatable to polite company. Couri said, "He told me: 'I don't want "billionaire pervert" to be the first line of my obituary.'"

Would I sit down with this creep, who was clearly hoping to use the press to launder his image? Yes, in a heartbeat.

Epstein was connected to leaders around the world, from Prince Andrew of Britain's royal family to Bill Clinton—it's always Bill Clinton with these guys—and Mohammed bin Salman, the crown prince of Saudi Arabia. I wanted to know what he knew.

Never one to think small, Couri had devised an audacious plan to restore Epstein's image. It involved spending a year in a rehab facility for sex addiction, seeking spiritual counseling from a rabbi, and donating up to $50 million a year to charities that addressed child sexual abuse. Additionally, he had to sign Bill Gates and Warren Buffett's giving pledge, which would liquidate his fortune to good causes upon his death.

But the rabbi's involvement was just the start. The strategy also included having Epstein confess and ask forgiveness from Pope Francis himself, never mind that he was Jewish.

To an outside observer, it might sound outlandish if not downright offensive to suggest the Holy Father could be dropped into a public relations plan to rehabilitate a man who had committed Epstein's crimes. But the dots did connect.

Couri's client Jean Shafiroff had met privately with Pope Francis just that February through her support of the Galileo Foundation, a charity closely associated with the pontiff. Unlike Epstein, Jean was a lifelong Catholic who had no crimes she was trying to sweep under the rug. But if the disgraced billionaire directed enough of his money toward church-related good works, it was entirely possible that a papal audience might follow.

After all, the Pope was in the business of forgiving sinners. And the optics would have been superb for Epstein. Who could question the penance of a man who had been forgiven by the highest human religious authority?

After an initial conversation in the spring, Couri called me again at the end of June to say the interview would take place in September. Epstein had told him that something was in the works—he didn't say what—that made that the right time to launch his comeback.

Just a week later, he was arrested by federal agents at Teterboro Airport in New Jersey, getting off his private plane after returning from France.

It turned out the absurd leniency he extracted from the Florida authorities had backfired, prompting an investigation by the *Miami Herald* into the true extent of his underage sex trafficking. The FBI took note and picked him up in a joint operation with the New York Police Department.

They stashed Epstein in the Metropolitan Correctional Center in downtown Manhattan, the same place I used to go and buy microwave sliders for my friend Ken Starr. One month and four days after his arrest, he was found dead in his cell under conditions as mysterious as many aspects of his life.

Who knows what Epstein would have told me in the interview, had it gone forward. He wanted to use it as a step toward once again being welcome aboard the mega-yachts of his famous friends, while my agenda was to string him up. Clearly, he felt it was worth the risk.

But that's how modern New York operates. It is a place where nobody carries shame and publicity is always the answer.

It all made sense, in the end.

In the late 1990s, the fashion industry in New York was at its peak, coming off a decade of unprecedented relevance. Models had become "super." Brands like Calvin Klein had trained mainstream media to cover advertising campaigns as if they were news. And cults of personality were everywhere—not only the models and designers, but even the editors were stars in their own right.

By the time I landed in New York, fashion occupied a greater share of popular culture than it ever had before, or would again. It was the natural subject for a striver to write about.

Fashion magazines of the 1990s also provide a uniquely quantifiable gauge for the rise of celebrity influence. For decades, they had chosen for their covers a procession of blue-ribbon models with names like Dovima and Veruschka, featuring a pop culture figure like Cher or Jane Fonda only every few years. But everything changed when Madonna appeared on the covers of British and then American *Vogue*, three months apart, in 1989.

American *Vogue* editor Anna Wintour later said the boost in newsstand circulation Madonna provided was "something extraordinary, like forty percent." The financial incentive for publishers to leverage the power of celebrity was suddenly clear.

In 1999, the *New York Times* ran an article marveling at celebrities' rout of models in women's magazines. Jennifer Aniston, Courtney Love, and Michelle Pfeiffer were the cover stars then selling at the newsstand; Wintour said she expected a circulation boost of five hundred thousand each for issues fronted by Oprah Winfrey and then–First Lady Hillary Clinton.

More than twenty years later, even catwalk stars who are crossover phenomena—like Gisele Bündchen, Cara Delevingne, or Gigi and Bella Hadid—are almost as rare on the covers of *Vogue* as celebrities used to be. Mere fashion models are no longer even considered.

Today, long after *Sex and the City* and *The Devil Wears Prada*, fashion's influence on broader popular culture has dramatically receded. The Marc Jacobs storefronts that came to saturate the West Village have disappeared. Celebrities no longer attend his—or anyone else's—Fashion Week shows in numbers that indicate they are major events.

Even the mighty fashion magazines, once institutions as revered as central banks, mostly either have been shuttered or are on life support and not expected to recover. They survive mainly as brochures for their websites, even as those sites are themselves diminished by social media and its unrelenting, pitiless feed.

As the tide went out on fashion, it was not surprising that a young reporter might be carried into the deeper water of celebrity. These things feel like choices at the time. But in reality, you go where you're invited and eat what's on the menu.

It was an unusual career path, to start online with "Chic Happens" and then move into wilting print. I think it had to do with the immigrant's yearning to climb the ladder, picking up associations with the *Daily News* and *New York Times* like scout badges of integration and respectability. Most people now are trying to forge their online brand; Horacio and I created one twenty years ago and then had no idea what to do with it.

But being a gossip columnist at a New York daily newspaper was spectacular fun. Even at the time there was a Walter Winchell nostalgia to it, and I loved the ink-smudged legitimacy it conferred. In a city where you are defined by what it says under your name on a business card, the job made me proud.

The newspaper gossip columns are all but gone now. The *News*, which ran up to three every day when I worked there, no longer has even one.

"Page Six," having cleaned up its act since the bribery scandal of the mid-2000s, still breaks news and benefits from being the last column standing. Its host body, the *New York Post*, hasn't been shown to turn a profit since Rupert Murdoch bought it in 1976; different analysts have guessed its annual losses may be between $20 million and $100 million. But as in *The Death of Marat*, the corpse continues to proffer its text.

I still believe that, when practiced with integrity, gossip journalism can be a power for good. After a decade out of the business, however, some added life experience has prompted me to reevaluate a couple of things.

In the mid-2010s, I sat on a panel of former gossip columnists held as part of a speakers' series at the Half King, a writers' pub in Chelsea.

One woman, who seemed politely skeptical about the value of gossip journalism to the common weal, raised her hand and asked whether a famous person was allowed to have a bad day.

I replied, "Yes, but if that person is a public figure, then their bad day is news."

But then she had a follow-up question.

She said that the problem with gossip was that it fixed its subjects at their lowest points. That we might all have our ups and downs, but the newspapers were more likely to print only the most embarrassing stuff.

"Don't we have a right to be known for more than just our worst moment?" she asked.

Huh. I didn't have an answer to that. For all my moral justifications of the practice, it's still the most cogent criticism of gossip culture I have heard.

I often think about what she said that night at Half King, especially as I get older and add to my own catalog of sins and mistakes. Would I want each new lapse to be all anyone knew about me?

I would not.

Anthropologists have long argued that gossip exists to reinforce community norms. But perhaps, on an industrial scale, it also diminishes the impact of shame in public life.

For the opportunistic, destigmatizing shame is a small price to pay for enjoying the upgrades in status, money, and power that celebrity can provide. And for those who are just having a bad day, it helps them move on with their lives.

Now shamelessness is morally neutral—it can be noble or despicable or anything in between.

Monica Lewinsky refused to carry the shame heaped on her by others. Instead, she designed a line of handbags, went on television, and wrote about her experiences. Her refusal to be erased was an act of moral heroism.

But at the other end of the moral spectrum, Jeffrey Epstein, the billionaire molester of underage girls, also sloughed off shame. Rather than hide from attention, he hired a publicist to arrange media opportunities. For him, an elevated profile was the best tactic to spin his way back into the corridors of power.

They had nothing in common, these twenty-first-century figures, except one thing. In a post-shame world, they both believed in the redeeming power of publicity.

# Acknowledgments

Thank you each to Melissa de la Cruz, who introduced me to Richard Abate, who became my agent and delivered me to the superlatively talented editor Eamon Dolan.

And I am grateful to the gifted copy editor Aja Pollock, for spanking the baby into life after Eamon delivered it.

Thank you also to the friends—Emily, Donna, Clare—who slogged through various drafts of this manuscript. Especially Matt, the genius behind *Pop Culture Died in 2009*, whose encyclopedic knowledge of 2000s gossip culture made him an invaluable fact-checker. He is also the only person I know who shares my crackpot theories about the importance of Paris Hilton.

# Index

Academy Awards, 102, 103, 109–10
Adams, Cindy, 128
Adolfo, 214
Adrover, Miguel, 61, 75–76
Aetna, 179–80
Affleck, Ben, 127
AIDS, 12
Ailes, Roger, 91, 264
Akiva, Richie, 126
Aktar, Alev, 101
Allen, Joan, 108
Allen, Woody, 98
Altchek, Chris, 240–41, 243
Amazon, 258–59
Ambrosio, Alessandra, 127
*American Horror Story*, 177
amfAR, 62
Amos, Tony, 9–10
Andrew, Prince, 266
Aniston, Jennifer, 102–3, 129, 268
*Annals, The* (Tacitus), 52
*Answered Prayers* (Capote), 52

AOL, 47, 140, 171, 174, 198, 201, 220, 228–30
appetizers, 40–43
*Apprentice, The,* 107, 201
Aquino, Corazon, 49
Archibald, Robert, 19
Armstrong, Tim, 228–29, 255
Arquette, Rosanna, 66
AsFour, 61
Astor, Brooke, 233, 246
Astor, Caroline Schermerhorn, 201
*Australian,* 64
Australian American Chamber of Commerce, 20
*Australian Art Collector,* 14
*Autobiography of Alice B. Toklas, The* (Stein), 52
Avedon, Richard, 225
Azoff, Irving, 189, 191
Azoff, Shelli, 189–91

Bacall, Lauren, 248
Baker, Gerard, 255

Balan, Nello, 95, 98
Balazs, André, 127
Banks, Tyra, 116–17
Barna, Hayley, 255
Barry, Maryanne Trump, 168
Barton, Mischa, 139
Basabe, Fabian, 145–46, 149
Bassett, Angela, 109
Basso, Dennis, 220
Bathing Corporation of
    Southampton, 209, 212
Beard, Mark, 58
Beatrice, Princess of York, 254
Beatrice Inn, 126
Beatty, Warren, 191, 192, 225
Beckham, David and Victoria, 80
Belushi, John, 187
Benza, A. J., 152
Bergen, Candice, 225
Bernstein, Alexander, 248
Bernstein, Leonard, 248–50
Berry, Halle, 102
Beverly Hills Hotel, 185
Beykpour, Kayvon, 255
Beyoncé, 121
Bezos, Jeff, 180, 197, 258–60
Bezos, MacKenzie, 259
Big Picture, 14–17
Billionaire Lane, 211–13
Billionaire's Row, 199–200
Bing, Steve, 63, 95
Black Panthers, 250
Blackstone Group, 227
Blanchett, Cate, 120
Bloomberg, Michael, 130, 133
Blue Note, 36–37
Blumenthal, Neil, 255
Boardman, Samantha, 135, 209
Boardman, Serena, 135
Bond, Justin Vivian, 13, 73
Borrok, Andrew, 237

Boyle, Peter, 105
Brando, Marlon, 58
Brett, Lily, 20
Briganti, Irena, 171
British Vogue, 118
Brody, Adrien, 103
Brokaw, Tom, 225
Brolin, Josh, 104
Brooklyn, 61–62, 77
Brown, Bobbi, 255
Brown, Laura, 80
Brown, Tina, 65, 67
Bruce of Los Angeles, 57
Bryanboy, 64
Buatta, Mario, 261–62
Bubby's, 10–11
Buffett, Warren, 266
Bungalow 8, 126, 148
Burch, Tory, 234
Burkle, Ron, 95–96, 110
Burr, Raymond, 75
Burrell, Paul, 117–18
Burton, Richard, 160
Bush, Barbara, 146
Bush, George W., 77, 128
Bush, Laura, 128
Bush, Sharon, 246–47
Bushnell, Candace, 30, 109
Butter, 126
Byrne, David, 108
Byrne, Gabriel, 108

Caesar, Julius, 52
Café con Leche, 13
Cailleach, Bronagh, 154–56
Campbell, Naomi, 118
Canal Street, 10
Capote, Truman, 52, 144, 247,
    256
Carey, Mariah, 121
Carey, Peter, 20

Carousel Ball, 185
Carradine, David, 103
Carter, Arthur, 198
Carter, Graydon, 198
Carter, Lee, 48–49, 81
Cassavetes, Zoe, 66
*Cat's Meow* (de la Cruz), 49
CBGB, 73
CBS, 258
Central Park, 199, 206
Charles, Prince, 128
Chateau Marmont, 187–89
Cheban, Jonathan, 62
Chelsea, 27
*Chicago*, 103, 104
"Chic Happens," 49–50, 60–64, 77,
    78, 80, 90, 96, 101, 269
*Chic Happens TV,* 78, 87, 89–90
*Chikatime,* 64
Chilton, Eve, 104, 105, 152
Cho, Ben, 61
Chou, Silas, 238
Christensen, Erika, 108
Chung, Connie, 15
*Citizen Kane,* 143
*City, The,* 147
Clegg, Bill, 31, 222–23
Clinton, Bill, 30, 54–55, 95, 110,
    173, 266
Clinton, Hillary, 116, 268
Clooney, George, 110, 256
Cobain, Frances Bean, 106
Cock, the, 13–14
Cocteau, Jean, 57
Cole, Natalie, 173
Collins, Joan, 150, 160, 163, 184,
    220–21
Combs, Janice, 166
Combs, Sean, 118, 138, 166
*Confessions of a Dangerous Mind,*
    110

Connery, Sean, 105
Cooper, Anderson, 220
Cooper, Ray, 60
Copperfield, David, 66
Coppola, Sofia, 65
Crisp, Quentin, 73–75, 183
Cronkite, Walter, 225
Cruise, Tom, 122–23, 129
Cruz, Celia, 36–37
Cumming, Alan, 109
Cunningham, Bill, 257
Cuomo, Andrew, 208
Cuomo, Chris, 208
Cuomo, Cristina, 208
Cuomo, Mario, 208
Curr, Judith, 20
Curtis, Colleen, 96–98, 132, 171
Cusack, Joan, 108
Cutrone, Kelly, 147

Dakota, the, 5–7, 35, 247, 249, 250
Dallesandro, Joe, 58
Damhave, Matt, 61
Dan Klores Communications, 138
Da Tommaso, 128
Davis, Barbara, 184–85
Davis, Brandon, 139, 185, 196
Davis, Jason, 185
Davis, Marvin, 185–86
Daye, Marvin, 170
Dean, James, 187
de la Cruz, Melissa, 49
de la Huerta, Paz, 12, 222
Demme, Jonathan, 225
Dempsey, Patrick, 108
Dench, Judi, 103
Deng, Wendi, 82, 84, 90, 237–40
De Niro, Robert, 120
Denton, Nick, 64
Dern, Laura, 108
De Vette, Lee Anne, 123

Diana, Princess, 75, 117, 128, 135
DiCaprio, Leonardo, 120, 127
Dickinson, Angie, 98
Dillon, Matt, 109
DiLuna, Amy, 101–2
Dimitri of Yugoslavia, Prince, 246
DKNY, 45–46
Dobson, Jill, 170–71
dogs, 206–7
Doherty, Shannen, 110
Domingo, Placido, 248
door people, 38–40
Dorff, Stephen, 66
Douglas, Michael, 104
Dressed to Kilt, 147
Drysdale, Clare, 72–73, 130
Dubin, Michael, 255
Duca, Lauren, 242
Dugdale, John, 56–59
Dunleavy, Steve, 94
Dunne, Ronan, 255
*Dynasty*, 185–86

E!, 142, 166
*Eat Pray Love*, 176–77
*Economist*, 228
Edelman, Richard, 255
Eichmann, Adolf, 17, 24
Elaine's, 109–10, 171–72, 228
elevators, 78–80
Elizabeth I, Queen, 197
Elizabeth II, Queen, 20, 172
email, 46–47
Eno, Brian, 196
*Entertainment Weekly*, 109
Ephron, Nora, 225
Epstein, Jeffrey, 95, 265–67, 271
Equal Rights Amendment, 264
Escuelita, 13
*Esquire*, 52
Estrada, Erik, 111

*Everyone Comes to Elaine's*
    (Hotchner), 109

*Fabulous Nobodies* (Tulloch), 9
Facebook, 114
Farrow, Mia, 98
fashion, 49–50, 62, 66, 267–69
Feinstein's, 221
Felder, Steve and Sara, 15–17
*Filthy Rich: Cattle Drive*, 149
Fish Bar, 73
Fitzgerald, F. Scott, 256
Fleiss, Jennifer, 255
Florent, 29–30, 78, 157
Follieri, Raffaello, 110
*Footloose*, 24
Ford, Harrison, 23–24
Foster, Jodie, 123
"Four Hundred," 200–201
Four Seasons, 130
Fox, 91, 169–71, 264
Fox, Vicente, 255
Foxy, 13–14
Francis, Joe, 169
Francis, Pope, 266–67
Franco, James, 176–77
French, Jim, 57
Froelich, Paula, 92
Fuld, Dick, 255
Full Picture, 127
Furnish, David, 64–65

Gable, Clark, 187
Gabor, Zsa Zsa, 160
Gabriel, Peter, 108
Galileo Foundation, 266
García Bernal, Gael, 104
Gastineau, Lisa, 165–66
*Gastineau Girls, The*, 166
"Gatecrasher," 112, 114, 116, 128,
    129, 138, 157, 167, 169

gatecrashing, 35–37, 64, 172
Gates, Bill, 266
Gawker, 64, 141, 191, 236
Geffen, David, 173
Ghesquière, Nicolas, 63
Gifford, Frank and Kathie Lee, 225
Gilboa, Dave, 255
Gilt, 231
*Girls Gone Wild*, 169
Giuliani, Rudy, 12, 14
Gloeden, Wilhelm von, 57
Golden Globe Awards, 258–60
Gong Li, 238
Gooding, Cuba, Jr., 131
Google, 27, 157, 229
Gordon-Levitt, Joseph, 254, 255
gossip columns, 49–53, 93–96,
        105–6, 111–16, 125, 129, 139,
        162, 195, 196, 231, 269–70
*Gossip Girl*, 145, 147
Graff, Zeta, 235
Grammy Awards, 80
Grant, Hugh, 120
Green, Denise, 20
Griffin, Kathy, 220
Grubman, Allen, 127
Grubman, Lizzie, 127
*Guardian*, 64
Guest, Cornelia, 144
Guest, C. Z., 144
Guilfoyle, Kimberly, 146, 256, 263
Gurung, Prabal, 73
Gutfreund, Susan, 247
Gyllenhaal, Jake and Maggie, 102

Half King, 270
Hall, Jerry, 118–19, 253, 264
Hamilton, George, 166
Hamptons, 207–12, 237, 247, 262
Hanks, Tom, 120
Harden, Marcia Gay, 103

Harlow, Jean, 187
Harry, Debbie, 65
Haskell, Nikki, 163–64, 166, 167,
        184–85, 220, 221
hate mail, 111–14, 243
Hathaway, Anne, 110
Hawke, Ethan, 126
Hay, R. Couri, 144, 146, 234,
        243–46, 248, 265–67
Hayden, Michael, 254
Hayek, Salma, 104, 105
Hearst, Amanda, 143–44
Hearst, Gillian, 142–44
Hearst, Lydia, 142–44
Hearst, Patty, 143
Hearst, William Randolph, 143
Hearst Communications, 143
heiress trend, 142–50, 222
Hemingway, Ernest, 52
*High Society*, 147
Hilton, Augustus, 159–61
Hilton, Barron, 161
Hilton, Conrad, 160, 161
Hilton, Conrad "Nicky," Jr., 138,
        160, 161
Hilton, Kathy, 150, 161, 166,
        168–69, 172
Hilton, Nicky, 135–36, 139, 143,
        150, 172
Hilton, Paris, 29–30, 110, 130, 133–
        43, 148–49, 162, 172, 196,
        197, 231, 234–36, 264–65
Hilton, Perez, 63–64
Hilton, Rick, 161, 166, 172
Hilton family, 159–62, 166, 169,
        172, 236–37
Hiltzik, Matt, 151
*Hint*, 48–50, 81
hip-hop, 137–38
hipster culture, 222
HLN, 171

HL Strategic Solutions, 238
Hogan, Hulk, 141
*Hollywood Medium,* 249
Holmes, Katie, 109, 129
Hooper, Catherine, 225–26
Horst, Horst P., 57
Hotel 17, 6–7, 9
*House of Mirth, The* (Wharton), 232
Howard, Ron, 225
Howard Rubenstein and Associates, 116
Huddy, Juliet, 170
Huffington, Arianna, 229
*Huffington Post,* 229–30
Hujar, Peter, 57
Hunt, Danny, 22, 24, 25, 57
Hunt, Helen, 24
Hurley, Liz, 63, 95

Iacocca, Lee, 164
Icahn, Brett, 255
Idlewild, 36, 37, 144
Imitation of Christ, 61
Independent Spirit Awards, 102
Instagram, 197, 228
*InStyle,* 80
internet, 46–48, 63, 115
*Interview,* 244
Irons, Jeremy, 163

Jackie 60, 28
*Jack Maggs* (Carey), 20
Jackman, Hugh, 120
Jacobs, Marc, 65–66, 268
Jagger, Georgia May, 264
Jagger, Lizzy, 264
Jagger, Mick, 118
Jain, Ankur, 255, 256
Jain, Naveen, 255
*Jalouse,* 77
Jay-Z, 116

*Jeopardy!,* 185
Jerrick, Mike, 170
Jews, 208–9
Johansson, Scarlett, 102
John, Daymond, 255
John, Elton, 59–60, 64
Johnson, Betsey, 38
Johnson, Beverly, 163, 185
Johnson, Casey, 144, 148–50
Johnson, Libet, 148
Johnson, Lulu, 38
Johnson, Nadine, 127
Johnson, Richard, 91–93, 95, 98, 126, 127, 164–65
Johnson, Sale, 150
Johnson, Woody, 148
Jolie, Angelina, 128–29, 156
Jones, Baird, 166–67
Jones, Randy, 73
Judd, Chris, 104

Kairos Society Global Summit, 254–56
Kane, Nancy, 131
Kardashian, Kim, 138–42, 195–97
Kardashian, Kourtney, 142
Katzenberg, Jeffrey, 151
Kaufman, Elaine, 109, 172, 228
Keaton, Diane, 120
*Keeping Up with the Kardashians,* 142, 166
*Kell on Earth,* 147
Kennedy, Caroline, 233
Kennedy, John F., 122
Kennedy, John F., Jr., 11, 233
Kennedy family, 233
*Kept,* 119
Kerzner, Sol, 166
Kidman, Nicole, 63, 103, 129
Kingsley, Pat, 120, 122–23, 138
Kissinger, Henry, 239

Klein, Calvin, 29, 62, 212, 255, 267

Klein, Marci, 255

Klum, Heidi, 127

Koch, Bill, 212

Koch, Charles, 212

Koch, David, 212–17, 263

Koch, Fred, 212

Koch, Julia, 213–15

Koch family, 58–59, 212

Koolhaas, Rem, 62, 123

Kozmo.com, 46

Krakowski, Jane, 109

Kurisunkal, James, 222

Kurkova, Karolina, 65–66

Kushner, Charles, 198

Kushner, Jared, 133, 198

LaBelle, Patti, 104, 200

*La Bohème*, 150

LaChapelle, David, 7

Lack, Andy, 255

LaForce, James, 40, 42

Lagerfeld, Karl, 220

Lane, Diane, 104

Langan's, 91, 94

*Last Samurai, The*, 123

Lauer, Matt, 225

Lauren, Ralph, 220

Law, Jude, 119

Lawlor, Norah, 37, 144, 237, 246

Lawrence, Jennifer, 238

Leach, Robin, 88, 166

Leake, Esther, 32–33

Ledger, Heath, 126

Leibovitz, Annie, 225

Leporc, Amanda, 7

Levin, Harvey, 180–81, 183, 184, 195

Lewinsky, Monica, 54–56, 65, 103, 270–71

Lewis, Daniel Day, 102

Lewis, Jerry, 121–22, 196

Lima, Adriana, 127

Linney, Laura, 108

*Lifestyles of the Rich and Famous*, 88

Lincoln Center, 212

Lippman, Elizabeth, 259, 260

Liu, Lucy, 114

*The Lives of the Twelve Caesars* (Suetonius), 52

Livingston, Jennie, 33

Lohan, Dina, 134

Lohan, Lindsay, 126, 133–35, 139, 196

Lohan, Michael, 134

Lopez, Jennifer, 99, 104, 121, 134

*Los Angeles Times*, 242

Love, Courtney, 106, 268

Love Saves the Day, 73

Lowe, Chad, 65

Luce, Henry, 232

Lucky Cheng's, 73

Luhrmann, Baz, 150

Luke, Tim, 255

Luna, Diego, 104

Lynes, George Platt, 59

Lyonne, Natasha, 66

Madoff, Andrew, 225–26

Madoff, Bernie, 219, 225, 227

Madonna, 105–6, 121, 268

Mafia, 97–98

Maidstone Club, 208

Mailer, Norman, 109

"Male Room, The," 169–70

Mangan, Dan, 94, 133

Manilow, Barry, 234–35

Mantle, Mickey, 98

Maples, Marla, 150, 153, 164

Mar-a-Lago, 157, 165, 202

Marcos, Imelda, 163

Marsh, Lisa, 94, 133
Martin, Dean, 121
Marx, Groucho, 209
Mason, Christopher, 233
Matisse, Henri, 52
Max, Peter, 244
Mayer, John, 236
Mayer, Marissa, 238, 239
McConaughey, Matthew, 103, 126
McDermott, Dylan, 108
McMullan, Patrick, 145, 147, 231, 245, 246
McQueen, Alexander, 49
Meadow Lane, 212–13
Meagher, Patrick, 169–70
Meatpacking District, 28–30, 65, 77–78, 80, 157
Mehle, Aileen, 244
Mellon, Paul, 173
Mellow Mouthful, 21–25, 35, 56, 57, 81, 250–51
Mendes, Sam, 225
Menuditis, 73
Mercer, Dabney, 147
Met Gala, 215, 237–40
Metropolitan Correctional Center (MCC), 226–28, 267
Metropolitan Museum of Art, 212, 215, 232, 237–39
*Miami Herald,* 267
Mic.com, 240–43
Miller sisters, 135
Milne, A. A., 89
Milstein, Larry, 247–49
Milstein, Morris, 248
Milstein, Toby, 247–50
Minnelli, Liza, 109, 163, 210–11
Miramax, 95, 103–5, 152
Miss USA, 167, 202
Mizer, Bob, 57
Mizrahi, Isaac, 225

Mohammed bin Salman, Prince, 266
Molloy, Joanna, 96, 98–99, 126, 130, 258
Moomba, 62
Moonves, Les, 258
Moore, Julianne, 80, 102
Moore, Michael, 225
Morellet, Florent, 29, 157
*Morning Show with Mike and Juliet, The,* 169–71
Morrison, Toni, 30
Morrissey, 188–92
Mortimer, Tinsley, 146–47, 234, 244, 245
Mortimer, Topper, 146
Moss, Kate, 29, 60–61
Mother, 28–29
Mulroney, Dermot, 108
Murdoch, Elisabeth, 78, 81–85, 89
Murdoch, Grace, 83
Murdoch, Lachlan, 80–81
Murdoch, Rupert, 78, 80–85, 90–91, 116, 153, 185, 217, 238, 253, 264, 269
Murphy, Ryan, 177
Murray, Jawn, 140
Musa, Mansa, 197, 245
Museum of Modern Art, 76
*Musician,* 196

Naess, Arne, Jr., 208
*Naked Civil Servant, The* (Crisp), 74
*National Enquirer,* 236, 244, 259
Neeson, Liam, 120, 225
*Neighbours,* 120
Neistat, Casey, 255
Netflix, 259
Newman, Paul, 121
Newsom, Gavin, 146
*Newsweek,* 200
*New York,* 64, 162, 200, 214, 250

New York *Daily News,* xiii, 96–99,
101–2, 105–6, 111–15, 129,
132, 134, 152, 153–57, 171,
243, 269
*New Yorker,* 128, 136, 151, 242
*New York Observer,* 30, 198–200,
213, 235, 236, 238
*New York Post,* 64, 83, 90–96, 106,
114, 128, 133–35, 142, 146,
148, 152, 153, 164–65, 237,
269
*New York Times,* xiii, 63, 64, 96,
130, 138, 141, 198, 201, 212,
214, 231–34, 236, 237, 240,
243, 248, 257–59, 263, 268,
269
*New York Times Magazine,* 215
Nice, Chuck, 169–70
Nicholson, Jack, 120
Nielsen, Brigitte, 166
*Nikki Haskell Show, The,* 163
9/11, 76–77, 133
Ninja, Willi, 13, 32–33, 130
Nixon, Richard, 239
"No Regrets," 258
Norton, Graham, 89
Norwood, Brandy, 140
Noth, Chris, 65

Obama, Barack, 133, 200
O'Connor, Billy, 57, 59
Odeon, 10
O'Donnell, Rosie, 236
Ogunnaike, Lola, 138
O'Hare, Sarah, 80–81
*OK!,* 165
Olsen, Mary-Kate and Ashley, 126,
140
Onassis, Jacqueline Kennedy, 199,
213
O'Neal, Tatum, 109

1Oak, 126
O'Reilly, Bill, 170
Orensanz, Angel, 72–73
*Orlando* (Woolf), 74
Oz, Mehmet, 255

Pacino, Al, 123, 173
"Page Six," 64, 90–94, 96, 98, 114,
127, 165, 170, 184, 232, 235,
246, 269
*PageSixSixSix,* 64
Pahlavi, Noor, 249–50
Palermo, Olivia, 147
Paley, Babe, 247
Paltrow, Gwyneth, 103
Papandreou, George, 255
*Paris Diary, The* (Rorem), 52
*Paris Is Burning,* 13, 33
*Park Avenue Peerage,* 145, 222
Parker, Sarah Jessica, 65
Parker Bowles, Camilla, 128
Pastis, 77–78
Pataki, George, 116
Patric, Jason, 108
Patz, Etan, 12
Pearce, Guy, 120
*People,* 236
Perhapsburg, Baron, 3–6, 161, 250
Peters, Bernadette, 109
Peterson, Karen, 175, 176
Peterson, Pete, 227
Pfeiffer, Michelle, 268
*Philadelphia,* 170
philanthropy, 244–46, 248
Phillips, Bijou, 148
Piazza, Jo, 131, 132
Picasso, Pablo, 52
Pissarro, Camille, 249
Pitt, Brad, 102–3, 128–29
Piven, Jeremy, 126
Plaza Hotel, 172, 247, 260, 261

Polo Lounge, 185, 186
Ponzi schemes, 219, 224–27
Portman, Natalie, 173
Post, Marjorie Merriweather, 165
Prada, Miuccia, 62, 123
Presley, Elvis, 94, 244
Presten, Sy, 127–28
*Price Is Right, The,* 182–83
Previn, Soon-Yi, 98
*Profiles in Courage* (Kennedy), 122
*Project Runway,* 127
publicists, 115–16, 126–27, 144,
    231–34, 237, 245–46, 248
Puente, Tito, 36
Putin, Vladimir, 201

Quartana, Joseph, 61

Rankin, David, 20
Raphael, Sally Jessy, 66
Ray J, 140, 141
Razor, 46, 77
Reagan, Nancy, 128, 214
Reagan, Ronald, 128
Reddy, Sameer, 63
Reed, Lou, 196
Reid, John, 59–60
Reid, Tara, 66, 150
Remm, Eugene, 255
*Resident,* 37
Rhymes, Busta, 107
Ricci, Christina, 102
Rich, Denise, 172–73
Rich, Marc, 173
Richards, Marty, 104–5
Richie, Lionel, 136
Richie, Nicole, 136, 139, 148, 196
Rivers, Joan, 62, 104, 188, 190
Rivers, Melissa, 62
*Robb Report,* 88
Roberts, Julia, 176–77

Robinson, Carl, 260–61
Rockefeller, Mark, 255
Rodgers, Nile, 173
Rolls-Royce, 263
Roman Empire, 51–52, 196, 201
Roosevelt, Franklin, 217
Roosevelt, Theodore, 205
Roquebrune, Micheline, 105
Rorem, Ned, 52
Rosen, Aby, 209, 212
Ross, Diana, 208
Ross, Hilary Geary, 261–62
Ross, Wilbur, 261–62
Roura, Phil, 98
Rovzar, Chris, 131
Roxy, 13
Rubenstein, Howard, 116, 127
Rubenstein, Steven, 127
Rubicondi, Rossano, 157, 164–65,
    168
Rudolph, Maya, 66
Ruffalo, Mark, 102
Rush, George, 96, 98, 102, 104,
    126, 131
"Rush & Molloy," 96, 98–99, 101,
    105–6, 110–11
Ryder, Winona, 106

Sabin, Andrew, 262, 263
Sacco, Amy, 126
Sachs, Shawn, 127
Sahagún, Marta, 255
St. Vincent's Hospital, 131–32
Salomon, Rick, 110, 136
Sanchez, Lauren, 260
Sand-Freedman, Lisette, 126
Sargeant, Bruce, 58
Sartiano, Scott, 126
*Saturday Night Live,* 235
Save the Music Foundation, 166
Sawyer, Diane, 225

Saxton, Catherine, 144, 166,
    171–74, 228, 236–37
Scharf, Kenny, 13
Scheindlin, Shira, 228
Schiffer, Claudia, 50
Schlossberg, Edwin, 233
Schrager, Ian, 212
Schreffler, Laura, 125–26, 131
Schreiber, Liev, 109
Schwarzman, Stephen, 200
Scientology, 123, 129, 224
Scorsese, Martin, 173
Sedaka, Neil, 166, 168
Seinfeld, Jerry, 29
Semel, Courtenay, 149
September 11 attacks, 76–77, 133
Serrano, Andres, 29
Seven, 61
Sevigny, Chloë, 61, 126
Sevigny, Paul, 126
Sex and the City, 30, 65, 136, 268
Shadow Lounge, 89
Shadow PR, 126
Shafiroff, Jean, 245–48, 266
Shakespeare in Love, 103
Shields, Brooke, 209–10
Shields, Teri, 209–11
Shine, 77–78, 82, 89, 90
Showbiz Tonight, 171, 174
Shuter, Rob, 138, 234–36
Silva, Horacio, 5–7, 9–11, 13, 14,
    22–24, 29, 32, 35–36, 49–50,
    57, 64, 71, 76, 77, 80, 82, 84,
    85, 89, 101, 130, 144, 157,
    187–89, 191–92, 198, 269
Silver, Mark, 255
Silver Hill Hospital, 220
Simmons, Kimora Lee, 66
Simmons, Russell, 255
Simon, Carly, 225
Simon, Paul, 225

Simons, Raf, 61
Simple Life, The, 136, 142, 149,
    196, 197
Simpson, Ashlee, 235
Simpson, Jessica, 134, 235–36
Simpson, Joe, 236
Simpson, Wallis, 74–75
Skull & Bones, 94, 96
Smith, Emily, 246
Smith, Will, 123
Smiths, the, 189
Snowden, Edward, 254
Socialite Rank, 145, 222
socialites, 244–45
social media, 114–15, 221, 241–43
Soho House, 80–81
Something's Gotta Give, 120
Sorensen, Ted, 122
Spacek, Sissy, 102
Spears, Britney, 133–35, 236
Spiegelman, Ian, 92
Spy, 50
Stalin, Joseph, 217
Stallone, Sylvester, 109, 173
Star, 63–64
StarCaps, 163
Starr, Diane, 173–75, 223–28,
    236–37
Starr, Ken, 173–75, 223–28, 236–37,
    267
Stassinopoulos, Agapi, 229
Stein, Gertrude, 52
Steinbrenner, George, 109
Stern, Jared Paul, 92, 94, 96
Stewart, Martha, 237
Stewart, Rod, 200
Stiles, Julia, 108
Sting, 64, 74, 235
Stone, Oliver, 254
store parties, 38–43, 51
Strategy Room, The, 170–71

Streep, Meryl, 119
Studio 54, 244
Styler, Trudie, 64–65
Subkoff, Tara, 61
subway, 53–54
Suetonius, 52
Summers, Alison, 20
Sunset Boulevard, 180, 187
Sunshine, Ken, 127
Sussman, Bruce, 234–35
Swank, Hilary, 65
*Sydney Morning Herald,* 139
Sydney *Star Observer,* 113
Symbionese Liberation Army, 143

*T,* 64, 198
Tacitus, 52
*Talk,* 65
Tavern on the Green, 116
Taylor, Elizabeth, 106, 138, 160
Taymor, Julie, 104
*Teen Vogue,* 242
Te Kanawa, Kiri, 248
Tennant, Stella, 66
Tequila, Tila, 149
Thanksgiving, 32–33
Thompson, Mark, 255
Thurman, Uma, 126, 173, 224
Time Inc., 232
TMZ, 180–84, 186–92, 198
*Town & Country,* 143, 234, 244
Transit TV, 183
Trebek, Alex, 185
Trescher, George, 232–33
Tribeca, 10–11
Trump, Barron, 161, 167
Trump, Donald, 66–67, 106–7, 138,
     147, 148, 152, 157, 160–62,
     164–67, 172, 180, 195–97,
     201–3, 213, 231, 257, 258,
     261–63

Trump, Donald, Jr., 107, 168, 263
Trump, Eric, 107, 168
Trump, Fred, 160
Trump, Fred, Jr., 161
Trump, Friedrich, 159–61
Trump, Ivana, 106, 157, 161–68,
     172
Trump, Ivanka, 133, 144, 162, 166,
     168
Trump, Melania, 67, 162, 167,
     201–4
Trump, Tiffany, 152
*Trump: The Art of the Deal* (Trump),
     164, 167
Trump family, 159–62, 166, 169,
     172, 216, 263
Trump Organization, 160
Trump Tower, 201, 261
Tulloch, Lee, 9–10, 13, 222
Tunnel, 13
Turlington, Christy, 65
Twilo, 13
Twitter, 114, 221, 240–42

*Us Weekly,* 128, 236

Valderrama, Wilmer, 140
Vanderbilt, Gloria, 220
*Vanity Fair,* xiii, 136, 148, 198, 254
*Variety,* 152
Veloso, Caetano, 104
*Velvet Underground & Nico, The,*
     196
Versace, Donatella, 106
Victoria's Secret, 127
*View, The,* 117
Village Halloween Parade, 30
Village People, 73
Villency, Eric, 146, 147, 256
Vivid Entertainment, 140–42
Vogels, Werner, 255

*Vogue,* 48, 50, 61, 65, 185, 215,
232, 268
Vojnovic, Natasa, 66
von S——, Charles, 3–6, 161, 250

*W,* 213
*Wall Street Journal,* 91
Walters, Barbara, 225
Warhol, Andy, 58, 145, 243–44
Wasson, Erin, 66
Web, the (nightclub), 13
Weinstein, Bob, 103
Weinstein, Harvey, 94–95, 103–5,
150–53
Wessel, John, 57, 59
Wessel + O'Connor Fine Art, 57–60
West, Kanye, 195
Westheimer, Ruth, 166
Wharton, Edith, 232
Whelan, Melanie, 255
*When We Were Very Young* (Milne),
89
W Hotels, 37, 134
Wilcox, Chris, 255
Will, Kelly, 131
Williams, Robbie, 80
Williams, Robin, 120
Wilson, Chris, 92

Wilson, Owen, 126
Wilson, Rita, 151
Winchell, Walter, 127, 269
Windsor, Duke and Duchess of,
74–75
Winfrey, Oprah, 268
Winslet, Kate, 120
Wintour, Anna, 61, 65, 215, 237–39,
268
Wojnarowicz, David, 57
Wolfe, Tom, 250
Wong, Kaisik, 63
Wood, Natalie, 160
Woods, Tiger, 184, 192
Woolf, Virginia, 74
World Trade Center, 11, 45–46
Wyler, David, 255

Xes, 148

Yambao, Bryan, 64
*Y Tu Mamá También,* 104

Zeifman, Brad, 126
Zeta-Jones, Catherine, 103–4,
237
Zucker, Jeff, 225
Zuckerman, Mort, 153